703

703

HOW I LOST MORE THAN A QUARTER TON
AND GAINED A LIFE

NANCY MAKIN

DUTTON

DUTTON
Published by Penguin Group (USA) Inc.
375 Hudson Street, New York, New York 10014, U.S.A.
Penguin Group (Canada), 90 Eglinton Avenue East, Suite 700, Toronto, Ontario M4P 2Y3, Canada
(a division of Pearson Penguin Canada Inc.); Penguin Books Ltd, 80 Strand, London WC2R 0RL,
England; Penguin Ireland, 25 St Stephen's Green, Dublin 2, Ireland (a division of Penguin Books Ltd);
Penguin Group (Australia), 250 Camberwell Road, Camberwell, Victoria 3124, Australia
(a division of Pearson Australia Group Pty Ltd); Penguin Books India Pvt Ltd, 11 Community Centre,
Panchsheel Park, New Delhi—110 017, India; Penguin Group (NZ), 67 Apollo Drive, Rosedale,
North Shore 0632, New Zealand (a division of Pearson New Zealand Ltd);
Penguin Books (South Africa) (Pty) Ltd, 24 Sturdee Avenue, Rosebank, Johannesburg 2196, South Africa

Penguin Books Ltd, Registered Offices: 80 Strand, London WC2R 0RL, England

Published by Dutton, a member of Penguin Group (USA) Inc.

First printing, April 2010
1   3   5   7   9   10   8   6   4   2

REGISTERED TRADEMARK—MARCA REGISTRADA

LIBRARY OF CONGRESS CATALOGING-IN-PUBLICATION DATA
has been applied for

ISBN 978-0-525-95137-7

Printed in the United States of America
Set in Sabon
Designed by Lenny Telesca

While the author has made every effort to provide accurate telephone numbers and Internet addresses at
the time of publication, neither the publisher nor the author assumes any responsibility for errors, or for
changes that occur after publication. Further, the publisher does not have any control over and does not
assume any responsibility for author or third-party Web sites or their content.

Author's Note: The names and identifying characteristics of certain persons included in this memoir have
been changed, and certain characters have been composited for the sake of protecting their privacy.

Penguin is committed to publishing works of quality and integrity.
In that spirit, we are proud to offer this book to our readers;
however, the story, the experiences, and the words
are the author's alone.

God knit together beautifully
The precious son who came to be
His handiwork that formed within
A child 'could make the angels grin
Good job, God.

Darling Son:

You were a blessing as a child, so easy to love. You have grown into a good man: hard working, a loving husband and father. You make me proud every day. I am still at a loss as to how that happened, how you turned out so well. It didn't come from my end of the gene pool, angel. Give your daddy a call to thank him.

For your love, your support, your loyalty, your acceptance and forgiveness of my many deficiencies, selfishness and missteps over a lifetime, I thank you. My path would be so lacking without you in it. I am a very lucky woman. I love you, Christopher . . . Oooooh, Eeeee, Ah, shucks. I wouldn't trade you for a million bucks . . .

CONTENTS

Contents

FOREWORD

My Son's Perspective

I enter the first set of doors at the building and give a courtesy buzz to the person I am visiting, then scan in with the lone key card issued to residents. The occupant I am coming to see doesn't need hers; she hasn't as long as she's lived here. I stand in the lobby waiting for the elevator, fielding various questions from the elderly residents congregated nearby. I enter the elevator and on my way to the seventh floor read the notices regarding the upcoming potluck dinner, the next feature film to be shown on movie night and the obituary notices of those tenants who've died this week.

The elevator door opens; I exit to my right and begin the long walk down the hall. Immediately, my dread starts to build. The corridor has a floor-to-ceiling window at its end, and I walk along, focusing solely on the windowpane as it comes closer, consuming more and more of my field of vision. The tops of the trees are now visible along with the clouds above them. I imagine that I'm a bird and can fly away from this place and the helplessness and pain I feel, intermingled with the bitter joy of seeing her again. I am visiting my mother's tomb the way so many others visit a dead relative in a graveyard's mausoleum, only *my* dearly departed answers. Will she answer me this time?

Or will I this time be left alone to tidy up one last situation, rearranging her clothing, smoothing her hair and positioning my mother in the most flattering position possible? In this way, when the firemen arrive, my mother can maintain that false sense of dignity we both worked so hard to uphold over the years. I say *false* dignity, only because, with her weight at 703 pounds, such a select few allowed her any at all. The protocol described may seem a macabre or insensitive way for someone to view the death of a parent, but I had been in training for this moment for so many years, it was just part of the drill. I'd had to be ever vigilant for years now; attempting to help my mother make the most inconspicuous entrance and exit possible on the rare occasions she left the building, thinking about where I should stand to block the view of the majority of prying, inquisitive eyes and, most important, trying to accomplish the task as quickly as possible. You have to understand: Her death wasn't a matter of *if*, but of *when*. So many times the two of us sat together, laughing and enjoying each other's company; every time I stood to say good-bye, it was with the silent understanding that this farewell could be our last. Only when this son's final duty was done, when I'd given my best effort as a layman mortician for my dear mother's exhausted corpse, when she'd finally drawn her last lonely breath, would I have time to cry; cry for a life so promising, yet unfulfilled.

The question I get asked most often is "Did you shop for her groceries?" It's more of an accusation than a question; the meaning behind it is so condescending. Yes, I *did* go to the store for her often, although cookies and chips had vanished from her grocery lists long before, back when the pain in my eyes had apparently caused her to stop requesting them. I guess if you put enough mayonnaise on a ham-and-cheese sandwich, or if your metabolism shuts down, or if you've become virtually stationary, as my mother had, there isn't much left to be done; you're going to die sooner rather than later.

In my mind I was a son, granting my mother the only bit of autonomy and control left to her; she still had the right to make the decisions she *could*. I was not her jailer; it was not my place to dictate to her, or anyone else's province for that matter. Maybe we should put pizza delivery workers on trial, or slap fines on those who work at drive-thru windows if they fill the orders of people weighing over a societally prescribed amount? These hard memories and agonizing frustrations filtered through my mind as I neared the end of my long walk down the hall. So with my mind doing its best not to think of any of it and realizing that I hadn't sprouted wings to take flight, I stopped at the last door on the right and turned the knob.

Chris Makin
October 22, 2008

PREFACE

A View from the Crow's Nest/My Turn

No one could be more surprised than I to find myself here tapping on this keyboard, pounding out these characters, building words, telling a tale that could never be; it is too fantastic. But I am tapping, and it *did* happen. I am alive, and that revelation still stuns me. This was not the plan, the blueprint that I saw lying there before me. Life is for the living; I was not alive, only went through the motions, and even those were streamlined to the very barest function necessary to keep my heart pumping and lungs filling in a heavily encumbered chest. My vacant eyes were still activated, watching all that bustled about me, all I had no part in. I marked time, waiting for the end.

My death would come; either slowly, incrementally, a wasting sort of degeneration, or in a swift manner, suddenly, taking me away in one fell swoop and releasing my misused body, my brain's unspent currency and saddened spirit.

My incarceration crept up on me over years, built not in a day, but in millions of moments, one upon the next, as if each were a single brick in some ominous structure of my own design. In every moment, I pressed firmly down each sturdy rectangle, applying a liberal layer of the mortar of worthlessness, then another and another heaped upon the last, till the walls of my prison were erected solidly around me.

I was a fine mason. There were no gaps between bricks, no air pockets in which to find a fissure, some defect that could later be exploited, tearing down my encasement and letting daylight shine upon my prisoner's face. There would be no escaping this mind-numbing cell. Yet this is the story of one woman's unlikely prison break. There alone in my confinement, I felt helpless to find a way outside. My liberation would come from the most unexpected source, and in my wildest imaginings, I never contemplated its arrival. I had resigned myself to this life sentence, although that was surely a misnomer. For truly, it was a death sentence I faced. And I ought to know, it was I who was prosecutor, judge and jury. I had imposed a sentence, the harshest possible. And those outside the dank walls would be my improbable liberators. I did not even know them, nor were they aware of me, not yet. Let me take you back to when it all began.

> *Pansy's petals, violet, yellow*
> *Cannot stand fierce rainstorm's bellow*
> *But mist's touch makes flowers flourish*
> *With its tender, gentle nourish*

Nancy

children were privy to. When I was older, my dad used to say that my mother and he "had agreed seven times," referring to the conception of us seven girls. The two just never meshed. The nine of us inhabited the same space, but never really were a unit, all this despite the outward trappings of dinner together every night, rosaries said on knees in front of brass stems holding green-glass-cupped votive candles, trips to Lake Sammamish for picnics and swimming, and the memory of many fresh-baked wild blackberry pies cooling on the kitchen counter.

Four of my sisters were much older than I, otherworldly entities I watched from afar, with their clip-on velvet bows adorning bouffant hairdos, and their plaid Catholic high school uniforms, white anklets and saddle shoes. They'd rush past in the early-morning race for bathroom space, to examine eyebrows lest a stray hair mar their teenaged symmetry and apply even *more* hairspray to their teased-to-attention coiffures that appeared to be more like helmets. Daddy said they'd die from the chemicals. They'd roll their eyes and silently brush past him every time.

I remember one morning standing next to my father in our long upstairs hallway. Dad was wearing his baggy boxer shorts and a sleeveless white T-shirt, and holding his shaving mug and brush, with soapy lather already covering his whiskers. He startled me by blurting out to anyone within earshot: "Four bathrooms, eight females, hell, we even own a female dog! Do you think a man could find a place to shave? Hell, no." I didn't quite understand the depth of Daddy's frustration on that long ago morning, but I do now. My father was heavily outnumbered; the poor man never stood a chance.

Although as an adult I do revel in my fairer sex status, my regimen was, and still is, far less involved than most of my gender's. Once my navy pleated skirt and short-sleeved white shirt of St. Anne School's dictate were removed in the afternoon, my mother played hell trying to get me into any raiment of femininity. Pedal pushers, I think they called them, Capri pants these days, and plain little cotton shirts were my play uniform of choice. And, Lord! How I detested shoes, still do. I'd dutifully wear them till I got out of Mom's eyeshot, then ditch them around the side of our large, five-bedroom home, under one of many enormous purple or white rhododendron bushes that dappled our property in the Queen Anne Hill district of Seattle.

I had an avid interest in slugs and would happily stroll alone along the sidewalk beneath a Seattle winter's drizzle-filled sky to watch and wait for the slick brown creatures to emerge. They always did. I'd squat to pick one up, place it on my forearm for further inspection and marvel at the slug's rhythmic movement.

I had use of a giant old Schwinn, long past its prime, in a rust and white color combination, with balloon tires and coaster brakes. I flew aloft its bulbous wheels down the incline of Kinnear Place with abandon. Gordon Capretto and Rusty Hokanson were my best friends, at least that's the way I felt about *them;* depending on the boys' mood, I was either a pest or a guide to new discoveries. We found excitement in the expanse of overgrown blackberry brambles behind our garage, or in looking through one of the telescopes atop Kerry Park and out toward the Space Needle and steady boat traffic on Puget Sound. We often went swimming in the Hokansons' above-ground pool, at the end of the plummeting driveway in Rusty's backyard. Everything plummeted in Seattle; all was on an incline.

My father never bought a new car, though we could have well afforded one on his engineer's salary. I can remember many a time riding up Queen Anne Hill with my mother and several of my sisters aboard, Mom giving the order that we should all begin saying the Hail Mary, as our car seldom made it all the way up the steep rise. Somewhere around "blessed art thou amongst women, and blessed is the fruit of thy . . . ," the car would sputter and stall. "Shit!" my mother exclaimed as we began rolling back down the hill.

Mom was a great organizer. She'd say that she *had* to be. She was a wife and the mother of seven girls. Mom called her method "overlapping," better known now as "multitasking." So as she made breakfast for her girls each morning, she'd overlap by exercising at the same time.

My mom's exercise uniform was as follows: hair in rollers from the night before, a sensible and pointy white brassiere, white cotton "granny" panties, nylons rolled down to form a "donut" at each ankle and regulation white nurse shoes completing her ensemble. She'd turn on *The Jack LaLanne Show* and, after pushing the first two slices of bread down in the toaster, would do a lap or two through the rooms of our large house, rounding the corner from the dining room back through the pantry to the kitchen just in time to apply butter when the bread popped up. I liked to watch her slice bananas into each girl's bowl, all of them set out on the counter in a production line. I tried for all I was worth to mimic Mom's precision, only to have my slices land in an unsightly clump in the bowl. Her longer fingers moved with great speed and accuracy. She'd stand there singing the Chiquita banana jingle as she sliced, her pantied hips swinging back and forth in tempo with the tune. . . .

"I'm Chiquita banana and I'm here to say, my bananas are ripened in a special way. . . ."

My mom prepared neatly packed brown bag lunches for us, too.

They always contained representatives of all four food groups and each was labeled with a daughter's name in her perfect penmanship. Our uniforms were pressed, our shoes highly polished and beds neatly made. Even Daddy's boxer shorts were ironed on the mangle in the basement.

I ASKED HER much later in life why she never sat with me to read a story or just plain hold me and whisper, "I love you." She welled up and said, "Honey, I was showing you girls my love in those neatly packed lunches and sharply pressed uniforms! I was trying to give you all a clean and ordered world, a stable environment to develop in. I was too busy to relax!" I couldn't help wishing that she'd left the peanut butter smear on my face or the bed unmade once in a while and just slacked off to play. I was only six years old when my sister Francesca brought me a daily schedule that Mom had asked her to type up for me. My routine from rising till bedtime was outlined on a piece of red construction paper.

My sister Julie (two years my senior) and I shared a room during those years, a double bed as well. We got in trouble for giggling over *Sea Hunt,* a TV program starring Lloyd Bridges. He wore a skintight wet bathing suit in nearly every half-hour episode. We had no brothers and thus no way of knowing what that bulge in the front *was,* and we never confessed to my exasperated mother exactly *why* we were laughing when she'd come into our room to put an end to the ruckus. I got into bigger trouble imitating Father Kramer by parading with the bedspread draped over my shoulders and pausing at the doorway of the bedroom to proclaim to my congregation of one, "*Oremus!*" This is Latin for "Let us pray!"

* * *

I LOVED MY PATERNAL GRANDPA, Kyle, dearly. He had moved to Seattle shortly after my parents did in 1952. Dad purchased a boat for his father, an older, fifty-foot recreational trawler that became Grandpa's home. The *Beachcomber* was a homely but well-built vessel that my grandfather had tied up to a pier on Lake Union. He seemed content in his life on the water. My dad and I used to escape "the women at the house," leaving to spend time with Grandpa on the boat, watching *Big Time Wrestling* on his small, rabbit-eared black-and-white TV after a day of fishing and a spartan evening meal of fried Spam and canned pork and beans. I remember many a time walking up the hill from the lake with Grandpa, to a small corner grocery where he'd buy a square pint box of cherry–black walnut ice cream for us to share back at the boat. The crusty old man, with a constant three days' growth of beard and his ever-present fishing cap, would remove the bowie knife from its sheath at his waist (the same knife he used to scale fish) and chop the box in half, handing me my "bowl" with a spoon. I'd sit on the sill of the huge open window in the pilothouse area, and when Grandpa turned his back, I'd spit the walnuts over the edge and into the lake. Every time, he'd spin on a heel and squint his eyes at me . . . "Nan," he'd bellow. "You aren't spitting out the nuts, are you? They're the best part!" I'd solemnly swear that I was not.

Grandpa taught me how to row a boat. He'd tie the dinghy to the pier with about forty feet of slack on the rope and lift me down inside. Then he'd stand on the pier with his hands in his pockets and a cigar stub between his lips as I rowed in and out, in and out, till my small, exhausted arms couldn't pull to take one more stroke. I felt so accomplished; he told me that I was going to be a real sailor. His impact on my childhood was indelible.

IT MUST'VE BEEN MY MOM who decided the family needed some counseling; Dad would have never thought of consulting with an outsider, and besides, Mom acted only on her ideas—nobody else's. Whatever the exact genesis of the decision, we girls were loaded up in the car one evening after dinner and ended up sitting around a conference table in a psychologist's office.

Mom sat at one end. Dad followed suit, taking his place at the opposing end. My mom fought in any situation as if she held all the cards, a moral royal flush. Most people, family or otherwise, chose to fold their hands and not do battle with her: It was akin to playing with the deck stacked against you.

As Mom laid out her case for the counselor, detailing all perceived slights, infractions and sins of omission committed by my father, the woman leading the discussion broke in with "Mel? Can you tell us what you feel your position in the family is?" My dad paused, being reserved and uncomfortable with articulating emotion, and asked the counselor for a piece of paper and a pencil. "Let me draw you a picture," Daddy said. From my seat beside him, I saw Dad make a large circle, one that nearly covered the entire page. He then drew a large circle within the confines of the first, and within that circle six small ones. The largest circle represented "the family." The large circle within it signified my mother. And those six small circles within Mom's circle were my six sisters. He then drew a small circle outside the largest circle. This represented my father's perceived place in the family unit. Lastly, he drew another small circle that straddled the largest circle, half in and half out of the "family circle." This small circle symbolized me.

Mom sighed audibly when my father was explaining his graphic to the counselor. "That's not the way things *are, Mel*," my mother said in an exasperated tone. "Why, it's just plain silly of you to think that way!" I heard this rationale from my mom throughout my childhood and on into adulthood. If you explained to her that what she said or did hurt your feelings or that you held a different opinion from hers, you were told that it was "a silly emotion to have" or "a strange way to think." No feelings were valid unless, of course, they were my mother's. Counseling didn't last long when Mom realized the therapist wasn't unconditionally on her side. But soon, bigger things would influence her thinking.

ROME STARTED RATTLING traditional Catholics' cages when they introduced changes in Church liturgy via the Second Ecumenical Council of the Vatican (Vatican II) sessions beginning in 1962. I remember Mom talking with friends from St. Anne's Altar Society lamenting that it portended the "end of the world as we know it." At about the same time my father was toying with the thought of opening his own business, casting his secure position at Boeing aside and venturing out on his own. Mom heartily disapproved. He did it anyway, starting a business called Ideas, Inc. And so began Mom's series of novenas to various and sundry saints involved in hopeless causes, offering up these prayers toward reforming the waywardness of both the Holy Roman Catholic Church and my poor father in the bargain. She prayed fervently for a sign from heaven as to what to do.

In midsummer of 1965, Mom's friends through church, Harry and Martha Bradford, told her about a place they'd heard of in Canada that had formed in opposition to Rome's new edicts. They'd listened to a representative of this community speak at a gathering of concerned Catholics. The Bradfords arranged for Mom to meet with this man; the die was cast. Our lives would never be the same.

AN ODD LITTLE MAN garbed in the brown, coarse wool tunic of a monk stood on the other side of our massive mahogany front door one afternoon. Brother Gabriel was a sixty-plus-year-old transplant from Belgium, with a thick accent, a grizzled beard and Limburger breath. He was looking to raise money for the small community he belonged to in Canada, but instead he lit a zealot's fire under Mom's sensible cotton muumuu that prompted her to sell everything and move everyone to this radical isolated community in the middle of nowhere in Quebec, thus saving her children (and husband) from an uncertain future. She received her sign in answer to her prayers. For me, Saint Teresa of Avila expressed it best: "More tears have been shed over answered prayers than unanswered ones."

CHAPTER 2

Dangerous Waters/Out of This World and into the Abyss

BY EARLY SPRING of 1965, my oldest sister, Laura, was already married and had a little boy, and my sister Cyndy was on her own and had established a career, so they were exempted from Mom's life-altering clarion call. The two eldest remaining in the home, Francesca and Diane, were told what the plans were, but the youngest three, Julie, Michelle and I, were kept in the dark. And so we believed that Daddy was being offered a job in New York and that we were going to attend the World's Fair upon arrival.

On the 31st of October 1965, a family friend drove us to the train station in Vancouver, British Columbia. We boarded the Canadian National Railway and set off on a four-day trip across the ever-changing terrain of Canada. I was nine and walked alone through the many cars each day, opening the doors between them and being welcomed by the jarring clatter of steel wheels on the tracks beneath, then heading into the next elegantly appointed and insulated passenger car. I climbed the steps to the observation deck and sat in awe

of the Rocky Mountains' snowcapped peaks and the great wheat fields in Saskatchewan and beyond.

I don't know what I imagined would happen once we reached New York, but what *did* happen was the last thing I would've guessed. We arrived at Montreal's main train station after midnight, a light snow swirling in the frigid air. I held on to Daddy's hand. And then they came into view.

The three men looked like carbon copies of Brother Gabriel, brown robes billowing in the chilly late autumn wind, enormous strands of heavy rosary beads attached at their leather belts clattering at their approach. The tallest one spoke to my father in broken English, gesturing toward two cars parked off in the distance. My mother and four sisters piled into the station wagon that held the two other monks, and my father and I took seats in the sedan with the English-speaking brother. It would be a long drive, beyond the famous Montreal lights, and off into a dark, foreign clime. I held my daddy's hand.

After what seemed hours, we approached a small wooden cabin with a logging chain strung across the road in front of it. I heard our driver tell my father that we had arrived at the monastery, outside St. Jovite, a tiny town nestled in the low, rolling and ancient Laurentian Mountains, and that we would all finally be able to get some rest. Another monk came out of the small structure and, as he unhitched the chain that barred our way, gave a greeting I would come to know well in future months. He said, "*Vive Jesus et Marie!*" To which our guide responded, "*et St. Joseph!*" "Live for Jesus and Mary, and St. Joseph!"

The monastery's buildings were spare and far between—only a few standing structures dappled the cold and silent moonlit scene

before me. The conditions at the compound were rudimentary in the beginning: The main form of heating and cooking was wood, both furnace and stove. Our "toilet paper" consisted of cut-up squares of newspaper that were deposited in a bin next to the toilet once used. We got out of the cars and were escorted into what I'd later learn was the visitor's center.

Mere Germaine, the mother superior, greeted us and introduced us to another nun, Soeur Marie Gerard. Mere Germaine looked like a kindly older woman; her underling, on the other hand, exuded harshness, not charity. I asked Daddy when we were leaving for New York and told him that I didn't like it here, but he would only say that he'd tell me more in the morning. The youngest three girls, Julie, Michelle and I, were led off by Soeur Marie Gerard. I wasn't holding Daddy's hand anymore.

The monastery of *Les Apôtres de L'amour Infini,* "The Apostles of the Infinite Love," was a highly regimented place. It was a "simple" life there as well. There were no choices with which to muddle your mind; every moment was planned for you, from early morning till night's clanging bell, signaling *"le grande silence."* Your duties were handed out and you followed your superiors' edicts without question.

The children were separated into age categories, and you worked, ate and prayed with only those in your group. There was no contact with others there except when passing single file in a hallway, and then you were told to keep your eyes on your shoes, as looking up was considered being curious—a sinful defect. Needless to say, I was the sinful sort.

My younger sister, Michelle, was only five years old when we arrived. She was sent to a group called "Nazareth," where newborns to eight-year-olds were housed. I was sent to a section called "St. Germaine Cousin," named after a French saint, along with my eleven-year-old sister, Julie. At least I had a familiar face to ground me in this maelstrom; some vestige of days past to which I could cling, back when things were normal. My two older sisters were placed in the group called *Les Aspirantes,* "Those Who Aspire." Just what they were aspiring *to* escaped my nine-year-old imagination. Married couples lived in trailers on the property; some eventually separated and became nuns and brothers.

I woke that first morning to the clanging of a brass bell in my dormitory room. Soeur Marie Gerard stood in the center of two stark rows of metal bunk beds, her dark, heavy, knitted eyebrows furrowing as she bellowed the soon-to-be all too familiar mantra, "*Vive Jesus et Marie!*" All but my sister and I responded with "*et St. Joseph,*" sprung from their beds and began to smooth the covers on their thin mattresses.

I lay in my bed and watched as these girls, a dozen or so, formed a line, each in a billowing nightgown, a seemingly disembodied, short-cropped head attached to five yards of shapeless drab fabric, each girl holding a pitcher and waiting her turn to fill it with water from a communal sink. No one uttered a word. Not one face wore a smile; just blank, bleary-eyed stares.

The girl in the bunk adjacent to mine returned with water and filled her basin, situated on a stand between the sets of bunks. She wet her washcloth; then her arms disappeared into the expanse of coarse muslin cloth. This was how we washed ourselves. No un-clothed body part was ever to show; it was forbidden. I would come to know this girl as Renee. She was from Montreal and not the most welcoming person you'd ever meet. She was older than me, probably around twelve, and was short and stocky, with dark, heavy features and a large black hole of decay prominently displayed between her two upper front teeth. She began to dress. This feat was accomplished in the same manner as the sponge bath, beneath the nightgown and away from sinful and "curious" eyes.

In the early days of the founding of this group there were no uniforms for the girls, as there would be later on. It was a poor order, surviving solely on charitable donations from businesses and other concerns, and what people gave of their worldly goods when they came to stay at the monastery. Consequently, all of the girls' clothing was a mishmash of colors and styles. They were ill-fitting to the wearer and intentionally so. I can still picture the dress I'd arrived in the night before. It was gray, with red smocking at the yoke, very stylish. Mom had bought this dress for me downtown at Nordstrom's for the trip to New York and I loved it. I began to put it on and Soeur Marie Gerard snatched it from me, saying something I could not understand in French, but I did comprehend the meaning in her tone. The dress she handed me to wear was light cotton, long-sleeved, covered in daisies and fell nearly to my ankles. The following week I caught a glimpse of the gray dress I'd arrived in; a little girl from my younger sister's group was wearing it as they walked by. It fit her as badly as mine now fit me.

It was still dark outside as we were escorted by the "scowl in a habit" through hallways lit only by candlelight, then down a set of steps and to the right. This door opened into a small refectory, or what served as one. Inside, there were two long wooden tables and rows of mismatched chairs. Each girl quietly took her place behind a chair and Soeur Marie Gerard began to sing. The song had the quality of music you'd have heard in a Catholic church back in the days of the Latin Mass. It was a pretty melody, if rather somber, and made even more so by the uncertainty of my situation and my not understanding the words. Julie and I would learn French very quickly; speaking English was heavily frowned upon.

Two girls from each table were dispatched to retrieve food from the kitchen. The "entree" that morning and for all the mornings to come was a thin, oatmeal-like gruel, gray and lifeless. Torn chunks of bread arrayed on a platter were passed around our silent group, with a gravy boat of molasses following. The girls would pour a puddle of the gooey black syrup onto a plate and then dip the crusts in it. The "pièce de résistance" that morning was a bowl of fermented oranges. To this day, when I catch a waft of spoiled fruit, I instantly think of the monastery. The same feeling washes over me when I smell a pot of navy bean soup simmering.

After breakfast, we all put on coats and were taken outside. There were several out buildings on the property, some holding farm equipment, another for the goats, which were kept for their milk; a few hogs that were raised as meat for the visitors were held in the next shed to this, and a small building on the end stored the wood for fueling stove and furnace alike. Next to this building was an enormous pile of split wood that the boys had chopped.

Two bigger girls stood near the pile to expedite and all the others stood in a line. Each in her turn would be loaded up with pieces of wood to her nose and sent inside the shed. There we would neatly pile the wood against the back wall. When the wood rose to a level beyond our reach, one of the smaller girls would be hoisted atop to facilitate further stacking; I was the "hoistee" that first day. Months later a child would fall from the top and break her ankle.

My memory of the rest of that first day is somewhat of a blur now, but it would have followed the pattern of all the days and nights that would come after. They each entailed work and prayer, followed by more work and prayer. We went to Mass every day, twice in fact, but it was a far different service from the ones I'd attended in Seattle at St. Anne's parish. *Père Jean de la Trinitie,* "Father John of the Trinity," who was our "pope," proclaimed that God had spoken to him in a vision and that one of God's edicts was that nuns should become priests. Our morning Mass lasted well over an hour. Unless we were singing, we were on our knees, which quickly went from being uncomfortable to painful on the bare wood floors. The children there were allowed to accept the host (once consecrated, it became Our Lord's body and blood) in their hands, which was not the case "out in the world" in 1965. My sister Julie and I were the exceptions. We would have to go through the same ceremony as the others had to bless our hands. It would be performed by Father John when it was deemed that we were ready to receive this honor, and so we accepted Christ's body on our tongues for the time being.

The only time pew seats were used was during Father's lengthy sermons. On Good Friday that year, we knelt through nine rosaries, three recited in Latin, with a like number recited in both French and English, each recital of the rosary's prayers taking approximately twenty minutes to accomplish. I was caught leaning back against the pew to relieve my knees and Soeur Marie Gerard gave me a sharp poke from behind. She favored the most compliant in our group. I was prone to ask "Why?" too often for this nun's taste.

I spent my first weeks there thinking that any minute now, Daddy was going to walk into the room, grab Julie and me by the hands, give the nun in charge a piece of his mind and whisk us away to New York. It had all been only a bad dream. I implored God in every prayer to please see that I was good enough now to see my parents. I must have been a very sinful little girl, as it would be well over two months before I saw them again, and then the visit would be far from the reunion I'd imagined it would be. And the meeting might not have happened even then, had I not been tenacious.

On this particular day, a young nun came running down the hallway—running was not allowed but in this instance was forgiven—to announce that Father John was on his way. This was a rare honor; he did not often visit our living quarters. People scrambled this way and that, whispering excitedly and hurriedly picking up anything that was out of place. As he entered the room, all present formed a line to each side and fell to their knees; I followed suit.

Father John had a twinkle in his eye and a scraggly, unkempt auburn beard. I had seen him pick up a baby and coo at it and, from my far-off vantage point, noticed him stopping to pet one of the mongrel dogs that roamed the isolated property. As his brown robes laden with long rosary beads swished past me that day, I grabbed at his garment and implored him to let me see my mom and dad. He spoke broken English, but I knew that he had understood my message's import. Mother Superior was at his side and stiffened when she saw what I'd done. Looking at the opposite sex was forbidden. *Mon Dieu!* I'd *touched* the man.

He brought me up off my knees, used his coarse robe to brush away my tears and, with a pat on the head, said, "*À bientôt, chère petite fille, à bientôt; je te promets!*" Soon, dear little girl, soon; I promise you. The brown robe and beads disappeared around a corner, and taking a cue from the look on the face of Soeur Marie Gerard, my superior, I knew I was about to receive yet another testament to the fact that I was possessed by the spirit of Beelzebub, the prince of darkness; I was heading for hell in the express lane.

Soeur Marie Gerard even punished me unwittingly. She used some pretty interesting, if ineffective, backwoods cures. I developed a huge boil on the top of my head. She placed half an onion and horse liniment on it, then secured the remedy with a blue and white striped ski mask, which I was forced to wear day and night for more than a week. The waft of rancid onion made me an unpopular companion in both chapel and work duties. I must have been a sight. Luckily, there were no mirrors in the monastery.

ONE OF MY FREQUENT DUTIES became picking up trays from *la petite cuisine,* "the little kitchen," and carrying them up the stairs to the visitor's refectory, where prospective "inductees" were fed upon arrival. I left the tray outside the door and knocked, alerting the nun inside without being seen by the visitors. The edibles I was transporting were nothing like our daily fare. Fragrant meat dishes, covered to keep warm till presented; the fruits and vegetables served to the visitors were fresh and varied. There were often cheeses on the trays, accented by clusters of grapes and crackers to enjoy after their meal. Our diet consisted chiefly of thin oatmeal, bruised and rot-pared fruit, most often mealy textured apples or wrinkly skinned, atrophied oranges, root vegetables, soups and bread. There was goat's milk served on occasion, but I never touched the stuff. It smelled too much like what the goats left on the floor of their shed's stall. We also ate navy beans; lots of navy beans. My stomach growled on cue when catching a whiff of what I carried on the visitor's trays but would never consume.

Meat had not passed my lips since my travel on the Canadian National Railway. On the train, cakes were served with gooey frosting; there were eggs, sausages and toasted bread with butter melting atop to consume. There had been roast beef with fresh vegetables and hot baked rolls. These things and so much more became a haunting memory—I thought in quiet moments about what had been left behind.

I sometimes secreted food from the little kitchen in my deep pockets and saved it for later. Once my prize was a banana, and I wolfed it down in the toilet stall located just off our refectory. I flushed the peel, and the next day the monks had to be called to fix a clog in that very toilet. The girls in my group were questioned, and threatened with sure damnation if someone didn't reveal what she knew, but no one confessed. I was just a little girl, one who needed to control *something* in her life; stealing food was one way I could poke my captors in the eye, nourish my body and comfort myself in one bold act of defiance. If I was going to hell anyway, I might as well make the trip on a full stomach.

The kitchen that fed the community was called *la grande cuisine,* "the big kitchen," and I spent most of my daytime hours there, helping prepare the food, wash dishes or clean in general. I was small, and the industrial-sized pots used for soups were huge and deep, so I was often lifted inside armed with a stiff-wired brush and large serving spoon to scrape off remnants of burned-on soup, the dreaded navy bean. I learned to scrub well, for if it was not done to satisfaction, I was told that I had the devil in me and sent to a corner to pray on my knees.

We girls became master bread makers. The first time I had this duty, I innocently rolled up my long-sleeved blouse to prevent dirtying it. The girl adding the flour stopped, walked over to Soeur Marie Gerard and whispered in her ear. The "bushy eyebrows with unseen legs" strode to my position and whacked me on the head with a spoon. She threw a pair of *manchettes* on the table, told me that I was a sinful little fool and, as quickly as she'd come, marched off again. My companion showed me how to put them on. A *manchette* is a tubular piece of cotton fabric with an elastic band at each end. You slip it over the sleeve of your blouse to prevent it from getting dirty, thereby keeping clean and leaving your modesty intact at the same time. Yes, elbows, even lower arms, could cause impure thoughts, I was told.

Our usual schedule required us to be in bed by eight-thirty each night. Sometimes our sleep would be unceremoniously interrupted by the clanging brass bell at midnight, or later if necessary, when a truckload of donated food was brought in from Montreal by the monks. If a perishable load came in late at night, we would dress and race down to the kitchen to help. Once case upon case of strawberries were delivered in the wee hours of the morning, with perhaps only one or two left edible out of each quart basket. We'd remove these precious items so that these delicacies could be taken to the little kitchen's freezers to "fatten the calf" of the visitors' bellies. Another time we received numerous boxes of freezer-burned éclairs. Unfortunately, these little delights were used as a treat for good behavior every Sunday for months after their arrival. They tasted horrible. It was enough to make you want to sin just to get out of indulging in the reward.

Renee, the unfriendly girl from Montreal who bunked near me, once told me that we were going to have fried chicken for dinner. I was elated! All day while working I thought about eating it. The dinner bell was sounded and I eagerly waited in my chair. There it was as promised, golden brown and delectable. I couldn't believe my good fortune. I picked up my piece and took a big bite. Renee giggled with another girl down the line. It was fried, all right. But, it was *aubergine*, thick chunks of fried eggplant.

IT HAD BEEN about three weeks since my encounter with Father John and still no parents in sight, but that day I was to be reunited, albeit briefly, with a glimpse of one of my older sisters for the first time since arriving in Quebec. Initially, I didn't recognize her, as she so seamlessly blended in with the "flock" that passed my station, where I stood on a stool at a sink full of dirty dishes. The religious there, the nuns, wore what I still believe to be one of the most beautiful and colorful habits I've seen. The nuns at my grade school in Seattle had been more conventional, wearing the black garb and wimple of the Redemptorist sisters. The nuns of the Apostles of the Infinite Love wore three different-colored habits, according to their current state in the order.

There were three levels. Postulants, beginners in the order, wore a white gown with a black belt and simple black veil that fell to their waists. A novice was at the intermediary level, and she wore a white gown, belt and veil. A professed nun, one who'd taken her final vows as a bride of Christ and had received her sterling wedding band, wore a beautiful royal blue gown with belt to match, iridescent blue rosary beads hanging from the waist that tinkled when in motion, and a blue veil with simple white edging just at the forehead. It was a pretty picture to see a group of them walking, gowns swirling as they floated past. And so I stopped my duties to watch.

My eyes focused and there she was. My sister Francesca was wearing the gown of a novice. This group of sober-faced older girls was chanting the words to the Hail Mary in French as they strode by my position. I dropped my dishrag and ran to my sister, so happy to see someone from my family. I threw my arms around her legs, but she stiffened, not responding at all to my entreaty. The nun in charge of the group grabbed my collar and took me directly to Soeur Marie Gerard, muttering that I was a disrespectful girl, full of the devil.

It was not the last time I'd be informed that I was in league with Satan. Why, he seemed to follow me wherever I went, according to those in the know. Apparently, I even *slept* like a devil. I turned and squirmed in my sleep. I threw off my covers, and my nightgown sometimes moved precipitously up my legs. Soeur Marie Gerard pointed out that none of the other girls slept like I did. Their arms lay straight and unmoving at their sides under neatly smoothed bedclothes. The nun harped on my defects day after day. *"Quel est le problème avec vous!?"* What is wrong with you!? *"Vous êtes une fille mauvaise!"* You are an evil girl!

CHAPTER 3

Thrown Overboard/Unhappy Reunion

ONE SUNDAY AFTERNOON some two months after St. Jovite had become my home, I was sitting in what was termed *la salle de récréation*. We didn't have much free time at the monastery, but what time was allowed for relaxation was spent as a group in this place. Your recreational options were reading the Gospel in French, practicing cursive writing skills, playing hymns on one of a few plastic recorders available or tapping on the piano in the corner. No worldly music was allowed. Julie found this out the hard way while playing "The Blue Danube" from memory on the keyboard one evening.

We darned socks for the brothers, created brown, woolen religious scapulars or made cards, always to be adorned in a religious theme. The older girls and a few talented nuns sometimes occupied themselves in making beautiful silk vestments for the male priests to wear.

We also made the hosts used for communion. The large, heavy

press looked similar to an outsized waffle iron. Inside, the smooth, stainless steel surfaces were engraved with various religious symbols—a cross, a sacrificial lamb—that would leave an imprint on the host. We mixed flour and water in a bowl and poured a puddle on the heated griddle, then closed the handled lid and waited for the flour mixture that oozed from the pressure to congeal. We made a lot of hosts. I often munched on the crunchy scraps.

I sat that day making a card for my daddy, as if when I completed the card, surely I'd then be allowed to give it to him. My endeavor was interrupted by my superior, Soeur Marie Gerard, when she strode over to my table, informing my sister Julie and me that we were to follow her, and right away. Her favorite admonition was "*Dépêchez-vous, vers le haut, vous!*" Hurry up, you!

Julie and I walked swiftly to keep up with her pace, my heart quickening as we made a right turn toward the visitor's center area of the monastery. I looked at my sister and began to grin. I said a quick Hail Mary, directing any graces proffered by its recital toward Father John's immediate delivery to heaven's gates when he left the earth's embrace. He'd listened to a little girl's heart.

Soeur Marie Gerard threw open the door. My mother, father and little sister, Michelle, sat together on a long bench at the other end of the room, the five year-old in Mom's lap. I bolted from my jailer's side and ran for all I was worth into Daddy's arms, burying my head in his large shoulder.

Soeur Marie uttered a few pleasantries in my parents' direction and then turned to leave, quietly shutting the door behind her trail of whooshing skirts and rattling rosary beads.

My mother's first comment was regarding how well I looked. I found this observation ridiculous, as if I were talking with a stranger not acquainted with my current circumstance or to someone un-aware of how different my life had been only a few months prior. Anyone who knew me, who loved me, would have to know that I felt worse emotionally than ever before in my life and looked like a ragamuffin to boot.

Daddy took a different approach. He told me about what he did there every day. He chopped down trees with the brothers, split the logs into the pieces I carried to the shed, worked on the monastery's old trucks' engines and took occasional trips into Montreal for supplies. I told him that I worked in the laundry occasionally, but mostly in the kitchen, and that he'd probably eaten some of the soups I'd helped prepare. He responded that he had, and that I had become a good cook.

I grabbed his hand and told him that I was ready to leave now; that we should have Diane and Francesca brought to us and head off to New York right away. I asked if the World's Fair was still going on there. He stared at my mother and then said that he didn't know if it was, but that we weren't planning to go to New York anymore. I found out years later that he and Mom had had many arguments over whether they should lie to us about our destination and the purpose of the move. Mother was the manipulator, always was. Dad could be gruff, and was many times, but he never lied to me that I know of. There is security in knowing what you face, however hard that truth is.

Now that Daddy had done her dirty work and dropped the bomb, Mom took the floor. She informed us that we had a good life here, that we were lucky to have been saved from the world before the weight of sins brought it all to a hellish end; according to Father

John's visions, our sect would be saved by God from the cataclysm soon to befall all of mankind. Mom said that she needed to leave the monastery for a while to go back and sign the closing papers on the sale of the house in Seattle and get our affairs in order.

She started to weep a bit when she began to talk about selling for a mere fraction of their worth her marble-topped buffet, her Spanish-influenced heavy marble lamps and coffee table, the Queen Anne mahogany bedroom set and the four sets of rattan tables and chairs that bedecked our forty-foot sun porch overlooking the city. But it was all for the best, for our souls' sake, and with her angst released, Mom drifted into a more reflective tone of voice.

She stated that Francesca was quite happy here, that she had decided to give her life to God and that I should follow her lead. Francesca had made Mom very proud; if only I'd put my heart and soul into this opportunity, if only I wasn't so obstinate, if only I could be more like my sisters. Francesca didn't want to leave this place, her heaven, my prison. Someday, Mom told me, I too would feel the way Francesca did. Never, I thought, feeling so adrift and alone. Not in an eternity. Not in *ten* eternities.

I was frantic. "Why, Mom? Had I been a bad girl? I'll change." I promised with all my heart. Tears streamed down my face. Daddy hung his head and wouldn't return my gaze. Mother just sat silently, stroking Michelle's silky dark hair and staring at the wall opposite.

When all seemed lost, I did what I thought was the only option left for me. I threatened to run away. Julie began to cry. "Please, Nancy! Don't leave me here alone!" Mother's favorite line came next, "Look what you've done *now*! You've upset your sister!" She terminated the visit and informed me that I needed time to think, to accept this news, and left me with the comforting thought that she'd try to arrange for me to see my father again in her absence. Thanks, Mom. Love you, too.

Soeur Marie Gerard appeared as if on cue and pried me from my daddy's waist. He asked for a moment alone with me, and we went into a corner. "Nan, you have to be strong. This is hard for me, too. I'll come to see you when I can, when they let me, but your mother thinks this is what's best, and God help the person who stands between that woman and what she wants. Help me out here, will you?"

I'm drowning, and he wants me to throw him a lifeline? Children want love above all else, and I felt I was quickly losing any worth I had, any value to anyone, so I bravely sniffled a defeated nod, and hand in hand my father and I walked back to the others. Daddy's brusque manner back in Seattle was cover for a man who was never really king of his castle. There was another power behind the figure-head's throne, and she stood stoically by the door, patting me on the head as I walked past. I never even looked her in the eye.

We were in physical proximity to one another, but my family might as well have been on Neptune for all the good it did me. Perhaps it was even worse knowing they were all so close by and that I still couldn't touch them, I don't know.

This much I do know. As human beings we many times become numb to pain and fear and simply try to blot out the memory of whatever it is that is no longer available to us to draw upon for nurture and survival. We exist in a state of denial and simply get on with the mechanics of living, but at great cost. I felt unloved and unwanted, but I wouldn't allow myself to lose my spark as did other newcomers, who would go soon from bubbly child to speaking in hushed tones with dread about what was in store for the sinners outside the compound. God's righteous arm was heavy, and soon no pleading for mercy from His Blessed Mother, Our Heavenly Mother, would be able to forestall the horrific punishment to be meted out to these earthly transgressors.

My rebellions during that time were small ones, but in the mind of a little girl, these infractions helped me hold on to my sense of individuality. I remember intentionally throwing fresh goat's milk down the drain instead of refrigerating it after a meal, within eyeshot of one of the chief tattletales of our group and then standing like George Armstrong Custer with clenched fists awaiting the arrival of Soeur Marie Gerard and the final arrow through my heart. She wasn't going to mold me into an obedient little automaton. I wanted to get out of that place and back to the sinners who were, at present at least, having a much easier go of it.

I waited for a second *parler*, as it was called, a "talk," with my dad to be arranged. It never came. My older sister Julie, who bunked above me, would whisper down to me at night that she thought perhaps we'd "see Dad tomorrow." I'd mutter back a "yeah," but I didn't hold out much hope. My childhood in Seattle had become a dream and this nightmare was the reality. The days and nights passed much the same as the ones before, working hard, praying harder and making cards for my father that would never be delivered.

One day after our kitchen duties were finished, we went outside for exercise. Our calisthenics sessions entailed reciting the rosary as we walked about the grounds in single file. It was early spring now, and though there was still some snow on the ground, no coats were required. I remember feeling happy that the snow was melting and something other than piles of the dirt-choked stuff filled my view.

The woods surrounding the compound were lovely, dense and deep green with pines. Weather permitting, as we fingered our beads our group was led to a couple of small, spare chapels built along trails in the woods. We'd enter, kneel on the rough wood floor to pray before a statue of the Blessed Mother or St. Joseph and then leave, continuing our meandering parade route back to the main building to resume our chores.

While returning that day, I heard a commotion off in the distance. We were told to avert our eyes, these were *men* involved in the fuss ahead of us after all, and curiosity was a sin. Of course, I looked over as we approached the site of the disturbance and saw several monks standing in a circle, mumbling to one another, with a couple of young boys sporting crew cuts off to the side. As we got even closer, I could hear a dog yelping, and soon realized it was a favorite of mine that was causing this concern. He was a larger animal named *Chien*, or "Dog," with a ratty black coat, a nipped left ear, and a tail that always broadcast his happiness to see me. I sometimes carried a slop bucket outside for the hogs after a meal, and if I saw him, I would stop and let him lap out of my bucket before I moved on.

Now he lay there on his side, one monk crouched over the animal with pliers in his hand. The dog's mouth seemed full of something spiny. I would find out later that he'd chased a porcupine and been shot full of quills for his exuberant curiosity: still more evidence that inquisitiveness held dire consequences for all of us. The monk was having no success in removing the barbs from the dog's mouth and snout, and soon another of the monks scurried off into an out building, returning moments later and handing something shiny and gray to the monk with the pliers. I heard a loud bang, and without a whimper, my friend lay still and silent on the ground, red beginning to circle his head on the white funereal blanket of snow beneath. Soeur Marie Gerard's response to this horrific display was to yell at us to move along.

We'd had a special treat one spring day, the first and last during my time there: We packed a lunch of peanut butter, molasses and bread ends and trekked up the enormous hill beyond the chain at the compound's entrance. The buildings looked so obscure and non-threatening from my lofty vantage point. Wildflowers carpeted the sprawling hillside. It was hot outside that day. We were allowed to remove the little white head scarves that covered our hair and dip them in the creek to cool off our heads. We were even permitted to take off our long woolen stockings and wiggle our toes in the gurgling waters. Some girls sat playing their instruments while others sang hymns after our meal.

I was dead tired after walking back down the incline. The sun was sinking behind the treetops in the late-spring sky. When we got back inside our quarters, a nun motioned to Soeur Marie Gerard, and as I was undressing underneath my nightgown my superior informed me that I was not to go to chapel with the other girls in the morning. She would be taking my sister Julie and me *elsewhere*. I lay in my bunk and tried to figure out where this nasty person would be escorting us and why. If I'd been singled out, I would have imagined that she'd seen me lift my gown above calf level at the river or perhaps heard me laugh too loud for her liking on that unusually festive day, but my sister Julie had been included, so I was stumped.

Julie and I waited for what seemed forever after the others had left for chapel the next morning. Soeur Marie Gerard was busy riding roughshod over the other girls at prayer, and so another nun was dispatched to take us to meet our fate. This nun was in her mid-twenties and had a cheerful disposition. She'd even cast me a quick smile one day when I was being sequestered for yet another horror I was guilty of committing there at the monastery. More than once I'd wondered why *she* couldn't be left in charge of the children. We were again being led to the visitor's area.

And there they were: Mom, holding Michelle, Dad, and my two older sisters Diane and Francesca. It had been months since the last time I'd seen my parents, and Daddy looked so different to me. He'd lost weight and was now sporting an auburn beard. I'd never seen my dad with facial hair before. I sat on his lap and ran my fingers through it. After a moment or two of small talk, Mom informed us that she'd been back in the compound for three weeks already and living in a trailer on the property with Dad. In hushed tones, she told us that she had decided that this place was not all that she'd expected or been told it would be and that we would soon be leaving. Francesca had decided to stay despite the rest of the family's departure, she said; my sister had embraced this new life and Mom seemed proud of her decision.

I started shrieking in joy and dancing around the room. I told Mom that I couldn't wait to see my friends and Grandpa Kyle again. My excitement was subdued somewhat by the revelation that we would not be going back to Seattle, but to Grand Rapids, Michigan, where my mom's relatives lived. Daddy had no job waiting for him back in Seattle, our house had been sold, and so, in Mom's words, there was "nothing there to go back *to*." Her brothers would take us into their homes till Dad could find a new job. Perhaps we'd have to split up the family between two households at first, her relatives' homes weren't huge, but it would all be temporary.

My father looked drained, pretty much emotionless as I looked up at him from his lap. I'd always thought of my father as strong, Herculean. He wasn't tall, only five-foot-six, but he had been stocky and muscular. My dad could do anything. He could handle a boat in choppy seas in the Strait of Juan de Fuca or, camping on a mountainside, make a tent for us out of a tarp fastened with rope to tree trunks, with pine boughs scattered beneath us to cushion our bodies as we slept. Dad taught me how to scale and gut a fish when I was four years old at Echo Lake. He made the youngest girls a child's-scale stove and refrigerator out of wood, painting it pink for Christmas one year. He could fix bikes and old cars and replace windowpanes and trim holly hedges. I didn't see the man of my memory looking back down at me that late-spring morning. This man looked resigned; no, it was defeat I saw in his ocean blue eyes.

Mom must've had reservations about monastic life *before* she returned to the compound, as she was now talking about retrieving some furniture and household goods that she had stored in Seattle. Good thing they didn't sell, she now proclaimed, almost as if she'd done a *good thing* by being irresolute. We'd make a fresh start in Grand Rapids. Daddy would find a job, no problem there, Mom went on. I'd like my uncle David, her younger brother, and his wife, Jill. They had two kids about my age; it would be a perfect fit. They had a spare bedroom that Julie and I could double up in. Uncle Dan and his wife, Dana, would help out if necessary as well. Mom had driven our old 1956 Ford from Seattle, and so she would depart from the monastery directly for Seattle, and Daddy would take the four remaining children with him on the train to Grand Rapids. Regardless of the uncertainty we were facing, I was getting out of this place, and that was all that mattered to me at the time.

Somehow the gray dress I'd been wearing the night of our arrival in early November of 1965 was located, and so, with the sun just beginning to creep over the horizon, I silently dressed under my billowy nightgown for what I thought was the last time, in the spring of 1966. There were no tearful farewells as we made our departure early the next morning. My sister Francesca wasn't even present. Mom was blubbering as she spoke with the order's superior, Mère Germaine near the exit of the visitor's area, saying something about coming back someday; but not knowing what her precise reasoning was for not staying at present, I could never imagine a situation where any of us would come back to this place, someday or *any* day.

I watched as the monks who had driven me, my dad and three sisters to the train station that day slowly became tiny brown, insignificant specks outside the train's window as we pulled out of the depot. We were chugging away from our confinement and off to a new life out in the world. Renee, the French Canadian girl who'd been my chief irritant among the group, had warned me as I was leaving that my whole family, which had been favored by God in being chosen out of millions to be saved from the coming holocaust, would now perish alongside all the other *cochons,* "pigs." I told Renee that I was not going to perish *with* them, but was going to *eat* one as soon as possible.

CHAPTER 4

A Fish Out of Water/Landlocked in the Midwest

JULIE AND I were planted at Uncle David's, and his wife, Jill, made no attempt to disguise her contempt for our intrusion. Their two kids were spoiled, in my estimation, and often tattled on Julie and me for things we didn't do. They loved to get their mother riled up enough to tell us how much of an imposition we were on her family life and just how unappreciative we were as guests in her home. "You should act more grateful! You could be out on the streets."

Daddy kept coming "home" from his job searches saying that he'd been told he was overqualified. You could see how devastated he was. At forty-six years old, he had earned a good living all his adult life, and now he couldn't support his family. He'd sit just staring off into space, resting in an easy chair in his suit with his tie loosened.

It had been weeks since our arrival in Michigan, and Mom was still gone on her mission to retrieve the few belongings that remained to supply our fresh start. She ended up staying in Seattle considerably longer than expected, rationalizing that she wouldn't be able to see Laura, son-in-law Peter and her little grandson, Eric, again for a long, long time.

Meanwhile, Dad decided that we should all move in with my uncle Dan and aunt Dana, who were already housing Diane and Michelle. No doubt, he sensed my uncle David's wife's attitude; she wasn't attempting to hide her feelings much, even in my dad's presence. With the addition of the three of us, it was a full house at Uncle Dan's, to put it mildly. The couple made space for us to sleep in a spare bedroom and in their finished basement. It was heaven compared to dormitory life at the monastery. No one was telling me that I "slept like a devil." And Aunt Dana was a fairy godmother. She treated us well, all of us. She was fair, not stern or shrieking over trivialities. Uncle Dan was a gentle man and a dedicated worker who toiled long hours each week as a soft drink salesman in Grand Rapids. Dan and Dana had three little ones of their own, two boys and a girl, so for them to open up their home to all of us was more than a small sacrifice.

I remember a birthday package that was delivered to my uncle's house for me that year, from my mom in Seattle. I received it in early June, a little late, but so welcomed by me. I sat on my bed alone and opened the box. There were several gifts inside. Some were labeled for me and others for my cousin who celebrated her birthday only a few days before mine in May. She and I were only one year apart in age. My gifts were pairs of lacy anklets and pretty pairs of panties. I then began to open my cousin's gifts as well. Hers were an exact duplicate of mine. I decided that I wasn't going to share my moment and my mom with a relative just then. I threw away the birthday card sent to my cousin and put her gifts along with mine in my top dresser drawer.

Dad then had what was referred to back in 1966 as a nervous breakdown. It happened just after Mom got back from her trip to Seattle. He got in the black Volkswagen Beetle he'd purchased for his job search after we arrived in Grand Rapids and left without a word to us kids, not returning for more than nine months; Dad's body would be present from then on, but his old spirit was absent. He would never be the same again.

Mom was forced to find work in Dad's absence. She'd been a telephone operator before she'd married, and she was hired at Michigan Bell. She worked crazy hours in those early years, some split shifts, too, a few hours in the morning and then again late afternoon into the evening. My older sister Diane helped with the kids, in addition to attending high school and working a shift at the Big Boy restaurant on Plainfield Avenue. Her teenage years were far from carefree.

We moved into a two-bedroom house in a lower middle-class area of town. It was cramped and badly in need of repair. Our belongings arrived in Grand Rapids from Seattle on a Mayflower truck one day. It was quite the feat getting those outsized pieces of furniture intended for far more spacious rooms up the cramped stairs and into the two small bedrooms. Once they were installed, there was barely room to walk between the double beds. We had to broom sweep the threadbare gray carpet in the living room. Mom had sold our vacuum cleaner.

I had only two dresses to wear both in fifth and sixth grades. My family's "fresh start" in Grand Rapids was so foreign to me, vastly different from the lifestyle and access to basic necessities that we'd taken for granted in our lives on Kinnear Place. We had no washing machine anymore, only a weekly jaunt to the Laundromat, which, at age ten, was my job on Saturdays, so during the week I washed out a dress at night to wear the next day. I was the target of a lot of snide remarks at school regarding my limited apparel as I entered the fifth grade in the fall of 1966.

And the nine-year-old child who'd gone into the monastery in Quebec with a perfectly normal and fit body was now overeating. I had developed a habit of sneaking food at the monastery and it didn't stop. It was the only thing I could control and I remember feeling comforted by it. But my habit was beginning to show. When I was weighed by the school nurse in sixth grade, she shouted out the number registered on the scale within earshot of my classmates: 121 pounds. The digits seemed to reverberate against the walls.

The boys tormented me the most. There was a girl in my class named Gayle who was far larger than I was and no one mocked her, they just left her alone. It was as if Gayle were invisible. Unlike me, she kept to herself. Sometimes my sisters and I would come home from school for lunch when Mom was there between shifts at Michigan Bell. I was often given the "diet plate" if the menu that day was deemed "unhealthy" for someone in my condition. I remember feeling left out, different from the others, somehow less worthy. I'd sit there eating my broiled lean hamburger patty with mustard, a dollop of cottage cheese and carrot sticks, while everyone else enjoyed cheeseburgers on kaiser rolls, dripping with ketchup and mayo and crispy homemade fries. I wasn't allowed to eat what I wanted when Mom was around, but I made up for her dietary restrictions by furtively grabbing snacks or leftovers out of the fridge and finding a spot where I could wolf them down in private.

Mom always bought donuts for the family to enjoy on lazy Sunday mornings. She bought the exact number needed for each of us to have two. One Sunday morning, I was standing at the refrigerator door in the pantry off the kitchen, looking for the milk, when from behind me, I heard my mother call out, "Hey, Nancy . . . did you eat an extra donut?" I was incensed by her accusation. "Why am I always the one blamed for everything in this house? Why don't you ask Michelle or Julie, Mother?" I slammed the fridge door and walked out into the kitchen to face my accuser directly, proclaiming my innocence in this donut debacle. As I ranted on about the injustices I bore on a regular basis, Mom's demeanor was changing. She began to grin, and this infuriated me further. "What's so funny, Mother?" She told me to go take a peek at my face in the bathroom mirror.

For all my rabid and heartfelt protestations of innocence, there before my eyes was some of the worst circumstantial evidence: My mouth was ringed by a dusting of confectioner's sugar from the donut I had snuck only moments before.

I was a mouthy kid. I was noncompliant sometimes and argued too much for Mom's liking. My sister Diane was left in charge while Mom worked, and my sixteen-year-old sister was ill-equipped to handle my obstinacy. And my foul behavior seemed to wear off on my sisters Julie and Michelle; everything they did that was out of line, I taught them to do. Why, I was a regular Bolshevik, to hear Mom tell it. She was going to put an end to this chaos and now. Something must be gravely wrong with me: I was sent to a shrink. I went alone week after week to talk with this odd man. He was a small, balding guy, with heavy black-framed glasses and a disconcerting habit of rubbing his chin as he spoke. I didn't *want* to talk with him; Mom wanted me to. He'd pull out the chessboard and we'd play game after game during our hours of "therapy." I often beat him, not only at the game of chess, but at his own game, that of exploring the deep caverns of the human mind. He'd ask how I felt about my "daddy" being gone, I'd casually respond, with my eyes cast to the chessboard to determine whether my bishop would be in danger if I moved it nearer my opponent's rook, "I think that . . . he's gone." It was none of his business what I thought about *anything*.

After eight or nine sessions our time together came to an abrupt end, and Mom informed me that she had wasted eighty dollars a session on something that didn't work. "We could've used that money for so many other things, Nancy!"

"Well, then, you should have," I replied.

My maternal grandmother lived on the northeast side of Grand Rapids. She'd been partially crippled in a car accident many years before, at forty-nine years of age. The motor control of her legs had been damaged, and as a result, Grandma couldn't lift her feet. She ambulated with the assistance of a walker. You could always hear my grandma coming; the soles of her sensible black lace-up shoes made a distinctive scraping sound as they skated over the old linoleum floor in her rented house at the corner of Ann and Coit N.E. She wasn't a very demonstrative person, but she wasn't mean either; Grandma just wasn't into light conversation. She seemed always worried about some catastrophe that could be looming just around the next bend.

flooring in the kitchen and bathroom and rebuilt the structure of the back porch, and the family's joint effort paid off after several weeks. Each daughter had her own bedroom; I relished the privacy and set out to decorate my personal sanctuary in my own style, adding candles and incense and rock 'n' roll posters to hang on the walls.

My father was a broken man; he never fully recovered from the events of the last few years and so didn't hold down jobs for long; finally, he simply quit trying. When Dad wasn't occupied in fulfilling the duties of one of Mom's legendary "lists," I recall him many times just lying on the couch and watching the news, with a far-off look in his eyes. He escaped from the house when he could, securing his green rowboat to the top of the car and taking off to an area lake to go bass fishing. He was featured in an article on the front page of the Outdoors section in the *Grand Rapids Press,* proudly displaying his "catch of the day," the photo showcasing Dad standing at the back of our vehicle with six plump bass lying in a neat row on the closed trunk.

He eventually began volunteering his services with the Michigan Department of Natural Resources. His chemical engineering background made him invaluable in assisting in the cleanup of various polluted lakes in our region. Dad was instrumental in bringing the waters of Reeds Lake in East Grand Rapids back to life from its abysmal condition due to the practice of dumping in decades prior. The accolades given my father by those who worked with him vexed my mother to no end. He had better things to do, according to her.

With her raises at work due to seniority, Mom was making decent wages at the phone company and had good insurance coverage, and so we lived a fairly decent life, monetarily at least. You could tell that my mom felt superior to my father; she never *said* that he had fallen short by not holding down a highly paid job as he had years before, but it was in the way she complained about how tired she was every night after work, or when she'd inform him that he couldn't have the money he needed for some project, as "my income just won't allow for it, Mel!"

It was Mom's decision to move the family across the continent to relocate in a religious cult, dislodging all of us from a stable life in Seattle, but she managed to blame my father. She wasn't able to accept her part in the damaging fiasco we'd all suffered through. Mom was painfully aware that I didn't buy her revisionist history. I was about to pay the price for not toeing the company line; the family's CEO was contemplating "letting me go."

CHAPTER 5

Hook, Line and Sinker/Swimming with the Sharks

MOM HAD NEVER LOST TOUCH with the hierarchy at St. Jovite. Letters arrived periodically from my sister who'd stayed behind in Quebec; even a few phone calls were exchanged. Mom sent Francesca bras and "sturdy shoes" once a year. She sometimes taped a note inside the shoe's upper so my sister could read a piece of mail without it being censored.

It was rare for members at the compound to travel back to their family home. Contact with family members who hadn't approved of the member's decision to enter the community initially, or even more so those who had departed from the monastery's embrace, were considered particularly dangerous to remain involved with. These family members were thought to have "lost their faith" or to be "possessed of an evil spirit."

During my stay from November of 1965 through May of 1966, family members, ranging from small children to runaway spouses, had been hidden in the woods on the secluded property to avoid either the authorities armed with a warrant, in the case of minors, or estranged family members properly worried about a relative staying at the monastery.

What was about to unfold in my case took me completely by surprise. I was living in Grand Rapids, Michigan, hundreds of miles and nearly five years away from the hateful grasp of Soeur Marie Gerard and living the life of an average fourteen-year-old girl, brimming with feelings of angst, insecurity, youthful bravado and rebellion. So far, my most outrageous revolt had taken the form of coming downstairs one day wearing a translucent vintage blouse I'd found at the Salvation Army Thrift Store and, visible underneath, a brassiere emblazoned with the stars and stripes of the American flag. I'd bought it with babysitting money earned by watching my aunt's children at fifty cents per hour. Mom made me march right back upstairs and remove the symbol of insurrection. "Why can't you dress normally like your sisters?"

One day after school it was announced that Francesca was coming home for a visit. I was elated. She had often been my protector who had been there to stand up for me when I got into trouble, take the blame at times or at least plead my case against the harshest judgment about to be meted out by Mom. Francesca was many years my senior, and unlike my other three oldest sisters, who didn't take much notice of me due to our age difference, Francesca took an active interest in my welfare. I felt close to her; I adored her.

It was February of 1971. Francesca would spend nearly a week with the family. Aunts and uncles came to visit; we held a big dinner in her honor. We played board games together. Mom made delicious homemade pies and cakes, rolling them out into the dining room on the long three-tiered maple wood cart she'd "saved" from storage in

Seattle. I had to be ushered off to bed each night of Francesca's visit, so I'd be rested for school the next morning.

I woke up and came downstairs late one night to use the bathroom and found Mom and Francesca discussing something at the dining room table. Mom asked me what I was doing out of bed. I told her and she said to hurry up and get back to my room. I could hear their whispered tones as I walked back up the stairs to my bedroom, but I didn't think another thing of it till months later.

My sister would be leaving in two days and I was feeling glum. Once the dinner dishes were cleared from the table that evening, Mom asked me to come and sit with her and Francesca to talk. Mom told me she knew how much I missed my sister and that they thought it would be nice if I could spend some more time with her. She asked, "Would you like to take a vacation for a couple of weeks and stay with your sister, Nancy?" Francesca had obligations back at the monastery that couldn't wait; I was doing well in school, and so a two-week interruption wouldn't cause havoc with my education.

I jumped at the chance! I could see my sister every day, get out of two weeks of school and could show the others living in that drab place just how cool I was, how I dressed, how I wore my hair, not cut short and covered with a scarf, tell them about the groovy music I listened to, show them that the world hadn't ended, nor had I gone to hell as predicted, not yet anyway. They were missing a lot by being shut away in that tomb, and I wanted to mete out a little retribution.

My younger sister, Michelle, would be making the return visit, too, I was told. She was ten years old at the time. So, in late February of 1971, after I'd packed up all my worldly fourteen-year-old's treasures in a duffel bag, the three of us left the driveway of my family's home and headed out on our great adventure. I didn't know Mom hadn't bought Michelle and me a round-trip ticket.

There had been major changes structurally to the monastery in the years since I'd been there. There were more buildings, bigger buildings, and better-constructed buildings. It was still a very spartan scene, but the monks had been working hard since I'd left in 1966. It no longer appeared to be a transitional place, but struck me with its feeling of permanence. My sister was now the nun in charge of the aspirants. These were the fourteen- to eighteen-year-old girls who were anticipating giving their lives to God. *That* selfless endeavor was the furthest thing from my mind, but when my sister suggested that if I wanted to be with her as much as possible I should just bunk with the girls in her group, I agreed that it made perfect sense. Michelle was told that she'd be staying in another group of younger girls, but that we two would be seeing each other regularly during our stay. The plan was for Mom to travel to the monastery in two weeks to retrieve Michelle and me. She would ask for time off at Michigan Bell. She'd never been denied vacation time before. Mom would be there. She had promised she would.

The first thing to go was my jeans. I was told they distracted the others in the group. OK, I could deal with wearing one of their uniforms. It would only be for a couple of weeks.

The sleeveless jumpers covered you to just below mid-calf, in whatever dark, neutral color of fabric had been donated at the time they were made, and were formless from the shoulder to the waist, then pleated in a full skirt beyond that point. You weren't supposed to be showing off your "form." The long-sleeved blouse was buttoned to the throat and at the wrist. I was supposed to wear a T-shirt underneath my brassiere, all the other girls did, but in their ridiculous attempt to avoid "ever seeing a piece of naked skin" the authorities there had gone beyond what I would accept at the time. I refused to wear the T-shirt. We wore heavy long stockings underneath the jumper in the heat and cold alike. Our heads were covered with a white scarf tied at the nape of the neck. I was the only one in the group whose scarf did not lie flat in the back. I pulled my long hair into a tightly wound bun. All the others had close-cropped hair. I declined when a haircut was offered.

A couple of days later I was told that my books and jewelry would be stored for me, so nothing would come up missing. Odd. There was thievery in the monastery? It seemed that new devils had come to replace the evil minions that left with me years before. Next, I was informed that singing my rock 'n' roll songs was disturbing and I should sing a nice hymn.

I was beginning to get nervous. It had been more than a week and there was no sign of my sister Michelle. I couldn't stop thinking I'd been abandoned again. Then Francesca told me Mom was having difficulty arranging for time off during the week we'd planned on.

There was a new girl in our group; she and the rest of her family had come to the monastery the day after Michelle and I arrived for our vacation. She had been a cheerleader back in Ohio, a lively and vivacious fifteen-year-old named Carol. In just under three weeks' time, she'd been transformed before my eyes from a spirited teenager into a subdued and restrained young adult. She was "aspiring," all right, and whatever it was she was hoping for, Carol was on the fast track to achieving her goal. This drastic change so disturbed me that I took her aside one day to investigate my unsettling observations.

I asked if she'd forgotten all the stories she'd told me when we first met. "Remember, Carol? Remember how much you loved practicing your routines and performing at football games? Remember telling me when you first came how much you missed your friends already?" I told Carol that if I was forced to stay there now, I'd run away. Nothing and no one could hold me in that hopeless place!

Her response stunned me. "What is there to go back to, Nancy? My friends, my home, all the places I once thought I'd travel to in my lifetime will be incinerated soon! My family was blessed by escaping God's judgment; we will all be safe in this holy place! Father John has promised that we will survive on the Holy Eucharist if our food supply runs out! Please stay, Nancy! I love you! I don't want you to die out in the world!"

Holy smoke, I thought. This girl was a goner. I stood and left Carol to her thoughts. It would occur to me later in life that so much of an outcome is dependent on personality. If people don't have a bit of defiance in them when tested in an emotion-numbing situation, their minds seem to take the path of least resistance and just go with the flow, accepting what comes as its new reality.

My sister Francesca called me out of the kitchen one afternoon and took me into our empty refectory. It had been a month since my vacation had commenced. She started on a happy note; what she offered seemed at least to make *her* happy. "Mom wrote to me again, Nancy. She is still not able to get any time off work. We think it would be a good idea if you and Michelle just stayed till the end of June and finished your school year here. Otherwise, with the time you've already been absent," she continued, "you may have to repeat the ninth grade." The thought of walking down the halls of junior high school next year with the half-wit eighth graders, my underlings, *did* give me pause; I was a good student. I didn't want to repeat a grade, but I would rather do *that* than stay here. I would've rather had bamboo thrust under my fingernails.

Suddenly, I didn't feel like I was on vacation anymore. I felt frantic, but tried to maintain a façade of control. I held all the cards, right? This was *my* decision. I told Francesca that I wasn't interested in her option and that I would fall behind anyway because there was no real schooling at the monastery. We honed our French skills by reading the Gospel and took fifth-grade math, but beyond that, nothing was offered by way of instruction. My sister argued that I would get a good education. I said thanks, but no thanks. "I need to go home, the sooner the better."

"I hoped you would've seen the logic in our plan, Nancy," she responded. "I'm afraid you really don't have any other option."

Well, there it was: the specter that I'd been trying to veil. The curtain had been pulled back to expose its obscene, leering form. *You've been duped again; how stupid can you get, Nancy?*

I lashed out at my sister. "We *do* love you, Nancy," Francesca pleaded. "We know what's best for you! Mom wants to save you and Michelle from the world's dangers before they consume your souls!"

I know now that Francesca really *did* think she was doing what was best for me. She truly believed in the mission of *Les Apôtres de L'amour Infini*. And there were those there who felt called by God to join that community. I am sure that they had the best of spiritual intentions in the decision they made. But no one can *force* someone else to choose that kind of life. It has to be a vocation, something you know in your heart is what God has in mind for you. God hadn't delivered any such message to me. Francesca told me I could go for a walk in the woods till I calmed down. I had no intention of calming down. I grabbed my coat and headed outdoors.

There was a large, dark and oddly shaped boulder deep in the woods that was the supposed site of a horrible vision received by Father John in one of his "ecstasies," which he apparently had with some frequency. In this particular supernatural event, Satan stood atop this boulder and tormented the priest both physically and spiritually, attempting to discourage him in his "end of times" holy mission from God. After this mystical experience, Father John preached to the community about being strong and resolute, for the devil could hear us; he watched us and knew which of us he could use to undermine the others of the flock. Whenever my group would pray the rosary in the woods, the person leading would always give this unholy stone wide berth; no one in their right mind would want to mess with the father of all lies!

I gravitated toward "Devil's Rock" that unhappy day; in fact, upon arriving at the site, I scrambled up on top of it and began to sing. It was a Grand Funk Railroad tune, popular at the time called, "Closer to Home"; I was moaning the lyrics through sobs. The tears just kept coming. I think I was singing so I wouldn't have to process my new life-altering information. A few minutes later I detected a faint, dull sound, a drone, really. I looked over my shoulder, and off in the distance, coming up the path, were my companions, walking in single file. The girls were singing, just like I had been. I heard, "*Je vous salut, Marie, pleine de grâce, le seigneur est avec vous . . .*" These were the opening words of the Hail Mary.

I sat rooted to the spot as the line approached, watching the leader veering sharply off about thirty feet from my position. Some of the girls turned their heads to look, befuddled by the sight of me atop Satan's perch. I felt suddenly consumed by a terrible rage-filled indignation, so much so that words from another song that mirrored my feeling came roaring out of me as the girls drifted from sight: *"When the rain comes, they hide their heads . . . they might as well be dead."*

Dinner had already been served by the time I finally went back inside; the dishes had been washed and put away. I sat alone on my bed and stared into space as others milled about me, silently engaged in myriad duties. There were no tears left; I'd used them all up. The brass bell rang to gather us for evening Mass. I went through the motions, falling into exhausted sleep soon after. I rose with the others the next morning, went to Mass in the chapel, ate breakfast and performed my duties, but I didn't talk to anyone for days.

I MAY NOT HAVE BEEN TALKING, but I was definitely thinking. I was planning my escape. It was late March in Quebec, officially spring, according to the calendar, but it was icy cold outside. I'd brought my gray wool "maxi-coat" with me from Grand Rapids and was sure that its heavy material would insulate me from the frigid winds and snowy fields as I walked my way out of my involuntary servitude. I could take extra pairs of woolen stockings with me and change into them as the pair I was wearing got wet. I had mittens. I had the striped knit beret I'd worn when I'd arrived a month before.

What about food? Lord, this would be an obstacle. We ate potatoes, carrots, oatmeal, bean soup, bread and the like. All these things were bulky, hardly portable. Perhaps I could steal the sleeves of crackers that were used for the visitors' lunches; those would have shelf life. Maybe, if I was careful, I could grab a wedge of cheese from the *petite cuisine*'s refrigerator and stuff it in the pocket of my jumper. Cheese would hold up for a few days, especially in this weather. But how would I carry away all the treasures I'd brought with me to the compound?

I had stuffed several favorite T-shirts, three pairs of Levi's, my favorite pair of overalls, the ones with the peace symbol patch sewn on the butt, into the duffel bag while excitedly packing for this vacation. My copy of *Wuthering Heights* and an anthology of Edgar Allan Poe stories had been confiscated. I didn't know where they were. It only made me angrier to think that I'd have to leave these pieces of myself behind; it also made me more resolute.

How would I sneak out of the dormitory late at night without being detected? It was quiet as a tomb in there at midnight, and some of those in my group would love nothing better than to be instrumental in collaring anyone who would try and escape their "sanctuary." And even if I did somehow get off the grounds and onto the snowy country road beyond the chain that contained us, where would I begin? Would I choose to go north, south, east or west?

Both times I'd arrived at the monastery, it had been in the middle of the night. I didn't know how far I was from the nearest village or town. The children never left to run errands off the property; those things were taken care of by adults. We were alone on our own separate planet.

And what would I do about Michelle? I hadn't been able to see her; how was I supposed to take her away with me? I'd leave her there and come back when I could drive a car. I felt ashamed at being so selfish, but we never saw each other. What was the use in my staying? My fourteen-year-old mind reeled at all the variables I faced.

I acted "normal" as I plotted my liberation. A mutinous, disobedient teenager would be put under a microscope and kept on an even tighter leash than our usual fixed schedule already called for. My plan would fall into place over time, and I'd have a better shot at executing it if I wasn't being watched too closely.

I told Francesca that I wanted to learn how to type. She smiled and said that it would be a useful skill to have; she was very pleased by my new attitude. What my sister didn't know was that I spent a lot of that time tapping out with two fingers the lyrics to any song I could remember. I was finding that the words were slipping from my memory and I felt a fevered urgency to put them on paper lest they be lost to me forever.

I was unloading a box of apples that had come in on a truck from Montreal one day. Each apple was wrapped in a piece of newspaper. I smoothed out a page and began to read the words in French. The paper was advertising an album by Three Dog Night called *Golden Bisquits*. Another one was Gordon Lightfoot's album *If You Could Read My Mind*. I neatly folded the paper and stuffed it in my jumper pocket. I pulled this piece of paper out of its hiding place many times during my stay. It somehow helped ground me; somehow if I saw that, I wouldn't forget the world was out there, too. I would keep this scrap of paper for years into adulthood.

We were given slivers of soap to keep with our washcloths in our cubicles. When a piece would get too small to use, it would be taken and put in a bin with others, which would later have water added to be boiled and the soaps were remolded into bigger pieces. My sister gave me a special present one morning. It was a new bar of

Ivory soap; the packaging was still intact. The writing on it was in French. I remember opening the paper gently, so as not to tear it. I folded it and kept it with the other things in my cubicle. I held the bar to my nose and took in a deep breath. I sat and stroked my gift. I ran my fingers over the indentation of the letters engraved in its top. I-V-O-R-Y. I didn't use it right away; I wanted to relish the fact that I *had* it. Over weeks, I watched the letters fade away as the precious bar diminished with each day's use.

My ESCAPE PLANS were put on hold; perhaps in my subconscious I accepted that the likelihood of making it out of that secluded location under my own steam was remote, but I never consciously accepted or entertained the thought that I'd be staying in that place in the long term. Our "school" year, such as it was, would be over soon. I'd see then what excuse would be given to forestall my departure. I never again asked Francesca if Mom had written. Who cared? I had other pressing matters to deal with. For one thing, my typewriter had been taken away. Francesca had found the pages of song lyrics that I'd secreted in my cubicle. From then on I made a concerted effort to sing the lyrics in my head while working, so the words wouldn't leave me. And neither would the words of a little boy named Mark.

I was sometimes sent to sweep floors in the area allotted to the youngest members of the community. Soeur Melanie was one of the nuns in charge of the smallest children during my second "tour of duty." These children ranged in age from a few months to eight years old. From my experience, this nun was pigheaded and nasty, totally lacking in compassion or any sense of fun. I never saw a smile on her face. Pairing someone with her "qualities" to the needs of little children seemed a horrible injustice to me.

It was early May of 1971, just a few days before my fifteenth birthday, and the windows were open to let in a light breeze. As I entered the dormitory with my straw broom, Soeur Melanie was wrestling with a small boy who looked to be about five years old. His little legs flailed against her habit; his resisting arms were out-stretched over his head as he struggled to escape. He was frantically calling for his mom and dad in English. The nun was screaming back at him in French.

After tossing the child firmly onto a bed, she violently flipped her veil back over her shoulder and stomped out of the room. I leaned my broom against a wall and approached the little guy. Sitting next to his hunched, sobbing frame, I put my arm around him and stroked his hair. The little boy grabbed my waist, looked up at me and wailed, "I want to see my mommy!"

"What's your name?"

"Mark," he choked out, in the way kids do when they are so upset that even their breathing pattern becomes erratic and halting. Mark told me that he and his parents lived in New York. He had arrived the day before. After a brief conversation with his parents at breakfast that morning, he had been made aware that his mom and dad were going back to New York and would return to him when their house was sold. *Oh. I'm sorry, Mark.*

The sight of him and deep empathy for his frightening, innocence-robbing circumstances overwhelmed me. As his fourteen-year-old psychiatrist, I did what I thought was best. I picked Mark up, put him on my lap and rocked him. I started singing an Elton John song that calmed me when I felt low . . . "*It's a little bit funny, this feeling inside. . . .*"

By the time I finished the last verse, the boy lay limp in my arms. I knew I would not be there to comfort him when he woke; I might never see him again. I could only hope that sometime in the future Mark could draw something good from the memory of another human being who had tried to ease his pain. I laid his small head on the pillow, covering his precious body with a blanket, then finished my sweeping before moving on to my next duty.

MY BODY HAD CHANGED over the months spent in Quebec. I was losing the "pudginess" that had blanketed my hips and tummy; Francesca held it out as evidence of how good the experience had been for me and told me that she would write to Mom and let her know how well I was doing. It would please her to know it, she added. Perhaps Francesca should also inform Mom that my menstrual cycle had ceased; the folded, reusable cloths that served us as poor substitutes for Kotex pads lay neatly stacked in the back corner of my cubicle, unsullied after only my first month back at the monastery. Was that a "good" sign, too?

Our workday on Monday, the 17th of May, my fifteenth birthday, was the same as any other. We were finishing our evening meal when my sister directed one of the girls to retrieve my birthday treat from outside the door. All lights were turned out, and when the door reopened, the only illumination came from the tiny candle atop my birthday dessert. Once the little bowl was placed before me, the lights were turned back on to reveal my gift in all its glory. In the bowl was a small mound of canned fruit cocktail, a delicacy reserved for the visitors' palates alone. On top of that was a pink icing rosette, with a single candle planted into the heap of mixed fruit. Judging from the rosette's rock-hard consistency, it had been removed from some defunct bakery item donated to the community.

After blowing out the candle amid the strains of "Happy Birthday" being sung to me by my companions in French (*"Bonne fête à vous, bonne fête à vous, bonne fête chere Nancy, bonne fête à vous!"*), each girl then excitedly handed me a card she'd made. These cards were decorated in a religious theme and contained a set of promises, all geared toward saving my soul. I was offered Masses and novenas toward the filling of my "heavenly bank account."

I *did* receive another gift that evening; it was one that Francesca must have had a part in securing for my special day. The smallest girl in our group was given the honor of handing it to me to open. The others squirmed excitedly in their seats as I removed the paper covering the long, thin box. It was a brand-new tube of Crest toothpaste! As I had with the bar of Ivory soap, I would keep the container that held the prized product; I actually kept these items for years into my adult life. I even kept the hardened rosette that had adorned the top of my birthday dessert.

I HAD HEARD NO NEWS from home, but back in the States, there was a lot happening. My eldest sister, Laura, and her family were moving to Grand Rapids from the West Coast. The job market in the Midwest looked better to them at the time, and so they had sold their home and were on their way to be reunited with the extended family and establish a home in Michigan.

When Laura pulled into Mom's driveway with all her worldly goods packed inside the trailer being towed behind the family car, she expected to have Michelle and me, along with the others, waiting to greet her. It seems that Mom had forgotten to mention our "vacation" to my eldest sister. I never found out what Laura's motivation was in doing so, or what she thought of Mom's tardy revelation of our whereabouts, but she asked Mom if she could go to the monastery to bring us home for what remained of the summer. Mom agreed to Laura's proposition, with the caveat that she should inform Michelle and me that we would be going back in mid-August. So, within a few weeks, once Laura had settled her family in a rental home on the southeast side of Grand Rapids and put her belongings in some semblance of order, my dad, Laura and my sister Julie, two years my senior, embarked on the trip that would change the path of my young life once more.

The feast day of Our Lady of Perpetual Help was upon us at the monastery. It was a warm summer day on Sunday, the 27th of June 1971. I had offered some special prayers to the Blessed Virgin in chapel that morning, asking her again for assistance in my current plight. It was now early evening; dinner had been eaten and the pots scrubbed and put away. I was walking alone toward the dormitory, when passing by a window I saw something that stopped me dead in my tracks. The sun was still fully illuminating the sky, but I felt positive that what seemed crystal clear before me must be an illusion of some sort; surely it was a trick of the light.

There, in a large parking area were two familiar forms, one my dad, the other my sister Julie. The third person's identity remained a mystery to me at the time. They were standing by my family's car and talking with two nuns. My heart was beating violently. I flung open the window and shouted down to them from my second- floor position. "Dad! Hello! Julie . . . I'm here! Yes, up here! Come in! *Please* come in!" They waved back smiling and shouted that they'd see me and Michelle soon. I didn't move. I was *afraid* to move. If I moved, coming back to the window later, I might find that I'd only *imagined* them being there, a cruel illusion. I waited at the window frame till my family disappeared from sight, entering the building beneath me.

I frantically searched for Francesca. The girls in the dormitory told me she had left for a meeting and would be back in a little while. I couldn't sit still. I pulled out my duffel bag and began cramming it with anything I had been allowed to keep when I arrived in February. Then I started a list of the things that had been taken away from me to be stored. Whether Dad was there to deliver a message of liberation or something to the contrary, I was getting out of this hellhole. If I had to argue, claw, grab Dad's car keys and break through the chain at the entrance myself, I was leaving and never looking back.

When I finally saw Francesca again I just about exploded. "When can I see them? When are we leaving?" She calmed me down, or tried to, and smiling said, "Nancy, you are leaving in the morning. Mom sent a message that you and Michelle can come home, but that you will be returning here on the fifteenth of August. I don't know if Mom knows this, but that day is the feast day of the Assumption of the Blessed Mother, a very special day indeed. We will be happily awaiting your return."

I played it cool. "That's great, Francesca. Sounds like a good plan to me. When can I see Dad?" I asked, "and who was that standing with him and Julie in the parking lot?"

"Oh, that was Laura," she responded. Wow; another bonus! I hadn't recognized my eldest sister at all. The last time I'd seen Laura had been shortly before the family left Seattle on the last day of October in 1965. Hairstyles had changed, clothing styles, too; so much had changed in so many ways in those nearly six years since I had boarded the train in Vancouver, B.C. I was anxious to make new memories, but couldn't just yet. I was told that Michelle was being readied, and Francesca said that she'd retrieve my sequestered belongings for me to pack. I would sleep in the dormitory tonight and meet with my family after chapel the next morning. I didn't sleep a wink. I must have repacked that duffel bag five times.

In the chapel early the next morning, the girl kneeling next to me leaned over and whispered that all the girls were praying for me and that one of them had caught a glimpse of my sister Julie when they had been ordered to deliver a tray of snacks to the visitor's area the night before. I was told by my wide-eyed companion that Julie's skin "glowed like brass" and that her hair was "wild like a witch." And to make matters worse, my sister's long dress (a peasant dress, a popular style of the day) had little cap sleeves; it exposed her arms, her throat and farther down to just above her breasts! And the dress had a fitted bodice! *Mon Dieu,* her form was showing!

Julie had been wearing a shawl over her long dress when I'd seen her outside from the window the evening before. I hadn't noticed any problem with her skin tone from that distance. According to my informant, the consensus was that Julie had become a "worldly girl" and would now need much prayer, if in fact she wasn't lost to the devil forever already. I told her to "keep praying" because now I was going back out there, too, and God knew what would become of the likes of me. She soberly nodded her head in agreement and resumed her pious pose.

I was startled by my fellow inmate and younger sister Michelle's appearance that morning. I had seen her only twice from afar in all the time we'd been there. Upon closer inspection, she looked frail, with a flat affect to her facial features and dark circles beneath her sunken eyes. I approached Michelle and hugged her tight. I felt her body trembling in my embrace. I felt pity and concern but in my teenage mind believed that all would be well the instant we left this "bad dream" in the dust.

Julie's appearance was another story. When you've been sheltered from exposure to fashionable clothing, when you've been told repeatedly how sinful it is to wear such things, then when you *do* come into rare contact with what would appear as unremarkable attire to an outside observer, your conditioning causes an extreme reaction. I knew my sister Julie wasn't "in league with Satan," but her appearance up close *did* startle me.

My seventeen-year-old sister had just gotten back from a trip to Florida with some girlfriends and had obviously been doing some sun worshipping. Her wavy, dark brown hair (most of my family has wild and difficult-to-manage hair as it is) had been adversely affected by a lot of swimming in salt water. With that contrasted against her deep tan, and wearing pink lipstick to boot, she certainly did stand out.

Francesca asked why I was taking my heavy winter coat with me. Michelle and I would be back in August after all. I told her that Michigan was known for freak summer snowstorms and I wanted to be prepared. There was no argument; we both knew it would truly take an act of God to get me to come back to this place. She kissed me; I cried a bit. I did love her after all. I had been allowed to get away with a lot of little things at the monastery because she was in charge of my welfare; any other nun could've never tolerated it.

ONCE THE MONASTERY'S EDIFICE was out of sight, I dug through my belongings and pulled out some clothes. I warned everyone else not to look and began dismantling my uniform bit by bit. I donned a brightly colored T-shirt and fed my legs into the faded overalls one by one. I still had on a pair of the "monastery issue" underwear that I'd worn every day in Quebec. It was made of heavy cotton and covered you from the waist nearly to the knees. My sister Laura was laughing in the front seat. "We can stop at a gas station when we get to a town to change, Nancy," she offered. "What's your hurry?" I told her that I'd just feel better if I changed now. I ditched my jumper, scarf, blouse and long stockings in a trash bin at the first gas station we stopped at.

The return trip to Grand Rapids was rather uneventful, but for the food and another unsettling event. Hamburger and French fries! And bacon and eggs! You can never imagine (unless you've lived it) what it felt like to be reintroduced to these old friends after having been without them for so long. I was one grateful girl as I plowed my way through any and every succulent item presented to me.

The second memory of the trip that will be forever with me is my reaction to seeing a mannequin displayed in a department store window; I began to cry. The model was wearing a micromini skirt; the upper half of the mannequin's form sported a halter top that barely covered her breasts. The words I'd heard so often filtered through my head, and tears slowly ran down my face. I made no sound sitting in the backseat of my dad's car that day, but I felt an ominous noise warring in my brain.

"The sinful people of the world are about to meet a cataclysmic end! God's arm is heavy; He will not be mocked. He cannot allow his children to commit further outrages and blasphemies against His Holy Name! People go about in their sinful, hedonistic lives blind to the upcoming catastrophe as they did in the times of Noah! The Almighty will mete out retribution for their transitory pleasures!"

I tried to reason with myself. *Come on, Nancy. Human beings have flaws, some pretty deplorable ones, but there is a lot of good in the world, too. God is all-merciful; He wants us to come to Him willingly, not under threat of eternal fire!* I calmed myself for the moment with these arguments, but for all my confidence-building proclamations, I still had many episodes of the monastery playing in my head.

It was a six-hundred-mile drive from outside St. Jovite, Quebec, to Grand Rapids, Michigan, a trip possible to make in a full day's driving, but we left the monastery too late. Dad had always preached that a person should never drive when fatigued, so putting his words of wisdom into action, he pulled off the road and we stayed the night at a small motel along the highway. It was wonderful to sleep in a comfortable bed with my sister Michelle and see her still there when I roused in the night to use the bathroom. She stirred when I got back into bed, pushing me away for a brief, groggy moment until she realized where she was. Our car pulled into the driveway in Grand Rapids before noon the next day.

Mom came outside to meet us. Dad, Julie, Laura, Michelle and Mom were busy talking on the porch, then drifted off inside to eat some lunch. I lingered outdoors for a moment, saying hello to a neighbor who was working in her front yard. She asked how my vacation had gone. "You and your sister were away longer than expected, eh? Say, did you lose some weight? Well, you look great, honey! Did you have fun on your trip, Nancy?" "Oh, yeah, loads of that," I responded. I smiled. "But it's great to be home again!" "Well, I'll be seeing you, Nancy." "Yeah, later!" I walked inside the front door with my duffel bag and laid it on the staircase leading to my room.

I could hear laughter coming from the kitchen at the back of the house. People were taking turns making egg salad sandwiches and loading their plates with chips and pickle spears as I walked into the kitchen. Mom made great egg salad. I grabbed a plate and began making a sandwich. "Do you really need all those chips, honey? You don't want to throw away all the good you've accomplished while you've been away!" Those were the first words out of her mouth. It was Mom's way of saying hello, I guess.

After I'd finished my sandwich, Mom asked to see me in the bathroom off the kitchen for a minute. We went inside; she shut the door and turned to me. "Nancy, you look so well," she said. "I know you're probably angry with me, but it's all for your own good. I wanted this private moment with you so I could reaffirm what I know was already told to you by your sister Francesca. You will be returning to the monastery in time to celebrate the Assumption of the Blessed Mother." (She *did* know the 15th of August was a feast day!) "Are we clear on that point, Nancy?" I was leaning against the sink's counter with my arms folded; Mom was sitting across from me on the edge of our old, claw-foot bathtub. An odd smile came

over my face as I contemplated my response. I began singing . . .
"*Wild horses, couldn't drag me away.*"

Mom's face was turning red. Yes, she was a master in the art of pushing people's buttons, but I was no slouch at it myself. She lost her cool entirely. "I knew you'd do this, I just *knew* you would." She fumed. "Now, listen to me, Lady Jane! I will not attempt to hog-tie you and transport your little butt back to where you need to be, you'd create such a scene, but by God, if I ever and I mean *ever* find out that you've been smoking marijuana . . ."

With that bizarre declaration issued—I had not even tried the stuff at that point in my life, nor would I till I was nineteen—Mom trailed off into a sputtering, out-of-control diatribe concerning the manner, method and specific punishment that would be doled out to her sixth-born child as a consequence of any number of inappropriate activities that the aforesaid offspring might choose to take part in. From what I could gather, if I could only just stop breathing, perhaps I stood a chance at living to adulthood.

"Can I leave now, Mom?" That was all I said. She stomped out with no acknowledgment of me. *Welcome home, Nancy* kept lilting through my head.

CHAPTER 6

Pike Place Market Special/Can Anyone Love This Day-Old Fish?

THE REST OF THE SUMMER of 1971 went by without upheaval. Mom worked afternoons and evenings at the phone company; Dad was left in charge of Julie, Michelle and me. Diane was long gone; she'd married and moved out of state. Mom took a hands-off approach with me during the months of July and August. If I wasn't making waves, the two of us didn't have to talk much, and so I was doing my damnedest to stay out of her way. Mom did have to wrestle with the problem of my school registration, however. I would have been starting at Creston High School that fall, my mom's alma mater, had events of the last months in Canada not intervened. It turned out, surprise, surprise, that the curriculum at the monastery was *not* acceptable to the Grand Rapids public school system after all. It looked more and more like I'd have to repeat the ninth grade.

I was hanging out at Houseman Field with a girlfriend one day late that summer, watching Creston's football team practicing on the grounds. When it was over and the team members were dispersing, a uniformed figure approached the two of us sitting on a grassy mound. He held his helmet in his hand and wore a smile on his freckled face. Egads! It was my old arch-nemesis from the school lunchroom, Curt. "Nancy, you look great. You look more than great, you look wonderful! Where have you been?"

"Thanks," I muttered, "I was gone on vacation to Canada . . . a little longer than expected."

"Well, I'm glad you're back! I'm sure we'll be seeing each other around Creston in a few weeks," he went on. "It was great seeing you again, Nancy!"

"Yeah, later, Curt." I was sure that I wouldn't be seeing him or anyone else for that matter at Creston that fall.

My sister Julie had attended an alternative high school the year prior. She'd done all right there; could I go, too? Mom finally agreed, and so I was spared the indignity of being labeled the first and only member of my family in all of recorded history to have to repeat a grade. Walden Village billed itself as an alternative to public education. They handed out T-shirts with the school's symbol emblazoned on the white front: two tree trunks with branches that intertwined in the middle like a heavy Celtic knot. Anyone looking at the school from the vantage of today would call it a hippy school. They hosted classes in fine art, sociology, philosophy, basket weaving, bread baking (which was taught at a local Seventh Day Adventist storefront), yoga and even a Bible class, with an instructor who looked like he had just stepped off the *Woodstock* album's cover.

To be eligible for state accreditation, Walden was required to teach a government class. The government class was the only thing you could call mandatory at that school. There was no dress code, smoking was allowed in class, unbeknownst to my mom, and the scent of exotic incense and the strains of students' acoustic guitar and mandolin playing laced the air. Classes convened in various buildings around the downtown area of Grand Rapids. Our yoga class was held in the Fountain Street Church, sociology studies in an upper level of the First United Methodist Church on Fulton Street, and on and on.

There was a very small, odd-shaped building that Walden had leased; the basement was used as a sort of staff meeting and student gathering site. This school headquarters used to sit on a narrow V of land bordering on Fulton Street to one side and Ionia Street to the other, but the building that stood there back in 1971 has long ago had its appointment with the wrecking ball. The main floor of this place was used to display the students' artwork. We sold the pieces in order to help pay the teacher's salaries. Our sand candles were a hot seller for a while, as were our origami creations. We were given lessons in watercolor painting, and some of the students' talent was obvious in the pictures displayed on the building's walls.

I was newly aware of what I'd only felt at the monastery, under my voluminous nightgown as I washed my body each night before bed in the dormitory. I had since seen myself naked in the mirror after my bath. I now had a pleasant shape, for the first time since becoming a teenager. It was nice to have boys look at me without making a joke. I started school in the autumn of 1971 feeling fairly comfortable with myself, or so I thought.

Bob was the fourth-born in a family of five; four boys and one older sister. His father was a minister in the Church of Christ and Bob was a rebel. His mom sold Tupperware and was quite a sales-woman. She was always winning an award for something. Both of his parents hailed from Alabama and still had traces of a lilt in their speech. Bob wore his long, silky blond hair in a ponytail, had a brown fake suede jacket with fringe dangling from it and wore boots. He even had the scraggly beginnings of a full beard, which I felt was quite debonair.

We hit it off rather quickly; soon we were inseparable. By the end of November, I was pregnant.

I couldn't get up the nerve to tell my mom for more than two months. I had a nauseating first trimester. I'd walk by Mom in the morning on my way to the pantry to get down a box of cereal, and from only the action of looking at the box, I would have to run into the bathroom off the kitchen to throw up. One night as I was loading the dishwasher, Mom came into the kitchen to talk. "Nancy, your father and I think that you're seeing far too much of that Bob person, and so before it goes too far you two need to slow down. Perhaps you should take a break from seeing each other for a while."

"Mom, you're a little late. I'm three months pregnant!" And then the one whom God put in charge of my earthly welfare did what she did best: She fell apart.

"Are you sure, Nancy?"

"Yes, Mom. I've haven't had a period since late October." She couldn't seem to absorb the reality of my words. After informing me that sometimes women skip a cycle, that this evidence could have some alternate explanation, she again asked me if I was sure. What she was really asking was, "Have you had sex?" Reiterating my position gave her the answer she dreaded. It was written all over Mom's face and in her pacing of the kitchen floor. Her fifteen-year-old daughter was no longer a virgin. Her floundering mind moved to the next pertinent question.

"Well, is it Bob's?"

That one really stung. "Yeah, Mom . . . it's his all right." I found out later that Bob's mom had asked the same question of Bob when he finally spilled the beans to his parents. "Oh, good God," Mom went on. "What will we do now?"

After a few minutes of her anxious interrogation, Mom made herself a hefty serving of the odd culinary concoction that I'd watched her create for years without fail when under extreme stress. It was what her mother had made her for dessert during the Great Depression. She got out a drinking glass, tore up several slices of white bread and dropped the pieces into the glass. Next she added cinnamon and sugar and poured milk over the ingredients to the top of the vessel. Once the milk had saturated the bread thoroughly, Mom used a long-handled iced tea spoon to ingest the dense, wet blend, mouthful by soothing mouthful.

Dad had to be told. The man would either explode with anger or take in this information as if I'd just asked for a buck-fifty to go to the matinee at the Creston Theater. "So, it's a shotgun wedding, eh, Nan?" He followed that with a little laugh. *Lord, what a weirdo,* I thought. Arrangements were made to go down to the court building to see the judge and sign the papers that would allow two minors to marry. Our parents met for the first time at the courthouse. Mom loved men; she was a terrible flirt. She walked ahead of the pack with Bob's dad, John, acting coy as ever. She asked him, "Are we being hasty here, John? What do you think?"

"Florence, I think the thinking's been done." We made plans to be married in early February, only a few weeks away; there wouldn't be much to organize.

* * *

BOB'S JOB SEARCH was going nowhere. When Christopher was about six weeks old, Bob asked me what I would think about his joining the military. We were kind of "make love, not war" people, so this thought had never occurred to me. The next day we went together to a couple of recruiting stations, while Bob's mom waited in the car with the baby. Within a week's time, Bob had signed the papers and was enlisted in the U.S. Air Force; his departure for boot camp was imminent.

It's strange how responsibilities can change your point of view, sometimes in radical ways. Our four years in the air force would become some of my most memorable. I also gained great respect for the group of people who volunteer every day to keep our nation safe. But that feeling came over me gradually. In those early days, I was pretty unsure of what all of it would mean for my little family's future.

Soon came the day that Bob had to leave us for basic training in Texas. I felt so alone for those six-plus weeks. I created a shrine of sorts in our bedroom during his absence. In a corner of the room I placed the boots he'd worn every day and out of the top of those boots was draped Bob's bound and long blond ponytail. I remember looking over at it in the night, weeping softly. We weren't just kids playing house anymore; we were adults with big obligations. But I was out from under Mom, on my own, in charge of my new family, and I finally had control over my destiny. Or so I thought.

Friends wanted me to come to a football game on short notice— no babysitter and Bob was at boot camp. I remember silent tears rolling down my cheeks as I rocked and breast-fed my little son that night, knowing that my friends were sitting in the bleachers and having a great time. I didn't resent my son; quite the contrary. I loved being his mother. I was mourning the loss of those normal teenage rituals. I would never go to a prom, never go on spring break with friends and never have Mom and Dad offer to help me buy my first car or attend college straight out of high school.

After Bob completed basic training in San Antonio, Chris and I joined him as his technical training began in Wichita Falls, Texas. Once he'd completed his schooling there, we received our first choice of air force bases listed on the "dream sheet" we'd filled out. We would be stationed at McChord AFB in Tacoma, Washington, only a short drive from Seattle, for the entire four years of Bob's enlistment. It was wonderful being back in my old stomping grounds, a place that held so many pleasant memories for me. We often took advantage of our close proximity to the rugged beauty of the Pacific Northwest and went camping from the time Chris was barely one year old. We were content with our simple amusements and the thrifty lifestyle that military pay afforded us. We had each other. And I felt safe, protected and just wanted to stay close to home.

We didn't hear much from our families in Michigan during those four years, but for Christmas gifts and a few calls, and that was probably for the best. We were on our own to sink or swim. I walked out to the apartment complex's mailbox on the 17th of May 1977, my twenty-first birthday, and found an envelope there from my father. I remember thinking to myself that Dad was demonstrating his engineer's precision in my receiving birthday greetings from him on the exact date of my reaching the age of majority. I expected to open the envelope and be graced with one of Dad's legendary professorial lectures, this one regarding the profundity of this particular

milestone in my life and the attributes I needed to exhibit to establish that I'd made the grade.

The thick envelope contained only a copy of my parents' divorce
decree. My dad was a blunt man with very few people skills. The
irony of receiving this on my birthday struck, and I laughed out
loud. I laughed at my dad's strange nature and I laughed with relief,
wondering what the hell had taken them so long. The two of them
had bickered and nitpicked their way through those thirty-two years,
and so the only surprise to me was that their holy union hadn't dis-
solved years before. My husband and I fought rarely, and even then
our spats were generally minor and rectified quickly. I remember
feeling a little superior to my parents as I walked back into my
apartment that day.

Bob and I were both caring parents. He was an attentive father,
loving to get down and play with his son on the living room floor in
Tacoma after work each night. He was good to me, too. He'd chosen
to train as an electrician, and so once our military service was
completed, Bob would be prepared to make a good living for his
family. He must've felt overwhelmed by his new responsibilities at
times, though.

I loved taking care of our home and family. Some of my girlfriends at the apartment complex we lived in, just outside McChord
AFB, thought I was crazy to get down on my knees to scrub the
kitchen floor. It felt good to do a thorough job. Laundry, dishes,
changing diapers (yes, cloth diapers!)—none of these duties felt like
drudgery to me; it was all extremely gratifying.

In spite of my active life, I never pared off the excess pounds after
Chris was born. Over the years in Tacoma, my weight gain only accelerated. I loved to cook, to feed my boys, but I was doing more

than my share of enjoying the fruits of my culinary labors. Bob's constitution was long and lean; he could eat whatever he wanted and not send the scale careening into cardiac arrest territory. Not so in my case. I couldn't excuse my taking another piece of fried chicken or chocolate cake by rationalizing that Bob had consumed a second helping, so therefore I should be able to as well. But that's how I *did* excuse my behavior. If I'd forced myself to take more than a quick glance in the mirror as I passed by with an armful of folded laundry, I wouldn't have been able to deceive myself into believing that it wasn't that bad. It *was* that bad.

I began making excuses not to go out to functions, to the movies, to places where I'd be on view by a number of strangers. I wanted to stay home. Bob didn't complain as my weight gain caused changes in our social life. By the time his military tour was over and we were ready to pack up and head back to our families in the Midwest, I tipped the scales at nearly three hundred pounds. But I was happy and comfortable nestled in the security of my own little family.

CHAPTER 7

Dropping Anchor/Landlubbers

THE RETURN TRIP to Grand Rapids in January of 1978 was a miserable one. The weather was foul and snowstorms followed us through Washington, Idaho, Utah and beyond. I spent four-plus days in the cab of an enormous Ryder rental truck, trying to entertain a bored and fidgety five-year-old son while Bob drove the behemoth through tight mountain passes, dreary lengths of highway and some frightening whiteout weather conditions. The family cat, Tigger, was ensconced inside our old and magnificent light blue Ford Fairlane 500, being towed behind. We arrived at Mom's place in Grand Rapids late at night, and after brief hugs and kisses all around, Bob, Chris and I went upstairs and hit the hay.

We stayed with Mom and the two sisters who remained at home, Julie and Michelle, for months, not an easy thing for any of us. To add to the underlying tension, Bob was having trouble finding a job and it was really affecting him badly. He'd come home from a day of interviewing and put on his headphones, relaxing with some Dave

Brubeck to escape the fact, if only for an hour or two, that he and his young family were living in his mother-in-law's home. It was nearly six months before his doggedness paid off.

Bob began his employment at Roskam's Bakery. The pay was not what we needed, but it was a good first step toward our independence. He was hopeful that one of the other applications he'd submitted would bear fruit soon, and one of them did. Bob was offered a position as an electrician at Interstate Brands, a bakery on the southeast side of town. We would now be able to afford to buy our own home. Within a few weeks, by late June of 1978, we'd found a sweet but compact, two bedroom, one-story house on Fuller Street N.E. that fit our small family's needs. There was a pleasant backyard for Chris to play in safely and off the one-stall garage a screened-in patio with knotty pine paneling decorating its walls. It would be a great place to entertain family and friends. There was a magnolia tree in the backyard and a long, dense row of pink and fuchsia peonies that bordered the side of the house.

I was so happy. I had a home of my own to make beautiful. Chris found several little children in the neighborhood to play with. There was always a nice hot meal waiting for my boys, and homemade cookies on the kitchen counter in our house. I was known in the neighborhood as the "cookie lady," and many times kids would come to the door when Chris wasn't even there, just looking for a tasty treat.

I would have been in bliss if it weren't for the image that stared back at me every morning as I washed my face in the bathroom mirror. My eating was out of control. I tried not to think about it, but my weight was affecting many parts of my life, of *our* lives. I was happy to spend all day in the garden, but wouldn't join the PTA no matter how important it was for Christopher. I would send home-baked treats for Christopher's classmates to enjoy, but I wasn't there to set up their Halloween party that autumn. I wouldn't agree to go to dinner at Bob's colleague's house. I hated myself for what I was becoming: a vortex pulling myself and my family into its darkness. I knew what was happening was terribly wrong, but I was at a complete loss as to how to fix it.

I became absolutely sure that Bob was secretly coveting the Black Velvet whiskey vixen/spokesmodel alluringly dressed aloft on a bill-board overhead in traffic. Or perhaps he had designs on the bronzed and scantily clad temptress beckoning to him on a sandy beach in the Coppertone ad on TV. How could my husband love *me* when so many examples of perfect women met his gaze everywhere he looked? I *knew* my husband was faithful, and I argued that point with myself all the time, but that observation was made with my intellect; my feelings of inadequacy reigned supreme over any logical examination of the facts. I was miserable, and I grieved my inability to control what I accused Bob of the second these false indictments left my lips. I loved him, but I hated myself more. And as a consequence, I made my dear husband miserable, too.

Things only got worse as I packed on more pounds and the activities I allowed myself to take part in became even more limited. It's not that I didn't go on diets or try to control what I was eating many times over the years; I did. But the compulsion to overeat was so strong that the moments of weakness far overwhelmed the temporary victories I achieved.

At twenty-three years old, I had reached a new top weight of 328.5 pounds and was miserable in the summer of 1979. The heat of August in Michigan is bad enough when you're thin, but if you're heavy, it's unbearable. My apparel, which I sewed myself, was composed entirely of long, loose-fitting dresses in lightweight fabric. They covered every bulge down to my heavy ankles. I'd always been hyperconscious of what others thought of my physical appearance, and at this weight, I was sufficiently humiliated in my own mind that I thought I'd save myself from as much unwanted attention as possible. I rarely went out for anything other than the necessary, but once in a while I was talked into doing something.

Earlier that summer, I'd ventured out to an International House of Pancakes restaurant with my mom for lunch. She ordered a hot fudge sundae after eating her meal. Mom was a large woman, though not nearly in my class, but what others thought of her physical appearance never stopped her from acting on what she wanted to do; I envied her that attribute. I hadn't ordered any dessert and asked Mom for a bite of hers. I reached my spoon into her sundae, and as I brought the ice cream to my lips, one of two women sitting at a table a few feet from ours said to her friend in a clearly audible voice, "Did you *see* her eating that? What a pig!" Then the ensuing giggles.

I got a call one morning in August of 1979 from my sister Diane. She wanted to know if I'd like to go with her, my mom and my sister Michelle to Frankenmuth, a city on the other side of the state. The two main attractions in Frankenmuth are the largest and loveliest selections of Christmas ornaments in the United States, at a store called Bronner's, and the Bavarian Inn. I'd never been there, but according to legend, they served the best fried chicken ever.

I collect ornaments and had always wanted to see if this store was all I'd been told it was, but the thought of exposure was holding me back. I was making excuses. I had nothing to wear. I would sweat profusely walking from Bronner's to the Bavarian Inn and be embarrassed by how I looked. There wouldn't be room for all of us to be comfortable in her compact car. I was finding any reason for this outing *not* to work. Some of my siblings had battled with weight to varying degrees in their adult years, gaining a few pounds, then losing them, but anything they experienced came in a distant second to the mammoth gains I achieved: Like anything else you could name involving me, I either went at it whole hog or not at all.

In the end, I did go, and visiting Bronner's, for me, was like a pilgrimage to Mecca. We shopped for a couple of hours and soon it was time to make our way toward the Bavarian Inn. We were chatting about various things at our corner table when the lederhosen-clad waiter approached. I sat with my back to the wall and a sister to each side and Mom opposite for protection from other diners' prying eyes. We'd ordered fried chicken, of course; what would a trip to the Bavarian Inn be without sampling their world famous chicken? We would have mashed potatoes and gravy, steamed vegetables, rolls and butter; the works, served family style.

Our young waiter brought our drinks to the table and we talked while waiting for our meal. Again, the lederhosen guy appeared, this time with our dinner plates, butter in a small bowl with a basket of rolls and a bowl of soup. He put the cereal-sized bowl with a soup-spoon toward the back of my place setting. As the conversation continued, I pulled my soup toward me and began to eat. Others casually munched on rolls and butter as the banter continued. It had gone unnoticed that no one else's soup had been brought to the table. A few minutes elapsed, and amid the talk Michelle's voice rang out above the others. "Oh! My Lord! Nancy has eaten the whole bowl of gravy!" For a moment, there was silence; then the air was punctuated by shrill laughter and threats of someone wetting their pants because they couldn't stop laughing.

My mistake dawned on me slowly, so sure was I that Michelle was in error. I thought it through and put the pieces together: the thickness of the "soup," the tiny bits of meat floating in it, and finally the fact that no one else had been given a bowl. It was only made worse when Michelle announced my faux pas to the waiter, bringing more ribald laughter among my confreres. My excitement over purchasing beautiful Christmas ornaments faded and I rode home that evening wishing I'd never thought I could have a normal day out. Ho-ho-ho, Nancy.

I joined Weight Watchers a couple of days after returning from the Frankenmuth fiasco. With every weigh-in and meeting, with every encouraging pat on the back given by another member, with each time I heard the applause when the number of pounds I'd shed in that seven-day period was announced, I felt better and better about who I was, and it gave me the confidence to carry on. My clothes were getting baggier; I even had to pick up some new undies. I smiled more often. I had Bob invite another family over for dinner and cards. I was coming to believe that I wasn't a gross, unworthy pig. I had already lost more than a hundred pounds and was now only forty pounds from my goal of one hundred and fifty.

CHAPTER 8

A Seismic Shift/Tsunami

IT WAS MAY of 1980 and I'd just turned twenty-four. My son, Chris, was about to finish the second grade and my husband, Bob, left for the bakery each morning and did not return till well after Chris was out of school for the day in mid-afternoon. I was living a life of domesticated bliss, even though just under the surface something was off-kilter. When you're young, you don't inspect things too closely and your needs are generally pretty simple. I was happy to cook, clean and care for my child and husband, to show love in the things I did for them and to receive their love in return. Bob and I *did* love each other, but we weren't yet fully baked. It would take more time for our differing views and goals to come to light.

Bob was quiet; I am anything but. Apart from occasional social events planned with family and friends, my husband was happiest when working on a project or listening to music and being lost in it. He enjoyed many solitary pursuits. I was and am most alive when surrounded by people and immersed in conversation. I needed people more than Bob did. I desired new things and challenges to fuel my fire while he was content with what had always been. This difference would be at the heart of our marital woes, now just over the horizon.

During that late spring, I was bored to death. I'd get Chris off to school and, after making sure the house was in order and dinner ready to throw in the oven, would often take lunch to Bob at work to fill my time. Some days I'd climb in the car and simply drive. Sometimes I'd drive all the way out to Lake Michigan, which was almost an hour away, and just sit in my car at the beach, looking at the water.

A girlfriend of mine named Mary Lou told me that Grand Rapids Junior College (now called Grand Rapids Community College) had created a new two-year culinary arts program. She knew how much I loved to cook. I talked it over with Bob and he agreed to it right away. While I'd made great strides in the weight loss arena recently, and my feelings had *improved* regarding my right to lead a full and active life, I was still overweight and still afraid of not being accepted.

Due to my pregnancy at fifteen, I had never completed high school at Walden Village and never had a chance to learn how to fully function in the world. In order to be accepted at the community college in September, I needed to take the test for my GED (general equivalency diploma). I passed the test in the top 92 percentile on my first attempt, even though my formal education had ended in the middle of ninth grade. I was to begin in my mid-twenties what many people experience straight out of high school. College classes were waiting for me, and the thought of being back in school was very exciting.

I wish I could find my old junior college student ID card to include in this book. I was smiling for all I was worth, but I was scared to death. If you looked closely, you'd see that my face was a bit sweaty. I was wearing a sweater on that late August day, as I believed it best veiled my figure flaws.

The excess pounds melted off me like butter in a hot sauté pan over those next few months. I was still overweight, but by Christmas break of that same year I'd lost all remaining forty pounds; many women would still appear a bit pudgy at 150 pounds and 5 feet 4¾ inches, but my body type wore it well. I was busty, with a twenty-eight-inch waist and rounded hips.

And mind you, I was around good food every day. We made our own dinner rolls in culinary school, and there were dozens of them in a warming oven, with a bowl of soft butter sitting right next to it, that we were free to munch on at will. That delectable combo would have thrown me off my food program at many other junctures in my life, but I was never tempted, not once. I know now what made the difference. I was happy, truly fulfilled in what I was doing. I wasn't avoiding the rolls and butter because I was dieting. I was gaining confidence because I was able to care for my family and expand my knowledge at the same time. I felt good about myself, and I felt good about making people happy with the delectable treats I served. I did well academically in this climate. I scored high on tests, both on paper and in the kitchen setting. It was a real eye-opener for me. I had not been exposed to a workplace environment ever before; I was a housewife before the age of sixteen, so this was all exciting and new.

I felt so alive at that time. I was seeing a new dimension of myself, both in being in the company of peers and by taking in knowledge independent of my identity in the home. I was becoming a full human being. I was going out after class with friends on occasion. I was having a social life for the first time since becoming an adult. I was beginning to attract the attention of other men as well. Bob had been encouraging during my weight loss, but he now seemed leery of the newfound confidence that went along with it. I'd come home excitedly talking about things we'd done at school that day or upcoming events that energized me, and Robert would barely acknowledge my words. He'd pay lip service, but that's all it would be.

The students served elaborate dinners for various college functions at a grand old home on Heritage Hill called the McCabe-Marlowe House. Participation in after-class-hours dinners offered extra credit, and often I signed up to help. Once I asked my husband if he'd like to come by afterward to meet my friends and instructors. We were planning on going out for a beer once we'd cleaned up from the event. Bob told me that he'd likely be too tired to come; I went anyway. This pattern repeated itself over many months, and it began to appear that we were switching roles. Now I was the one who wanted to go out: I'd ask and he'd decline. I felt a chasm opening between the two of us, and I did not understand that what was being left unsaid could build to explosive levels later on.

ONE OF THE PUBS we students frequented was called Snug Harbor. It was a small neighborhood bar with a couple of pool tables, a jukebox and a Pac-Man electronic game standing against a wall. The bartenders were all friendly, and so were most of the clientele. It was also a big hangout for softball teams during the spring. One Friday night I begged Bob to take me there: It was only about three blocks from home. We could just have a couple of drinks, listen to some music and maybe play a game of pool and come back home. He finally relented and off we went.

Snug Harbor was packed. There was no place to sit, and so I stood shoulder-to-shoulder in the crowd while Bob wended his way to the bar to order our drinks. I felt a sharp push behind me, causing me to lurch forward against the person in front of me. As I was apologizing to the guy, I felt a hand on my shoulder whirling me around. "Hi, I just needed to see if the front of you was as beautiful as the back view." What a line. The guy was sloppy drunk, still in uniform from his softball game and celebrating or crying, I wasn't sure which, into his beer(s). He was asking me if I needed something from the bar when Bob pushed through with our drinks and, overhearing this guy's offer, blurted out, "Hey, bozo! The lady is with me; she's my wife!" Bob was red-faced and agitated. I was embarrassed by his overreaction to this man's few drunken words, and noticing a party of people standing up to leave just behind us, I pulled Bob by the arm over to the table to try to defuse the situation.

I was stunned by the emotion I'd just seen displayed by my meek and mild husband. I tried cajoling him, making small talk about most anything, asking him to play a game of pool with me. Nothing I said could erase the grimace or the clench of his jaw. He would only shake his head and tell me we needed to leave. We'd just gotten there! This was the first time we'd been together in a bar during our entire married life of over nine years. We'd been out to dinner many times, to friends' homes to play cards; we'd gone to parks or to the beach, but never to a bar. And it would be our last visit. Bob would only say that he didn't like that guy talking to me and that I should've done something to stop him. I felt that it was only a cover for some deeper kind of upset. I remember thinking that if he didn't talk to me about whatever was really bothering him, then we were heading down a bad and uncertain path.

I felt afraid and lonely as I drifted off to sleep later that night, as I'd been so sure that Bob and I would beat the odds, that we would show everyone who'd said we'd never last. My son came to me one day in the summer of 1981 to talk about his friend's parents' divorcing. "Why does that happen, Mom? Will it happen to us?" I hugged Chris close and told him that it only happens when people don't talk about problems and that it was not going to happen to us, ever. I felt uneasy the moment those words left my lips and only held him closer. By Thanksgiving 1981, Bob and I were separated.

Bob and Chris stayed at home on Fuller Street. I was going to school full-time and living at my mom's. I'd come to tuck Chris into bed many nights after class; second-year culinary classes were held from three to nine in the evening. I also took Chris to school many mornings.

Chris was a very mellow child. He had never been devious or destructive; almost always obedient. He was a pleasure to be around. Chris didn't say much when something was bothering him; you had to coax it out of him. With all the turmoil in my life at the time, I am ashamed to say that I didn't inspect my child's emotional condition very closely. What shame I feel now to know how much that decision hurt my little boy's trust and innocence. If I had it to do over again, I hope I would think more about the aftermath and perhaps work harder to mend my marriage; I'll never know if it would've worked.

My friend Mary Lou was married to one of Bob's fellow workers at the bakery. We sometimes discussed the details that she became privy to through her spouse. She said that Bob was dating a woman named Rachael who worked in the day-old bakery outlet in the front of the building. I was kind of surprised, as he hadn't mentioned anything about it to me. One night when I came over after class to see Chris, I asked Bob whether it was true and he became very defensive, asking me if he didn't have a right to date and angrily asserting that I had no claim on him. I agreed and the conversation ended there.

Chris came over to my mom's to be with me one weekend and was sitting on the couch, watching cartoons. He looked rather distant, almost sullen. I sat down next to him and asked if he needed to talk with me about anything, anything at all. He broke into tears and told me that he had had a bad dream the night before, and when he woke up to climb into Daddy's bed, he was told to go back to his own. It came out that Bob's girlfriend and her two year-old daughter were sleeping in the bed and Bob had told Chris that there was no room left for him. I was furious. In hindsight, I see things more clearly. Bob was a good man, a very good father to Chris, but like me, was sometimes unaware of the effect his needs and actions had on his son. Speaking for myself, I was very self-absorbed during that time. It was a whole new world for both of us.

This incident began a series of verbal batteries between the two parents, but, to our credit, at least never within earshot of our son. I told Bob I wanted full custody of Chris. He said that I could have custody if I could take over the mortgage payments on the house. Of course, this would entail me quitting college and getting a full-time job to support my son. I felt that time was of the essence, and so I lied. About a week later, I told Bob that I had found a position cooking at some fancy restaurant and would now be able to take care of our son.

I was still living at Mom's, waiting for the "vacancy" to open up on Fuller Street. Bob kept putting off getting his things out of the house, and so one day, having "insider information" that he and his girlfriend had gone to the racquetball club after work at the bakery, I let myself in to await their return. There were half-packed boxes lying everywhere. I spent the time alone finishing the packing for my soon-to-be former spouse. When there was nothing left to do, I sat at the kitchen table reading a *Newsweek* magazine awaiting their arrival, but I couldn't concentrate on the text.

I've always had a dramatic flair, especially when nervous or angry, and so as the two lovebirds walked in the kitchen door, Billy Joel's "Movin' Out" was blaring from the stereo speakers. Bob's jaw took a decidedly set position when he saw me, and his friend just stood there agog in her snow-covered boots, holding a six-pack of Michelob Light in her hand. I informed him that his possessions were packed and that today was moving day. I went on to say that if his things weren't out of the house that night, he'd find them in the snowbank out back in the morning.

Rachael chimed in, saying that she couldn't understand how I could treat such a good and decent man this way. She opened the refrigerator door and, while preaching her heartfelt sermon on the topic of my husband's finer attributes, lifted each beer bottle one by one from its holder, placing them all on a shelf of *my* refrigerator to keep cold. As she went on and on, I walked over next to her and picked up the discarded beer holder from the floor. I handed it to Bob's outraged defender and began replacing the refrigerated beer bottles one by one back inside the carrying case.

"Darling, you of all people should keep any thoughts regarding the sanctity of marriage to yourself, having already divested yourself of more than one husband by the ripe old age of thirty." Rachael proceeded to make a flurry of phone calls, finally securing a truck they could use to move Bob's things. I sat at the kitchen table to monitor their progress. There was nothing left of Bob's to throw out in the snowbank as the winter sun rose the next morning.

It was February of 1982; on the eighth, Bob and I would've been celebrating our tenth wedding anniversary; I was twenty-five years old. In May I was set to finish my culinary classes, but that was not in the cards for me, not now anyway. I had come so close and done so well, but with all the stress I was under at the time, I didn't feel I was able take on the triple threat of caring for my son, holding down a job and squeezing in a six-plus-hour block of time daily for college classes.

My chef instructor gave me a glowing reference, and I took that piece of paper and walked out into uncertainty. I had never had a job outside the home and it was a frightening experience to look for one. I applied everywhere I could think of and prayed for a call. I went for interviews and was kindly advised at one place that I needed to dress differently if I wanted to be taken seriously by employers. I liked to wear bohemian clothing; anything with flowing layers, vivid colors and tassels with bells. I was unprepared for the working world, to say the least.

My first job was waitressing at a place called Granny's Kitchen on Twenty-eighth Street. We wore what looked like white nurse's uniforms, with shoes to match. All I had were some low black shoes that I'd worn serving food in culinary classes. I was broke, beyond broke, and couldn't afford to run out and grab a new pair of shoes. The manager was a nasty man. He'd sit in a booth chain-smoking and scowling, sipping an iced tea and just watching for anyone to make an error, real or invented. He was hypercritical of all of us, but some employees seemed to have developed a thick-skinned approach to his abuse; I was new and it really got to me. I spent the first few weeks' break times standing in a phone booth downstairs pretending to be on the phone, when in fact I was only trying to find a place to cry.

A friend from college called me to say that there was an opening for a production person in a deli he worked at, so I jumped at the chance. Knowing I would never receive a recommendation from the rotten man at Granny's Kitchen, I worked one last shift, told him what I thought of his people skills and walked out the door.

My hourly wages stunk, but Chris and I got by on my income; just. Months later, the friend who had helped me find work at the deli was leaving for a position in New York City. I was offered his manager's position and took it. It would be a salaried post. I thought nothing of the difference between hourly and salary. I only knew that I'd be making two hundred and seventy-nine dollars per week after taxes, and that was all I thought of when I said yes. It was a set amount I could depend on. My naïveté would be short-lived.

After one fourteen-hour workday, I looked up at the owner and suggested that she should buy a cot to keep back by the chest freezers so I didn't have to drive all the way home and back again in six hours; I was only half-joking. I brought my son to work with me early each morning to start heating the water in huge stockpots for the gallons of soup the staff and I made every day. I fed Chris breakfast there and was given a little time off in the lull before the lunch crunch to take him to school, coming back to the kitchen afterward to continue my work.

Sometimes I went out after work and drank a glass of wine or three. I'd had to absorb a lot of changes over the last months, and alcohol allowed me to forget about my fears and new commitments for a while. I had made a number of friends in college whom I was still in contact with, so we'd meet up for a little frivolity after hours. Cooks are a strange lot; some might say crazy. We worked hard, got burned and cut, withstood high temperatures and long hours on our feet, and consequently a lot of us seemed to like to belly up to the bar to unwind. As time went on, I was gradually gaining the belly.

My crowd became fixtures at Snug Harbor. Sometimes I'd buy a martini with double olives. As the night wore on and the alcohol worked its magic, I would decide that it seemed a good idea to use the olives as missiles. No bartender was safe when in my alcohol-saturated presence. I'd stuff one of the juicy morsels up a nostril and, using my forefinger to hold shut the alternate nostril, would yell, "Incoming!" before forcing the olive out and in a trajectory toward the middle of the unfortunate barkeep's shirt. Other times you could find me entertaining the crowd with my rendition of "New York, New York." I'd unscrew the handle on the beer tap to use as my microphone. My life was crumbling around me, and all I knew to do was keep dancing. It was getting harder to convince myself that I could keep up the pace. My hours at work were killing me and left me very little energy for my son. I drank more at home with Chris; I drank wine during the evening and soon on my days off, sometimes taking my first drink by noon. I now needed alcohol to cope with *living*.

I cannot blot out the image of Chris at ten years of age sitting next to me on the couch, reading me a story before his bedtime. I was drifting off after several glasses of wine, and he had to nudge me time after time to ask if I was still listening. Caution: These memories will never leave you, no matter how you change or try to make amends for past behavior; no matter how much you apologize and wring your hands.

The damage has been done, and you cannot turn back the hands of time to erase a child's undeserved pain. If this story rings true for you, get help. Get it now. The haunting pain, recurring memory and the knowledge that you allowed such harm to come to the child you said you loved more than anything in this world, has no equal.

Because of the actions of an unstable male coworker, I had to quit that job; I was truly in fear for my life. I was granted unemployment payments, as it was determined by the National Labor Relations Board that I had legitimately quit "under duress." Regardless of fault or circumstances, however, it left me with far less money to pay the same number of bills. With stress mounting, I determined that more drinking was in order.

As with so many alcoholics, my life's path was heading downhill and fast. I was a mess physically and in every other way. My self-worth was at an all-time low. I didn't like being seen outside my circle anymore; in fact, over the next couple of months I stopped going out to drink with friends, too. I now did my drinking exclusively at home. I was ashamed of my appearance and was steadily gaining weight. I was back up to two hundred and fifty pounds.

SOON MY MORTGAGE PAYMENT was in arrears, putting the security of Christopher's childhood home in jeopardy. I made a mean cheesecake. It was a glorious New York–style cake, incorporating forty ounces of cream cheese, orange and lemon zest, heavy cream and a handmade lemon-infused butter cookie crust. I thought that if I could sell it commercially, I might be able to salvage our home with the profits, so I bought industry-type cake boxes, made up some samples of my cheesecake and mustered every ounce of courage to go into restaurants to try and sell my cakes. I was so self-conscious; apart from my size, drinking—though not inebriated when in these establishments—did nothing to enhance my self-esteem or reasoning abilities. I felt paranoid, nervous and sure of failure each time I walked through the door to peddle my wares. Over the next few weeks I did get a contract to make ten cakes a week for a restaurant in town. They later closed their eatery in my city, and so I had to make deliveries to their other outlets, in Ann Arbor and Lansing.

But the bottle won in the end. I remember having to concentrate just to follow the recipe. I had made these cakes hundreds of times, and it would seem that I could've done it blindfolded. That was not the case when I was working while wolfing down cocktails. My drinking menu had many evolutions. I began my career with Jack Daniel's and chasers of Tab diet soft drink in college. Then I went through my white wine days, followed by gin and tonics, then gin martinis, then the finest combo ever, Smirnoff vodka and Diet Coke, even lowering myself to using Popov vodka in the end, the bottom-of-the-barrel kind of stuff, when I and my bank account were really in the dregs.

I'd stand there feeling so proud, such a woman of accomplishment, in that I'd buttered the sides of the springform pans and set out all of the required ingredients for my cakes. But before you knew it, I was trying to remember if I'd already added the pinch of salt to the dry ingredients or whether the vanilla had been added to the cream cheese, heavy cream and eggs. I hated myself. *What an ass, and this will be the last time I'll put myself in this ridiculous position; I'll quit drinking tomorrow, damn it all.*

I've been told that most alcoholics lose their appetite for food. Most eat very little, ingesting the bulk of their calories in liquid form. I was obviously the exception to the rule; I over-imbibed *and* overate. Each ounce of liquor contains on average one hundred calories. If you figure that on most days I could easily put away a pint or more, I was adding thirteen hundred calories or better to my already bloated daily diet.

The restaurant that was ordering my cakes first cut down the amounts ordered, then closed up shop entirely at each of their franchise locations within the next few months. I lost our home to foreclosure. Each failure brought more worry; more worry fed my feelings of worthlessness and told me it was time for another drink. A friend down the street from our place on Fuller, named Joelle, opened her house to Chris and me, and so we sold some of our furniture and other remnants of our past life. We left there in the house some possessions that we had no place for and boxed up other things and stored them in Joelle's basement. My son didn't have a place to call his own. I despised myself.

My sister Diane was in Grand Rapids, visiting from Chicago. I talked with her about all that was going on in my life. She told me she thought that Chris should go back to Chicago to live with her and Chris's two cousins, Tommy and Alex, till I got my life back on track. My former spouse was in Kansas at that time, involved in a six-month training course required by the company he was employed by. Bob offered that Chris could stay with his stepmom and stepsister in Grand Rapids in his absence. Chris chose instead to go stay with his cousins in Chicago, with whom he shared both similar ages and a close relationship.

My son soon left for what would turn out to be nearly a full year in the Windy City. I hated to do this to Chris, but I felt it was really for the best. He would be living in a stable home, and for me then it

CHAPTER 9

Pinewood Estates/Have I Finally Found Dry Land?

MY LANDLORD, DOTTIE, was about fifty-five years old and a pleasant person, always ready with joke and a laugh when she and her husband would come to collect the rent or make repairs on the house or mow the lawn. One day late in August of 1987, she dropped in and was complaining about how hard it was to find suitable workers for her businesses. She owned three adult foster care (AFC) homes in the area and was again in need of a manager for one of them; she was desperate to fill the position right away. Dottie had been manning the helm for the last few weeks, as the last person in the position had given her only two days' notice before flying the coop.

Dottie soft-soaped the job description pretty well over coffee that day at my kitchen table, leading me to believe that my duties for the most part would be cooking, cleaning, passing out medications, filling out charts and doing the laundry for twelve souls. If I'd only known the emotional toll the job would take on me and how much more involved it all was, I don't know what my decision would've been.

Something tells me I would've bitten the bullet and gone along anyway; it was a good place to escape from what I didn't want to face.

Chris and I would be provided with separate quarters, in this case an airy, walk-out basement apartment with two bedrooms, living room and dining space. The salary was livable, though nothing more. The only major drawback I could see was that there was no allowance given for paid time off. You were on the clock seven days a week. She told me that I could find college students in the area who would sit for me if I wanted to leave for a while, but I would later find that not to be the case.

In my muddled frame of mind and with my feelings regarding my acceptability in the "outside" workplace, this offer seemed like an answer to prayer. I talked about it with my son that night, and Chris, as usual, with his mellow nature, desire to please and reticence to open up about his feelings, agreed that it was probably the best thing to do at the time. The decision was made to leave our new home and venture out beyond the city limits to a job and environment completely foreign and new. And we didn't have a lot of time to question our decision. We had to pack and go.

The week of the move was crazy, by anyone's standard. Things Chris and I would be using right away were haphazardly thrown into boxes and bags; the rest was packed nicely, as it would have to be stored. The basement apartment we'd be living in was much smaller than the place we were currently renting. The owner promised storage space for us at one of her three properties; the truth turned out to be that many of my boxes and furnishings were left in her garage and later placed in an old barn for the three years I worked there. When I finally did leave, my movers found that items I'd stored were missing, including an ornate, solid cherrywood mirror that had hung in my childhood home's foyer. Other boxes had been rifled through and left to rodent infestation. When you don't take charge of your life, others step in to fill the vacuum and you are left with the sometimes demoralizing results.

Chris locked up the house, loaded up our car, and we headed out of town. The new house sat on a nice piece of land about twenty minutes outside the city. This AFC home was called Pinewood Estates. It was a tri-level home, with six bedrooms on the two upper floors. Two residents shared each room, with twin beds and two dressers; the space was quite spartan, but for the few personal touches each had brought when he or she came there to live. A few farms dotted the surrounding landscape, gravel crunching under truck tires as they rumbled past the front porch deck. That first day, the owner and I sipped iced tea and discussed various odds and ends, while Chris walked off to explore the woods behind the house.

Several people living there came out to introduce themselves. One of them was Charlie. He was sixty years old, but from my observation over time had the mental capacity of a child of about six years of age. He was tall and almost ethereally thin; his sunken cheeks and eyes, graying hair and long bony fingers adding to the eerie effect. He had a reedy voice and ready smile and shyly extended a hand to greet me. One by one my new companions took their turns in saying hello and then just stood around nearby trying to look casual or otherwise occupied, meanwhile sneaking sidelong glances at the woman who was to become their next chief cook and bottle washer. They were like children in so many ways, and children had always treated me better than most adults I'd known. I liked my chances.

I was up to bat to make dinner that evening, no time to process the whole thing or sort out my possessions. Chris flipped burgers on the grill out back as I sliced tomatoes, pickles and onions. I cut up some potatoes and made home fries in the deep fryer for the group. They were all thankful for the meal, drifting off afterward to watch TV or sit outside while I washed the dishes.

Dottie had left the evening meds in tiny paper cups with names attached on Post-it notes, and so after giving everyone their pills and saying good night, I descended the stairs to my apartment and collapsed on the couch, staring at the piles of boxes to be unloaded and put in place and praying that I hadn't just made a huge mistake in coming here.

The next few weeks were on-the-job training for me. If I didn't know where something was kept, I'd ask someone living there and be shown. Many liked to help me with chores, so if someone was capable of vacuuming, and it pleased him or her to do it, the Hoover belonged to that person. I did laundry two times a week. If they were physically able, the residents would carry their loads to the basement and retrieve them, clean and folded, that night after dinner.

Charlie loved to go to the mailbox and pick up the newspaper for me each day. He'd come back singing and muttering to himself, knocking at the kitchen door and saying, "Honey, I've got your paper!" He was a sweet guy, but you had to watch out. One afternoon he came upstairs after lunch to thank me for the great meal. He sidled up behind me at the sink and, wiggling his bony fingers in my direction, summoned me closer for a kiss of gratitude. I turned to find his thin lips stretched to reveal a toothy smile complete with cottage cheese curds wedged between incisors and canines.

There were also the know-it-alls who took pride in telling me that they would help with a certain task as (fill in a name) was not competent to do such a thing, usually within earshot of the other guy. These same people would be the tattletales of the group. If any infraction was committed, large or small, these do-gooders would be on tap to inform me and then hopefully witness any outcome that humbled another. I've always had great distaste for bullies and sycophants.

Chris, who had just turned fifteen, seemed to be adjusting well, at least from outward appearances. He had already found friends to hang out with, and once school started, he had a pretty busy social life. The people living in the house loved my son. He played horseshoes with them or let them help him grill something for dinner or carry in groceries when Dottie would go shopping for us; most of them loved to help. Chris listened to them talk about how their day had gone or an upcoming trip they were going to be taking with their family. A few of the "girls" (remember, they ranged in age from mid-thirties to sixty-plus) had what I'd call a crush on Chris. They got all giggly and silly when he singled them out for attention. One asked me when he'd be old enough to marry.

MY SON AND I lived in this large tri-level house on the edge of woods with twelve people who had a variety of mental challenges that well . . . challenged me. Many didn't have any sense of boundaries. I was hounded at all hours of the night with what they thought of as emergencies, ranging from reminding me not to wash their new shirt in hot water because it would surely shrink, to imploring me never to serve zucchini (I hadn't as of yet) as they had always hated it and didn't want to ever see it again in this lifetime. Another person knocked at my door after two in the morning to inform me that his roommate was snoring and that therefore he needed to come into my apartment to sleep on my couch. I finally installed a notice on my apartment door that asked questions: "Is it after eight P.M.? Is this an emergency? Is the house on fire? Is someone hurt or in physical danger? Are you bleeding from a main artery? If the answer is no, don't knock! It can wait till morning. Please! I need some rest, too!"

Marlene, sixty-two, came to my apartment door after ten one night, pounding for all she was worth and calling my name. I said through the door, "Marlene, what do you need?" She responded, "Well, I *think* I have a headache!"

"Marlene, are you *sure* you have a headache?"

"Yes, Nancy, I think I do." There followed a five-second pause, and then "Yes, I do!" I opened the door with the aspirin bottle in hand and she started giggling. "I fooled you, Nancy," she said. "I really only wanted a kiss good night!" Well, I was not in the habit of giving kisses good night, especially to women with chin hair and a tendency to scratch themselves in untoward places before wanting to hold your hand, so I gave Marlene a *light* hug, shut the door and went back to what I'd been doing. These guys may have had mental difficulties, but they weren't stupid.

Jenna and Molly were in their mid-thirties and worked for a local business geared to the capabilities of the disabled. These two did line work, simple assembly jobs. They worked hard and sweat a lot in the heat of the factory.

Molly was a very caring soul, quick to anger, fast to forgive and first there to console or stand up for another person in trouble (as she perceived it, and whether they solicited her help or not). She was loud, and when she got excited and talked fast, you might get a spit shower if you were standing within range. She got off the bus after work wearing a scowl almost every day. Someone had pissed her off again at work or on the bus and she needed to talk with me about the injustice. Once the venting was taken care of, I'd tell her it was time to take a shower while I cooked dinner for her.

It was as if you'd told her she had to shower in liquefied monkey dung. She'd protest, stamp her feet, request that you smell her armpits (they really weren't so bad, she'd say) and, after many minutes of quibbling, see the resolute look on my face and march off to the upstairs bath to face her doom. I'd swing open the kitchen door when I heard her lumbering back by, to make sure she'd changed into clean clothes as well. Her gait was distinctive, loud and plodding, and after her shower she'd be recognizable also in that she would be muttering aloud over her victimization and abusive treatment at my hands.

Jenna had some interesting quirks. She loved to go shopping with the money she'd earned at her job and would bring home clothes from the store, remove the labels, put the labels in her top drawer, neatly fold the clothing items or hang them up and almost never take the items out of the closet again, ever. Jenna did love the tags, though. I'd come into her room to say good night and often find her sorting and looking at these tags with pictures of ladies on them. She was fairly mellow, unless somebody accused her of something she either didn't do or didn't want to confess to doing. Her face would turn bright red in protest. Only one other thing really upset Jenna. And that was when I needed to launder her purple Garfield sweatshirt. She would cry and cry till I returned it to her clean and folded. The thing must have been five years old, had come apart at the seams in spots, and Garfield was chipping off badly. But, man, it stank after a hard day's work and I was going to wash it.

Jenna's family picked her up on weekends to go out for dinner and shopping. One Saturday night she returned with a big box that she took into the TV room to open. Molly sat there on her knees like a kid at Christmas, watching Jenna open the packaging. It was a boom box and really deluxe, as she pointed out. She could not only listen to cassette tapes, but could record her voice as well. It had an AM-FM radio function, too. Molly turned off the lights in the living room to be able to see the dials glow in total darkness. She was transfixed and Jenna knew it. I stood at the edge of the room to watch, neither woman knowing I could see their interaction.

Jenna gave Molly a cassette to put in the machine. Molly's eyes got wide with this generous offer, but as she attempted to get it in the proper slot, Jenna grabbed it back, saying that Molly would only screw it up and damage her new boom box. Jenna added that Molly would never own something so nice, because *she* couldn't save her money! Molly was exasperated. She flung herself onto Jenna with a fury. I flipped on the lights and charged into the melee. Fists flew and I was struck inadvertently, but mostly it was feelings that were injured in the brief attack. Within a few days, I'd see the two of them out on the expansive back lawn, playing music and dancing and recording themselves singing duets. Then, another storm floated out onto the horizon in the form of a man.

Yes, these two women were smitten with the same hunk o' burning love, a guy named Bernard who had recently come to work alongside them on the factory line. This guy was a real keeper; he had greasy, long blond hair and bad acne and wore a Detroit Tigers ball cap that hadn't been laundered since the team won the World Series in 1984. Salt marks rimmed the crusty cap. Bernard mostly grunted, though he was perfectly capable of speech. He was brought as a guest to the dinner table many a night, and I once heard him ask to have the basket of rolls passed.

Jenna and Molly's rivalry over this fine specimen was kept below the roiling level until Bernard made a bold move. Until this time he'd been stringing them both along, sitting first with Molly at the lunch table at work, then alternating the next day with Jenna. These two would argue over whom Bernard *really* liked till the day Jenna came home wearing "the ring." She ran into the kitchen, her arm extended right under my nose, which was over a pot of steaming beef stew at the time. "Look, Nancy! Look what Bernard bought me! We're engaged!" I told Jenna that it was beautiful, but over her shoulder I could see Molly walk in the door, head lowered and sporting a frown. She thudded by down the hall into her bedroom and slammed the door. Jenna pretended not to know why Molly was upset. I told her she knew darn good and well why she was upset, turned off the stove and went off to talk with Molly.

In my experience, many people with disabilities get over disappointments more quickly than others do. Within days, Molly was waltzing in after work, telling me that Jenna was a fool, Bernard was a loser, and besides, Jenna had informed Molly that Bernard made her buy his lunch and snacks and also pay for movies they went to or anything else they did as a couple. A few weeks later, the engagement was off; perhaps Jenna's frugal nature finally kicked in and she realized the folly of diminishing returns on her investment. She gave Bernard back his Walmart diamond chip and seamlessly fell back into single life. However, Bernard's Svengali-like charms must have still held sway with Molly, because only one week after the dissolution of his nuptial pact with Jenna, it was Molly who came home wearing the very same priceless token of Bernard's affection and everlasting commitment.

One night in late summer I was doing dishes after dinner, when my son, Chris, and one of the more alert residents, Sam, knocked on the kitchen door, saying that I really should come out into the back-yard to see what was happening. We walked out onto the deck at the back of the house. About fifty yards from our position I spied an undulating mound of humanity in the grass near the woods that spanned the property. A smaller mound was positioned nearby. I didn't have my glasses on, so I asked what and/or who was out there, and just what were they doing?

Chris paused and looked at Sam for support. . . . Sam hesitated for a moment and then began slowly, "Nancy, they're uhhh, well, they're procreating, I do believe." God Almighty! I knew then it was Molly and Bernard, up to bat, with Jenna squatting in position as umpire, I supposed. Sam and Chris were doubled over laughing at this point; I was not. "Molly, Jenna! Get your butts in here this instant! Bernard, you too, mister! And I mean now!" I had faced many odd situations since I moved in here, but this one really took the gold medal.

Thinking about the whole episode later, I felt torn. After all, these people were in their thirties and had natural urges like anyone else. Of course their chosen venue and the addition of an observer were less than prudent, not acceptable in our circumstances, but I still felt bad about having to come down so hard on them for what had hap-pened. In fact, when any resident of an AFC home is involved in an act such as this, very strict protocol must be followed. The police must be summoned, each party's case manager has to come to the site and make a report, and all families involved are notified. I also had to fill out an incident report for my files and send a copy to the pertinent county agency.

I think the cops made a big impression on Bernard. The officers took him out into the garage to talk for a while, and once he was told he could leave, Bernard took off in his parents' car and was never seen at our home again. Jenna and Molly told me that the next day at work, they saw Bernard coming into the cafeteria, but once he saw the two of them sitting together, he laid down his lunch tray and left the room.

THAT HOUSE, THOSE PEOPLE, had become my world. I rarely stepped outside the door or looked out the windows much: It would only be a reminder of what I was no longer a part of. The owner took everyone to doctor's appointments and bought the groceries, and a bus picked up the workers every morning, so there was no need for me to leave.

One morning I had to go out on the front porch for some reason. Pinewood Estates was located on an old, tree-lined country road with few neighbors and beyond those few dwellings, only fields as far as the eye could see. I couldn't put my finger on it right away, but something didn't seem right to me that morning. Something was amiss in the scenery. All at once it dawned on me. It was the trees! It was now autumn, and the elms had all but shed their leaves. Their bony, finger-like branches danced in the cool breeze. The last time I'd been on this porch was springtime, with new foliage to greet my eyes. Each of these revelations added another layer to my numbness, to my detachment from the outside world. I went back inside and closed the door.

My companions at the home loved my homemade soups. In the autumn, with the temperature falling, chicken with vegetables and egg noodles really hit the spot. That fall day was spent slicing mountains of vegetables, cooking whole chickens, straining broth, adding seasoning and noodles and making sure there was space for two twenty-quart stockpots to cool in the refrigerators that were in the basement.

It had been a long, hot day inside the kitchen, but after serving everyone soup, a salad and crusty French bread, I was left with a feeling of accomplishment. I only had one last mission to complete before calling it a night. I needed to get those vats of soup down the seven steps from the kitchen level to the dining room level, turn the corner and head down the last eight steps to the basement and set them into the fridge to cool and later be repackaged for the freezer.

I was and am a very careful person in general, and particularly so when I was an obese person. Balance is a problem when you're that overweight; the slightest nudge can knock you on your keister, and the consequences can be far more serious than for the average person. Another of my "qualities" is stubbornness. Pair that trait with the candidates I could call on to help me with this task, and perhaps you can see why I chose to do it myself. I didn't want anyone else to get hurt or ruin my day's work by sloshing the contents of those huge, heavy pots onto the floor. The transfer of the first pot went off without a hitch. *Slow and steady wins the race*, I thought, as I headed back up the stairs to the kitchen to retrieve the second pot.

Several people were seated playing cards in the lower-level dining room. I asked a girl named Shanna to hold open the basement door for me again as I lumbered past with my aromatic pot. I stepped gingerly onto the first step, then another. Around the middle of my descent, I felt a tug on the back of my skirt's elastic waistband, followed by guffaws and snickers from above. In that instant, I lost my balance and began my plummet to the bottom. I was still grasping the pot handles when gravity had completed its task and planted me firmly on the tile floor at the base of the steps. Still stunned by this treachery, I glared at the collected humanity above me on the landing.

No one was laughing now. A resident named Darla came barreling down the stairs to help. I told her to please leave me there; I'd be all right on my own. I was sitting in an enormous puddle of broth, noodles sticking to my hair, and a piece of carrot nesting in my ample cleavage. I didn't want to try to get up with everyone watching, so I asked them all to leave. They shut the top door, and there I sat, proud, stubborn and wearing a heavy dose of poultry cologne. I did manage to stand up on my own. I grabbed the pot handles and took what was left inside of my day's work to the refrigerator, trying to pretend that nothing had happened. My ankle hurt, but not so badly that I couldn't walk. I would be A-OK.

After cleaning up the crime scene, I went back upstairs and took a shower. Molly approached me and said she needed to talk. She was crying, and confessed that it had been she who had grabbed my skirt. She said that others had encouraged her to do it, and that she was sorry I had fallen. After a little preaching regarding having your own mind and ability to makes choices for yourself and following your own conscience, I hugged Molly and slowly went back down the stairs and off to my bed.

Yes, it was a new day when I awoke the next morning, but the pain I now felt in my ankle was not about to let me forget the events of the night before; it was throbbing like mad. But I didn't feel the full impact of my injury till I tried to get out of bed. Sure, my body was sore, my hip and upper arm ached, but I wasn't prepared for the excruciating jolt I felt as I stood and put my full weight on that left ankle. Yet I had to get up. People needed breakfast and their medications, and there were lunches to pack; they were getting ready for work, and so must I. I put as little pressure as possible on the left foot as I hobbled to the straight-back chair near the kitchen table in my private quarters. I just needed to limber this thing up was all. I stood there sliding that chair in front of me as I hobbled back and forth across the room for more than thirty minutes, believing that eventually the problem would work itself out.

The alternative was unthinkable; I would have to go to a doctor. Not only had most of my experiences with doctors been less than helpful, but the humiliation I had gone through can never be truly understood by anyone who hasn't felt it personally. Irrational as it seems, I would have rather trudged feebly with that chair for an eternity than have to expose myself to the staring, unflinching and judgmental eyes of those whom I would encounter on my way for help. The pain ebbed slightly as I continued to move across the room, and it was past the time I had to get upstairs, so up I went.

Every morning for weeks I went through this ritual with the chair. Within an hour or two of getting up, the pain was bearable, but still quite pronounced. After a night without pressure on it, I was back to ground zero and had to begin anew the next morning. I simply learned to live with it. The pain subsided eventually, to the degree that the memory of the chicken noodle affair was mostly forgotten. Months later I noticed two knobby areas on my leg; one midway up my shinbone and the other at the side of my left ankle. Just another couple of war wounds. My body was so beyond help that it didn't affect me to see these. I hadn't felt proud of my physical appearance for so many years that nothing about it mattered anymore.

LIFE WENT ON; mine always did. And with the change of seasons came the rain. I became particularly sensitive about rain during my time at Pinewood Estates. You would think I'd be used to it; I was born in Seattle, after all, but the rain in this case made my basement apartment turn from an oasis of peace and relaxation into something that looked like an Indonesian island after the monsoon waters recede.

I called the owner to tell her what had happened. She was from Alabama and in her slow and easy way tried to assure me, "Oh, honey, it's *only* water! I'll bring the shop vac and it'll be fine in no time!" She and her husband showed up, and as I prepared breakfast upstairs, I could hear the hum of the machine sucking up the contents of my indoor pool. I stood there buttering toast, realizing how helpless I was. I wanted to quit. But where would I go? Who would hire someone who *looked like me*? This place had been a godsend in a way; I could hide from the world and still take care of my son financially. I felt stuck. I had to stay. But . . . it would only get worse.

The flooding happened over and over again. The owner ended up leaving the shop vac there in a back room so I could haul it out and use it as needed. All my wood and wicker furniture had discoloration at the bases. Some things warped horribly. My son and I always had to remember to pick up whatever was on the floor before bedtime. Woody Allen's book *Without Feathers* still bears the trademark wavy pages from being dropped to the floor one night when I fell asleep on the couch.

My weight was increasing steadily. I didn't need to weigh myself—nor could I on the house floor scale, it only registered up to two hundred and sixty pounds—I could *feel* it, in my body and in the way I moved. The elastic-waistbanded skirts I'd sewn for myself a few years prior had been stretched so far by my increasing waistline that the elastic, well, wasn't so elastic anymore. I still wanted to free myself from this body that shackled me. Many people don't understand how many times an obese person starts over again. How often they make a plan to control their food and *do* stick to that plan for a while, only to resort to the drug of choice when things got difficult.

I found the number for an Overeaters Anonymous chapter in my area and made plans to go that week. I called my mom, and she said she'd come for a couple of hours to watch over the residents with Chris. That afternoon, my mom, Chris and most of the other residents stood out on the front lawn next to the drive to watch my departure. Molly and Jenna both cheered as I grabbed on to my son's car door handle. Chris had moved the seat back to the farthest setting for me. I hadn't driven in a couple of years—not since I'd driven us to Pinewood Estates two years before. I put my rear end down onto the seat and attempted to swing my legs around. I'd performed this motion thousands of times over the years; as natural as breathing, right? Well, not this time. I couldn't fit my belly behind the wheel. I sat there for quite some time in denial, fidgeting and squirming to wrestle my bloated abdomen behind that damnable plastic circle, but to no avail. I got back out and, without comment, waddled past my well-wishers in total disgust. I felt completely defeated. A desperate woman risks humiliation by going to town for help and is stopped by the very thing she needs help controlling. Mom stayed that night and cooked dinner for everyone. I was in no mood to do anything; not anything at all.

Each resident had a caseworker who'd come out periodically to check the person's records and so on. I got to know them quite well and we'd sit, drink coffee and exchange "war stories" sometimes. One named June informed me that the average "shelf life" of a resident manager was six months; I had been there well over two years. She asked how I did it; where did I get my stamina? I told her there was a simple explanation. I had *become one of them.*

CHAPTER 10

Crying Uncle/Giving Up the Ship

CHRIS WAS SIXTEEN NOW and had things to do besides help his mom out with chores. He was growing up. We got along all right, as well as any rebellious, sixteen-year-old person and ancient (thirty-two-year-old) know-nothing mother can be expected to. Though Chris went through growing pains and was not always happy with my rules or restrictions on his freedom, he was a good kid in general and earned good grades in school. He was very bright and absorbed knowledge like a sponge. He made me feel very proud, and I had hopes of a wonderful future for him. It was sad to think that even in 1989, the year before he would walk out on stage to receive his diploma, we both knew that I would not be sitting in the audience to see this important milestone.

I also knew he worried about me, about my health. One night Chris was sitting alone at the kitchen table downstairs in our living quarters when I came through the door from work. I sat down next to him to chat and he started welling up. I've always hated to see anyone cry, but especially my son. I asked him what was wrong and moved closer to put my arms around him. He whispered, almost moaning, "Mom, I'm so afraid you'll die, you're getting worse and worse. You always promise me you'll do better and then I see you eating something I know you shouldn't. It's horrible to watch you slowly killing yourself!"

I had deluded myself into thinking that I was taking good care of my son; I bought him an expensive black leather jacket, I paid for his prom, bought him a nice drum set, helped him with a down payment on his first car and his second . . . you name it, if he asked for it I would move heaven and earth to get it for him. He had things; but he was desperately afraid that he'd lose *me*.

It cut me to the bone and I begged him to believe once more. I vowed that I'd change; I'd change *for him*! We all know how that promise panned out. With every extra bite of food, I hated myself for being so weak, for hurting my son, for being a failure on every front. And my malignant thoughts became a self-fulfilling prophecy; I was further cementing my belief that I was beyond redemption, a lost cause.

But still, every day I got up, kissed Chris as he went off to school, trudged slowly up the stairs and prepared breakfast for the twelve souls in my charge and began another workday. There were loads of laundry to do, appointments to set up for residents, paperwork and charts to fill out, beds to strip, questions to answer, bickering to put a stop to, lunch and dinner to prepare, and so it went day to day, month after month. A time bomb was ticking, but my state of denial was complete.

* * *

I LIKED TO BATHE in the bathroom at the end of the upstairs hall. There were three bathrooms in total. This one was located farthest from the living room, the place most likely to be populated during evening hours when I'd finally have the chance to do something for myself. There were only two other doors in this area, and both led to the bedrooms of some of the more tame, less nosy patrons. They kept to themselves, and I didn't generally have to worry about being interrupted while trying to get cleaned up. Peace was at a premium in this job.

I ran the water while I started to undress, putting my fingers in to test the temperature. It felt good and my body ached all over. I lowered myself slowly, using the rail installed on the wall for support. It had always been a tight squeeze for me in that tub. I was finished washing and grabbed onto the rail to lift myself up. I tugged and tugged; no movement at all. I had become a giant suction device. My hindquarters made a great seal. At first, I was only annoyed. After several attempts, panic set in: Would I have to call to a resident and have them phone the cops or fire department? I could see the headlines now, "Obese AFC Manager Extricated from Bathtub by Jaws of Life."

I sat there kneading, cajoling and desperately trying to wedge my hands between myself and the tub to break the vacuum. Bit by bit I worked my way to victory, but it was a long, hard slog and one I could not afford to risk repeating. I looked at myself dripping wet in the mirror after my exhausting dislodgment. I was disgusted by what had just occurred. That would be the last tub bath I would have for many years to come.

*   *   *

MY SISTER DIANE had recently moved back to Grand Rapids from Chicago, in 1990. She came out to visit me one day soon after arriving home. I was standing in the kitchen preparing lunch for the residents as we chatted. Diane was distraught. "Nancy, you can't go on this way, and if you stay here any longer, with this workload and trying to meet all the emotional needs of these people in the bargain, the owner will find you dead on the kitchen floor one morning. You'll have a heart attack making scrambled eggs."

If anyone but Diane had brought me this kind of message, I wouldn't have listened. My sister had finally put into words what I could never admit. I slumped down into a chair and wept as I hadn't in a very long time. I was finally free to admit defeat. I was so ashamed. I'd let myself down, my family and, now, the people at Pinewood Estates who needed me. Diane finished making their lunch for me and then set her plan into action.

She called the owner of the business and told her they needed to meet. Diane read her the riot act, telling her that she was negligent in allowing this situation to go unchecked for so long and in not allowing for any time off. I countered that it was not Dottie's fault that I'd become so heavy. I was embarrassed to be treated like a child, as if I had no control over my situation; but the truth was that I was completely out of control and it had to stop or I would die. Diane gave the owner two weeks' notice and said that she would be taking over my duties for that time.

And what about Chris, what was going to happen to him? He had finished high school that May, so next year's classes weren't an issue, but I wasn't going to just unceremoniously uproot my son, saying, "Sayonara, baby . . . it's been nice, but I've got to fly! See you around!" He wasn't quite eighteen yet, or ready to be out on his own, far from it.

I was humiliated to admit to Bob that I'd gone over the edge *again* and was unable to take care of our child. We were rarely in contact, hadn't been for years, and this wasn't a conversation I wanted to have with him. Bob had remarried years before; he still saw Chris on weekends, but he just pulled up in the drive on Saturdays and Chris ran out to meet him.

I talked with Chris about all of it, crying so hard that I couldn't even string sentences together, and we both were aware that our lives were going to be different from that moment on. I deserved every bit of this pain and more. I had created this situation, and just as when the divorce had come about, or when my years of out-of-control drinking had caused him such turmoil, Chris was again powerless to change anything about what was about to happen to him.

My son called his father the next day, unbeknownst to me. It certainly wasn't his obligation to do so; I only know that when Chris told me that he had, and that his dad had agreed to help, I was relieved. Humiliated, but relieved. And Bob was actually very decent in the way he handled everything. He never berated me or tried to make me feel worse about the situation than I already did.

I stayed in my basement apartment while Diane took care of things upstairs. At night we'd talk about where I wanted to go from there, and of course my options were limited. She brought up the fact that I would most likely qualify for Social Security disability payments, but I initially balked at the idea that I couldn't take care of myself and tried to counter with the suggestion that I could make crafts to sell. I was a good seamstress, I could crochet afghans; I was desperate and it showed. I had to come to grips with reality, and I didn't like it one bit.

The first thing on the agenda was finding me a place to stay. My niece Fiona offered me a room in her home. She had a husband and two small children at the time, and though I loved her and knew she was an easygoing person, I frankly thought of how uncomfortable it would be having her and her husband see me walking around and struggling to do everything. I declined my niece's kind offer.

My eldest sister, Laura, and her husband, Peter, asked me to come and stay with them, just as their daughter Fiona had. They owned a condo with a finished basement. She and Peter both worked during the day and had no children left at home, so I'd have the place to myself during work hours and be able to shower, cook a meal or get a bit of sun on their enclosed patio out back without disturbing them or vice versa. The basement had a bedroom and living room, and so I would be quite comfortable space-wise. It was my best option and I gratefully accepted.

The only encumbrance I faced at my sister's was the set of stairs leading to my quarters. They were rather steep and numbered fourteen in total. You remember things like the number of steps when you're heavy. I used a plastic-handled grocery bag to carry things in one hand, resting my back and rear end against the wall opposite the railing and then holding the railing in front of me with my free hand, slowly descended to my rooms below, one foot landing and then being met by the other on the same step, repeating this slow and careful process till I reached the basement level. This task alone would leave me exhausted and out of breath.

I had applied for Social Security when I moved out of Pinewood Estates but was told it might be as much as a year till I heard whether or not I'd been approved. I had to apply for food stamps to subsidize my living expenses, but Laura and Peter's generosity made up the lion's share of my survival during that time. I had to go in for a physical assessment as part of the criteria for SS. Both Laura and Diane went with me for moral support that day. I was in dread of the whole process, but it had to be done.

I was rolled into a room in a wheelchair to be weighed. My sisters were with me as the numbers were called out. Four hundred and two pounds echoed across the room. There it was: numerical evidence of what I'd done to myself, written out in big bold print on the nurse's clipboard and in my mind. I was next sent for X-rays. Lying on a stainless steel table is probably uncomfortable for a normal-sized person; for the obese, it is pure torture.

"Lie flat on your back and hold completely still." I could *not* lie flat on my back. I was encased in a shelf of fat that did not allow for such a thing. The ledge of fat surrounding my buttocks wouldn't permit the base of the spine to lie flat against anything. The spine then had no support and so was left in a contorted position, causing great pain. I was sweating and making every attempt not to cry out. I also had difficulty breathing well in this position. The pressure bearing down on my chest only allowed for shallow breaths. I was then asked to turn on my side so they could get shots of other regions of interest, which caused similar types of problems for me.

It was during this visit that I first found out that I'd broken my ankle back in my tumble down the basement stairs with the pot of soup at Pinewood Estates. The calcified bone shown on the X-ray bore evidence to what I'd denied out of a deluded sense of emotional self-preservation in refusing to see a doctor.

I was escorted into an exam room and met there by a doctor who bore a striking resemblance to Richard Milhous Nixon, poor man. He ticked off the requisite items on his clipboard's checklist as he went along. The doctor peered into my eyes, nose and throat. He banged on my knees with a mallet. And then he asked me to do something that common sense, physiology and the laws of gravity forbade my obedience to perform. He said, "Do a squat for me." I wanted to say, "What are you, nuts?" But instead, I said, "I'll tell you what, Doc. I am sure I can descend momentarily into the squat position for you, but once down, you will have to lift me back up. You game?" Without uttering a word of acknowledgment or displaying any change in his countenance, the man in the white coat ticked that item off his list and went on to the next.

After what seemed like an eternity of prodding and scrutiny, and reams of papers being signed, I was released from my bondage and wheeled by my sister Diane outside to her car in the parking lot, where I squeezed my tired butt onto the bench seat in the back. I wanted nothing more than to go home. I craved human attention, but not the kind I received even while sitting in a car at a traffic light. People do turn and stare, sometimes even yelling foul things out of their windows to make sure you know of their disgust.

I didn't have a personal physician at that time. My sister Laura said she had one that was very thorough and kind and that maybe she could help me with a good weight loss plan. I wanted to lose weight; really I did. I asked Laura if she might ask if this doctor would make a house call in my case. When she told me the doctor had agreed to come, I was surprised and delighted. It gave me reason to believe that this woman must be compassionate or she wouldn't have extended herself by visiting me after hours.

The afternoon of my appointment, I took a shower and put on

my nicest skirt. I made sure everything was tidy in my room and waited for Laura to bring this doctor down to me. Finally, she was there. She was a thin woman, probably in her mid-thirties, with long, dark hair and a warm smile. I was sitting on the edge of my bed as the doctor entered the room. She checked my pulse and the usual things, and then we began to talk, about family, life in general, small talk mostly. I then told her how desperate I felt, how alone and out of control I'd become. I told the doctor that I was ashamed of being about as old as she was and probably about to start living on a government subsidy. I had a good mind, but here I sat, wasting the life and opportunities that could be mine. She said that all I had said was true, that if I didn't get a handle on my weight, nothing good could ever happen for me, in fact I would more than likely die prematurely. I knew she was right and told her I agreed.

I was hoping she'd give me a decent food plan and a limited exercise program to follow and come back to see me once a month to check on my progress and encourage me. I had already begun to eat healthier and showed her a food journal I'd been keeping over the last few weeks. I certainly knew a bit about nutrition; I'd read enough charts and calorie counts by this point in my life and had built a plan that limited me to about twelve hundred calories per day. She looked it over, shaking her head as she read. She told me that in order to lose any appreciable amount of weight, I'd have to stick to a five- to six-hundred-calorie a day diet, no more than that. That amount of nourishment wouldn't support a newborn infant and I knew it; I wondered why *she* didn't seem to. I was shocked by her prescription, but uttered not a word in rebuttal. I just kept nodding. Soon she rose, told me that it had been nice meeting me and wished me luck. I kept my smile till she turned the corner and headed up those fourteen stairs to the main floor, but as the door at the top was pulled shut, I felt tears beginning to trickle down my cheeks.

I RECEIVED A LARGE, thick envelope from the Social Security Administration. I was nervous as I slit the edge to take a look. While approval for receiving benefits would be no cause for celebration, rejection would bring far more anxiety over what my future would hold. The letter read something like this: "It has been determined that you are ineligible for SS. You do not meet the criteria for enrollment. If you wish to dispute our findings, you must appeal this decision within the specified time frame. You may contact our office at the following number with any further questions."

I was devastated. It was just one more brick in my prison wall. What, pray tell, did they think I was capable of doing to earn a living? I had no office experience or even legitimate typing skills, barring my two-fingered pecking back at the monastery years before, and even if I was able somehow to wrangle some kind of placement where I wouldn't have to move around much, perhaps only answering phones, can you imagine the problems attached to trying to accommodate a woman of my size? Seating would be a nightmare, as would narrow pathways between desks, and any stair climbing would be a liability.

I thought back on the time I'd gone into a well-known, out-of-the-way restaurant near Cannonsburg Ski Lodge to apply for a cooking job that had been advertised back before I'd taken the placement at Pinewood Estates. This establishment was located inside an old farmhouse. It was a quaint, beautiful setting in and out, had a wonderful, innovative menu, but the kitchen area was very cramped.

The production table was located in the middle of the small room, refrigerator on one side, stoves on the other. As the manager led me through the maze of equipment, I remember the humiliation of having to turn to walk sideways between the counter and stove area. I could tell what he was thinking, too. How in the world would I move quickly and safely while doing my job, a job that I was more than qualified to perform? I had even brought an example of my baking skills for him to sample. It was a turtle cheesecake; New York–style, laced with milk chocolate in the mix, pecans, chocolate and homemade caramel drizzled over the top. He loved the cheesecake, I think he even liked *me,* but as I turned to shake his hand when finishing our interview, his words of "getting back to me soon" didn't match the unspoken message in his eyes. No harm, no foul. It wasn't this guy's fault. My body size simply made it unfeasible to hire me. I had to appeal the decision from SS.

I FELT ALONE AND ISOLATED, but talking to God helped. Even if He didn't answer right away with the proverbial bolt-of-lightning epiphany, prayer at least gave me a sense of calm as I waited for the celestial lightbulb to come on. One day it dawned on me that it had been fifteen years or more since I'd last been to confession, and I was feeling a strong urge to wipe the slate clean. I called the parish nearest me and asked if the priest was available to come hear my confession and bring me Holy Communion. We set up an appointment for the following Saturday. My brother-in-law Peter hauled my huge upholstered ottoman—the only seat in their home that could accommodate me—up from my room in the basement and placed it in their dining room so I could comfortably greet Father upstairs. He and Laura made plans to go shopping that afternoon, so I was left alone with my thoughts.

As the time of my meeting approached, I looked over the three pages of sins I'd enumerated on a large yellow legal pad over the last few days. No one could ever accuse me of being vague; I hammered at my memory, specifying location, instance and other players injured by my misdeeds and general nastiness.

Father rang the bell outside the open door. From my position on the ottoman, I called for him to come inside. I heard the screen door open and shut, and as he rounded the corner from the entryway to the dining room, he stopped for a moment. I assumed he was shocked by what he saw, so I steeled myself for the usual reaction. He said, "My, you bear a striking resemblance to Jean Simmons in her role as the crippled girl sitting at the well, the girl that Jesus healed!" Well, I love old movies and knew that Jean Simmons was a very pretty woman, and while I was not familiar with this particular film, I ate up his comment like manna from heaven.

We exchanged pleasantries for a few minutes and then he said, "So, how on earth did you let this happen to yourself, you have such a pretty face?" Strike the "manna from heaven" comment. Would I never be able to have a single normal conversation with someone? This question came not only from a man of God, but from one whose mortal coil appeared before me in the form of a sixty-year-old, pudgy and balding guy in bifocals whose left eye twitched. *Let he who is without sin cast the first stone*, I thought, inwardly seething. Guess that biblical phrase doesn't apply to the sin of gluttony.

After ten or more minutes' recital of my failings as a human being, Father called a halt to the proceedings, saying there was no need to go into every sin, especially considering the number of years we were covering; that a summary and true sorrow for having offended God was all that was necessary. Perhaps the copious tears and the pile of used tissues gave the priest the impression that I was sincerely remorseful, so he gave me absolution then and there, telling me to "go and sin no more." This was a tall order, but I promised to do my best.

I found out a couple of years later that this same priest had taken a leave of absence from his parish around the time of my marathon confession to go into an alcohol treatment center. I prayed that the shock of my "sinful" appearance and lengthy confession had not been the catalyst for his over-imbibing. Hey, I wonder why he let that happen to himself.

Chris called often to tell me how he was doing. He was still living with his dad, but saving up money from his earnings at Meijer's gas station in order to move into an apartment with a buddy from work. His love for Leane—a wonderful young woman he'd begun dating—had only grown stronger since they'd met three months before. She was still living in Mount Clemens, a three-hour drive from Grand Rapids, but he'd drive down often to visit her and they talked every day on the phone as well. There was something about Leane that Chris had not confided to me right away, but he finally did one night on the phone. Leane was four months pregnant with another man's baby.

Some parents would have probably tried to persuade their child not to get involved, especially at such a young age, in taking on that kind of responsibility. I knew Chris; even if I had protested, he would've stepped in and done what he could do to help. After listening for quite some time, I told him that I understood. To say otherwise would have done no good and caused a breach between us. I wanted Chris to know that he could talk to me when he found the need to do so. And he loved her. She had many endearing qualities and was very vulnerable. Leane had at times a difficult relationship with her parents. She and the father of the child she would give birth to had parted company well before Chris came onto the scene. It seemed that Chris was traveling down a path that I was all too familiar with. He would be eighteen when dear Ian was born; I had been sixteen when Chris had come into this world.

I settled into my new home and daily rituals over the next few months. I came upstairs each morning for breakfast after my sister and her husband left for work, and weather permitting I'd sit out back to recite the rosary or read a book. I always made sure that I was downstairs by the time Laura and Peter came home from work in the evening.

One night Laura came down to see me with a list of government-subsidized housing units available in our area. She told me that there were waiting lists at most of these places, so I should start making calls to get myself a place in line. I hadn't received an answer about my case from SS disability yet, but getting on a list was a reasonable first step. I really would've liked to be in my own place, but the thought of the move, of even meeting the people in the offices at these buildings, scared me to death.

For a couple of months, I lied to my sister and told her that I had made some calls, even put my name on a list or two, but nothing would be available for a long time. I never did find out for sure, but it seemed to me that she wanted me out of there, just a feeling I got from her. And I can understand that. I didn't want to be a burden or invade her and Peter's privacy, or moreover be a drain on their finances; I just felt so threatened by the outside world, so threatened, in fact, that I would lie to a sister, something I was not in the habit of doing.

Laura must have suspected I was stalling, as one day Diane came to see me. She said that she was moving into a bigger place and that there was room for me if I'd like to come. She thought I needed to get out of that basement and be able to see the outdoors just by glancing out a window. Her place was on the second floor of a house, but since I almost never went out, stairs would be a rare obstacle to overcome. I agreed, and plans were made for the move. Diane also took the list of subsidized housing options and made some calls herself. I was now on the list, like it or not, and would sooner or later have to face my fears and the people outside my comfort zone. I knew it was for the best. One of these options was the building my mom had lived in for the last year, and according to Diane, it was a very nice place.

Diane's landlord had agreed that I could come and stay with her, but had not met me as of yet. My family came and moved the things I was taking from Laura's, leaving me with my trusty ottoman to sit on till I left. I wanted to show up later that night, hoping that fewer neighbors would see my arrival. It was dusk when we pulled up to the house. I was relieved to see no one sitting on porches nearby.

My nephew Alex took my ottoman upstairs ahead of me, as I knew I'd need it immediately after I reached the summit of the stairs. My son, Chris, stood outside the car door to support me as I lifted up and out of the seat. A wheelchair was on the sidewalk so I could travel up the thirty-foot path to my new home. I needed to reserve all my energy just to get up those stairs. It was an older home, and as the side door opened, I could see the narrow, steep flight before me. I held the railing with my left hand and began my deliberate ascension. Chris came up right behind me to help in case I felt woozy and unbalanced. I always joked that the guy behind me anywhere I went must really love me; he had to be ready to die for me!

Finally reaching my second-floor destination, I sat down on my ottoman, which had been left next to the door. I was really out of breath and so just concentrated on cooling down for the moment. Once my heart stopped racing, I began to drink in my surroundings. It was a pleasant room, with a large set of windows facing the front of the house. There was a huge tree outside of them, its spring leaves dancing lightly in the warm breeze.

THE LANDLORD, JULIUS, AND HIS DISABLED WIFE lived downstairs, and I was told that they were both very nice. He was about eighty years old, but he still had the stamina to putter away for hours in his garden. Those first couple of days I spent my time reading at my bedroom window and glancing out on Julius hunching over in the yard beneath my window, planting, weeding and watering his beautifully colored friends.

Diane left for work early one morning, and I noticed how tired she looked when she was saying good-bye. She did so much for those around her, rarely taking time for her own care. I decided that I'd make a nice meal to greet her when she returned home that night. I was always careful to walk as lightly as possible, as this place had all hardwood floors and I didn't want to disturb Julius and his wife downstairs. I grabbed the salad ingredients I'd need and sat down at the kitchen table to prep the vegetables.

Then I remembered that the chicken breasts were frozen. I'd have to get them out to thaw now if I was going to be able to bake them in time for dinner. I found them wedged under some other items in the freezer and so had to move stuff to get to them. I had placed some items on the edge of the freezer compartment while I yanked the chicken out at the same time, and the breasts slid from my fingers and onto the hardwood floor. I cringed to think of the noise it must have made down below, but I continued with my task, moving the other items back in place and shutting the freezer door.

There was a door in the kitchen behind which were steps that led down into the landlord's level of the home. Within a minute of sitting back down to make the salad, I heard slow, shuffling steps approaching. Next came the unmistakable sound of the clatter of keys.

Julius looked surprised to see me. "Where's Diane?" he demanded. No niceties, no "Hello, I'm Julius. Are you Nancy?" I told him that she was at work and that I was preparing our evening meal. He told me he didn't care about dinner, and neither should I from the looks of me. He was there because he'd heard a god-awful noise and thought someone had fallen. I showed him the slip-and-fall victim lying there on the counter thawing and said I was sorry that I had disturbed him. He responded with "Diane told me you were large, but my. . . . You're enormous!"

I didn't know it at that moment, but it wasn't that night's chicken I needed to be worried about; it was my goose that was about to be cooked.

Diane walked into our apartment at the usual time carrying a manila envelope; my sister Laura had called her at work to let her know that a letter had come for me from the Social Security Administration. It was good news. My case had been reconsidered and my verbal jousting seemed to have done the trick. The letter said that I would be receiving benefits, and retroactively from the moment

I'd applied months before. I waited till after dinner to tell Diane about my odd introduction to our landlord and what he had said. She left to go downstairs soon after and didn't return for more than a half hour. I was on pins and needles as the minutes wore on, and though I couldn't imagine what was to come of my brief encounter with Julius, I worried that I was being a bother to my sister, and that thought upset me greatly. This caused another round of self-recriminations and heightened feelings of worthlessness as I sat and waited for news from Diane.

She looked drained when she returned. Finally, she began. "All right, Nancy . . . Julius seems to believe that he is at risk by having you stay here. He said that any number of catastrophes could ensue, including you having a heart attack, or falling down the stairs, and beyond that, he thinks it is possible that if you fell up here you might just go through the floorboards. He protested that the house is old, the boards aren't what they used to be, and he can't afford the risk that your weight might do damage to the home he and his wife worked for years to pay off. He is giving you two weeks to find someplace else to live."

Diane was crying now. "Guess this is God's way of telling me that I shouldn't hesitate in fulfilling my heart's desire, my long-wished-for dream any longer," I said. She asked me what I was talking about. "Well, to join the circus, of course! I can sleep in the quarters of the other elephants and will surely make friends with the bearded lady and Lobster Boy, don't you think?" She had to laugh. What else was there to do?

CHAPTER 11

A Cook with No Galley/Out of the Frying Pan and into the Fire

MOM OFTEN SAID that she was fortunate to have been blessed with so many daughters—married daughters, that is. Their husbands made perfect workhorses in situations like the one that faced me then. She would call on her labor force anytime she required a little muscle.

I was not gifted with Mom's sense of entitlement, however. It really bothered me to have to ask for help in any way or from anybody. I felt like such a failure. I should be able to do these things for myself. I was a young woman and quite strong. Back in the days when I cooked for a living, I heaved fifty-pound sacks of potatoes or onions easily. Asking for help only cemented in my mind how dependent I'd become. I wanted to be an asset, not a liability.

I wanted to be able to drive a car to a family function, pick up my contribution to the meal from the seat next to me and walk into the house to hear people say, *Hi, Nancy! Oooooh, you made a cheesecake!* And I could say, *Hey, what still needs to be done in the kitchen? Can I help with anything?* I was all take, take, take and not someone people were thrilled to see anymore. My family told me otherwise, of course. They liked having me with them, but it was all so complicated. Is there a place for her to sit? No, we'll have to bring something from her house. I couldn't fit in most family members' cars, and neither could my ottoman. If those with larger vehicles weren't able to attend, neither was I. And if I was playing cards or a board game, and the person who had driven me there needed to leave, well, the party was over for me, too. I had lost all control.

Where would I plant myself now? Mom called one day to talk about the situation and offered that I could stay with her for a short while. I couldn't see how it would work. She had only one bedroom and we often argued over trivialities. Plus, she wasn't allowed visitors for more than two weeks at a time. This was subsidized housing, and there was a raft of rules and regulations to follow. But I was running out of time and options, so we hatched a plan for me to go and stay with Mom for the duration. I still had an active phone line at Laura's place. I forwarded all my calls to Mom's number. I had the boys take all my things back to Laura's, except for what I needed day to day.

Julius, the landlord at Diane's, had become a frequent visitor since the infamous frozen poultry incident. He'd come upstairs almost every day to ask how the moving plans were coming along, and as he chitchatted, his eyes roamed the apartment for signs of structural damage caused by my tonnage. When I said that I would be moving in with my mom, he broke out into a wide Polident smile. He even offered his sons' services. Julius went over to the steps that led to the street below and, after a moment's perusal, informed me that he'd already consulted with his sons regarding my problem and that they were both handy with carpentry, had lots of plywood lying around and would be willing to fashion a slide of sorts for me, using ropes under my armpits to slowly lower me down to the ground floor. They were "big boys," and he was sure they could handle the task at hand.

Diane was sitting with me during this discussion, and her eyes apologized for Julius. I only smiled, thanked him for his concern for my welfare and said that we'd be in contact with him soon. I was planning on leaving within the next few days, but this charming interlude accelerated my scheduled departure.

Mom had two recliners in her living room; one was an electric power-lift chair, designed for people who had trouble getting up from a seated position. The other was the standard type. Mom was heavy, though not nearly as large as I, but she had arthritis in her knees and that made it difficult for her get up from a chair. She used the lift chair, leaving the other one for my use. Her couch was only a love seat; it was low to the ground and rocked as well. Sitting on that piece of furniture was out of the question for me, so the recliner became my new, cramped home. I ate, read books, watched TV and slept in that chair for the entire length of my stay in Mom's one-bedroom apartment. There wasn't room for my ottoman.

My mom worked as a foster grandparent in a government program that paired young kids in school with a retiree. They helped the children with their homework and read to them. She was given bus tokens, lunch and a stipend for performing this service, so she was gone for a good part of the day. Imagine trying to sleep in that recliner while Mom, fresh from her early morning bath, would sit in the chair opposite mine, spritzing twelve sprays of cologne (I began to count them) on various parts of her anatomy. Two behind each knee, one behind each ear, one at each elbow, one at the nape of her throat, one on each wrist and on and on and on.

These rituals of hers (there were many) were some of the things that brought out the worst in me. Mom was oblivious to her effect on others much of the time. When informed of someone's discomfort, she'd usually respond with "Why, that's just silly. . . . Why would anyone feel that way?"

Another unflattering quality my mom exhibited was her take on physical perfection. She'd whisper criticism of complete strangers' appearance; her standards were even higher and directly voiced in my case, as they sometimes were in the case of my sisters. My lips were fat, not lady-like, as Mom's were. (Hers were exact duplicates of Elizabeth Taylor's.) My hair was unruly. When I was a child in Seattle, she'd stand behind me in front of our foyer's cherrywood wall mirror, raking through my hair with a wet brush and bitterly complaining about its noncompliance. Why, my hair was as much of a rebel as I was! Even the freckles that dappled my nose were considered blots on my otherwise fair complexion. I never quite measured up. I sometimes wonder whether I took the opposing view to my mom's so often, whether I rebelled against anything she liked or wanted me to accede to, in some subconscious attempt to poke her and her scale of beauty, of perfection, right in her sea green eyes. . . . Mine were blue like Daddy's and commonplace, so nothing to write home about. External beauty truly is in the eye of the beholder, but is only skin-deep after all. It, too, fades with age. It's up to each of us to find that pleasing *internal* quality within the other, that lasting quality, and let them know how wondrous it is, how unique they are . . . how glad you are that they are in the world.

There were times, however, when we got along magnificently. I truly loved my mom, and she loved me, but she was so critical and self-absorbed and I was so stubborn that, unlike my sisters, who generally accepted what she dished out without much comment, probably the wiser move, I took umbrage at each and every disparaging observation, believing it to be a direct challenge to my personhood. "Oh, I wouldn't do it *that* way; funny how different people can be, isn't it, Nancy?" "Yeah, Florence," I'd drone out. "It's hilarious just how different we all are, and what's even more astounding is that my way works just as well as, if not better than, yours. Just leave me alone."

Every month a newsletter would come to each apartment in the building, including a column titled, "Welcomes and Farewells." This piece listed those who had recently moved in, others who'd entered the hospital or moved to assisted living placements, and finally those who were now "in the presence of the Lord." I was on the waiting list to get into this very same building, and when my number had finally come up, I felt like I'd won the lotto! I arranged to meet the administrator in her office the very next morning at eight to sign the necessary papers. I knew I would encounter fewer people in the lobby at that hour. She asked if I had directions to their building. I told her I'd have no trouble finding it.

DIANE MET ME at Mom's at seven the next morning to go over how to handle my entrance. The office was located at one side of the lobby and had large windows on every exposed side. I was particularly worried about the ones facing the elevators. Mom's apartment was located directly next to the elevator on the fourth floor. I knew I could make it that far unassisted. The office was only about twenty feet from the elevator doors, but it would be a long haul for me, especially after standing in the elevator on the way down. I was determined, however, to get there under my own steam. Diane rode down with me, and as the doors opened, I stood against the wall till she checked to see if anyone in the office was looking our way. The coast was clear, so I moved with deliberation toward the door. Diane carried my shower seat with her in case the chairs in the office wouldn't work for me. Good thing we brought it. Chairs with arms are the enemy of the obese.

The office manager's name was Karen. She was in her mid-twenties and had a kind face. I could tell that she was a little surprised by my appearance, but who wasn't? She began with small talk, then settled in to go over the amenities offered in the community. There was outdoor grilling available, a screened gazebo and shuffleboard court out back, ceramics classes, basket weaving instruction, potluck dinners and the celebration of each month's residents' birthdays at a gathering in the community room; singing, cake and all.

Karen cheerfully asked me what my hobbies were. Diane's look said, *Nancy, be good.* I couldn't resist. My new apartment would be on the seventh floor, and so I replied, "I enjoy bunny hunting and balcony bungee jumping!" The poor fledgling smiled nervously; I assured her that I really didn't like killing bunnies, didn't even like eating them. We listened as she filled us in on all the rules and regulations of residency and signed some papers.

Then Karen asked if I'd like to go up and see my unit. I wanted this place desperately. I had been told my apartment number the day before and, from the configuration of the floors, knew that my unit was the last one at the end of a ten-unit hall. Diane, Karen and I walked to the elevators in the lobby. I could already feel my legs cramping up, my lower back forming a painful fist as I stood erect, but I plodded along as best I could. I was afraid that if I used my wheelchair to get there, I'd be ineligible to have this particular apartment and have to wait till one located closer to the elevator was available. I had to be able to take care of myself, and I wasn't going to fail the test.

As the doors opened on the seventh floor, I looked down the long expanse of hall before us and felt like a scuba diver who finds herself five hundred feet beneath the waves with a sliced oxygen tube. I motioned for Diane and Karen to go on ahead of me. Even with holding the handrail installed along the side of the wall for support, my breathing became audible after I'd passed only a couple of doors. By the time I had passed three of the five, my legs were severely cramping, I was sweating profusely, and the tension in my lower back was becoming unbearable. I knew I couldn't make it any farther.

I leaned on the railing and had to call to Diane, asking her to please bring back the shower seat. I was only two doors from my unit, but it could have been a hundred miles for all that mattered. I had to sit down, and it had to be now. The door before mine opened a crack; I was about to meet my next-door neighbor. An old woman poked her head out and, seeing me sitting there, asked, "What are *you* doing here?" I told her I was her new neighbor, Nancy. She looked puzzled, stared blankly a moment longer and then, without another word, closed the door. Her sentiment echoed inside of me; I wanted to go inside and shut the door.

After Karen had left us, Diane went down to Mom's apartment to gather the bags I had packed the night before. She was going to be late for work, but she was worried about leaving me there alone. I had just my shower seat to sit on, a comforter and a cooler left next to me with water and some fruit and cheese inside. My son, Chris, was coming after work that evening to bring me my ottoman from Diane's. For the rest of my belongings, I would have to wait till the weekend, when people had time off work to help.

My waterbed had been thrown out when I left the AFC home, and I had used the beds (with the addition of cement blocks installed beneath) in the places I'd stayed since then, so someone was going to have to help me find another one. The same story applied to my old couch. When you're dependent on the charity of others, it's hard to complain. The guys told me when I'd moved from Pinewood Estates that not only was my couch heavy, but it was worn and ratty-looking, not worth saving. When I needed it, they'd pool funds to buy me a new one.

I WAS ELATED to be sitting alone after having lived so long in someone else's place; this was my new home, my sanctuary. After I'd rested for a few minutes, I got up and surveyed my new space. It was freshly painted and had large windows that looked out over a field with woods in the background. A large high school was to the left, and a tennis court stood right over the fence of my building's property line. There were plenty of closets and ample kitchen space for a single person's needs.

The balcony was lovely; I was lucky to be up high enough that I couldn't see the parking lot traffic beneath where I'd sit, only trees, the school and downtown's skyline to my right. More important, no one would be able to see *me*. But the best discovery of all was the moment I hauled my shower seat into the bathroom and realized it fit in the bathtub. Not every tub's configuration meshes with a particular shower seat. One more obstacle conquered. I had a book in one of my bags, and so I sat in the living room, reading contentedly into the afternoon.

By three my butt was aching and my legs and ankles felt like they were on fire. A shower seat is not built for comfort; at least not for a very long period of time. My comforter was lying on the floor next to my cooler. Every few minutes I'd look up from my book and ponder stretching out on that plump spread, but I knew that this idea was a dangerous one. Perhaps I'd be able to get down there, but would I be able to get myself back up when I felt uncomfortable again? I mulled over the pros and cons. Finally, the pain over-whelmed my reason. I scooted to the edge of the seat, put one knee on the floor and slowly sank onto the comforter.

First, I sat, legs stretched out in front, wiggling my toes and revel-ing in my freedom. Next, I lay down on my side and stretched some more. My back felt great relief. I sat back up and read for an hour or more, till the bones in my derriere began their protest. The com-forter was not *that* thick, after all; it was time to get back up onto my stool. I braced myself with my hands flat on the floor to one side and attempted to pivot onto my knees. I made it that far, but when I applied the necessary pressure to lift myself, I felt incredibly sharp pain in my knees. So I tried again, and regardless of the pain, I got back onto my knees and pushed with my arms for all I was worth. After a couple of attempts, I managed to get vertical, if wobbly from the exertion, and sat back down on my shower seat, wheezing and sweating and vowing never to do something that stupid again.

My son showed up around six with my ottoman, and it was one of the most beautiful sights I'd ever beheld. Chris and I celebrated that first night in my new home with a toast of Diet Coke and cheeseburgers. It dawned on my son as he was leaving that I had no place to sleep. I didn't even care. My particular body configuration, a wide foundation, allowed for me to sleep sitting up if need be, as long as I had a comfortable seat to situate myself on.

Soon my sister Laura procured a 1960s crank-type twin hospital bed for me from her church. A big drawback to sleeping in a hospital bed was positioning. Imagine an enormous body that covers the entire mattress side to side. The effort to turn onto your side for comfort is exhausting. I would reach across my body with my left arm and around the side of the mattress to the heavy frame, and grab on to it as I tried to wrestle myself onto my side. My heavy belly hung slightly over the edge of the bed in this position with my butt pressed against the wall behind me. A lot of times I'd wake up and feel uncomfortable, but the thought of exerting the energy required to turn was just too much, and so I'd drift back to sleep without having moved. I was never completely comfortable, no matter where I sat or lay. Before my couch arrived, I spent many a night catching my zzzzz's with the ottoman pressed against the wall upon which I propped my weary head.

Human beings get used to almost anything if they have to. Once my couch was purchased, I usually slept there, removing the back cushion and sitting up in the corner with one leg thrown up onto the couch and the other resting on the floor. I did this to help the circulation in my legs as best I could. I had edema (water retention) that produced horrible swelling, lending a lovely reddish tinge to my lower limbs, with my little, round purple feet attached beneath.

YOU HAVE A LOT OF TIME to think when you're in that condition and alone. I hadn't unpacked myself, so few of my things were where I might have wanted them. Often I would sit frustrated, staring straight at an item and wishing that I could reach it and move it to a place that would better suit it. I didn't sit around and weep; I mostly thought about what an ass I was to have let it get this bad.

And so I settled into my new life and home. My son came over one day with a large floor plant as a gift. He was riding up in the elevator with a group of older women who lived in the building (almost all of the residents were retirees) when one asked him who the plant was for. He told her that it was for his mother. "Oh," asked one, "is she new in the building?"

"Yes," Chris responded, "she just recently moved in."

"Who is she?"

"Nancy Makin," my son said. "She lives at the end of the hall on the seventh floor."

"Oh," one woman said to another, as if Chris wasn't even there, "*she's* the one who wouldn't answer the door for the Welcoming Committee!"

THERE ARE BIG DRAWBACKS to being an unknown entity. People make assumptions, and you can find yourself a scapegoat for things that might go awry.

It was my first Thanksgiving at the complex, and I wasn't going to go to our family gathering that day, so I thought I'd make the best of it by immersing myself in the newspaper. I opened my door to get the paper and noticed an envelope taped to it. Inside the envelope, I found what looked like dryer lint. The note read: *This lint was found in the dryer after you washed your clothes! The notice clearly posted says to clean the lint trap after each use! Make sure this is done in the future!* No "love and kisses" and no signature. Welcome to the neighborhood, Nancy. My laundry was taken out every week to be done by my daughter-in-law, Leane. It was never washed in the building.

GOING OUT WAS LOGISTICALLY DIFFICULT and physically taxing. After sitting for a short while, I would become uncomfortable and need to move around, with all the attendant and involuntary grunts and groans, which was embarrassing for me, even in front of my family members. As much as I missed them and all the fun, the costs began to outweigh the benefits; I was not myself anymore.

I told others not to worry about me when they'd ask me to come, saying that they missed me at these functions, I'd been the life of the party. There wasn't much life left in the old girl. I told them that I'd be fine, but nothing could have been further from the truth. I was dying, and I knew it somewhere in the recesses of my cholesterol-choked consciousness. So I stayed home instead, distracting my mind and emotions with food and reading, watching politics, an old classic movie or some inane television program. I even used the escapism of sleep.

I spent many hours with my grandson Ian, especially, in those years. Whenever Chris, now twenty, and Leane needed a break for a few hours, they had an eager babysitter waiting to smother their wee lad with kisses and love. Ian was a wonderful little child, so alive . . . and he loved bugs. I would hold him under his little butt, pressed against my lapless body, and he would reach up near the light on the balcony's wall and ever so gently press together the wings of a moth and place it in his tiny open hand. It was remarkable to me how many times these moths would just sit there when

Sailors Nancy and Daddy atop the Beachcomber in the spring of 1958

Nancy, age seven (*center front*), my sister Julie grinning to the right, with baby Michelle partially obscured behind me

Dad, Michelle, and me days before my second trip to Quebec in 1971

Back home from Tacoma with son Chris, age six, in our new home on Fuller Street in 1978

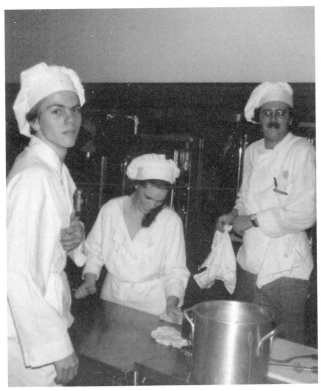

Wiping down
the counter in
culinary school
in my fetching
cook's togs

Early 1981: I thought my life
had finally come together;
that's what you get for
thinking.

My weight begins to climb, Christmas 1984

At a family function with niece Fiona a few months before my move
to manage Pinewood Estates in 1987

Holding my
grandson Ian in
my double-wide
wheelchair

My dear son, Chris, comes for a visit

A rare trip out, with Mom at daughter-in-law
Leane's baby shower in 1996

Exhibit #1: holding up
my old 108-inch waist
denim skirt

I am reborn, moving in for a kiss from grandson Isaac
at a picnic in the park

Nothing comes between me and my Levi's.

In the garden of my friends Mark and Frank

their wings were released, as though the insects knew this child was harmless. In the summer I'd sit on the balcony and let him spray me all over with the plant mister. The cool of the water felt good on my swollen feet. Ian thought this was deliciously naughty; something frowned upon by most adults, while I was his willing victim.

MY GREATEST INTEREST was and is history, especially that involving conflict, the great wars, those who fought them and those who commanded the troops. I spent many hours reading; the people and places within the pages took me out of my isolation and into their world of excitement, if only for that period of time.

As time wore on, hope ebbed away. I began giving away my possessions, including furniture that I'd inherited and nice pieces of jewelry I loved but never wore, as I wished these things to be enjoyed before I could no longer see their impact on loved ones. I never said, *I'm going to die soon. I want you to have this,* but I believe I was preparing to go.

There came a time when I rarely even went out onto my balcony anymore because I was unsure of my footing when navigating the threshold plate. Instead, I'd sit on my couch with the balcony door open to see a little nature and smell spring's waft in the air. I could see the steady stream of early-morning traffic push down the steep hill beyond my building. They were all off to their jobs, rushing to take their kids to school or on the way to tend to some errand. I remember thinking that not only didn't they know I even existed, but if I died at that very moment, no one's car would screech to a halt, there would be no moment of silence to mark my passing; no one would know that I had ever *been.*

I had not yet made my mark in this world. I love to learn and grow, but all of that was gone for me; it had been for years. I had resigned myself to the fact that life could never be mine, that happiness and love were somehow only for other people.

I even lost my sense of womanhood. I am a very earthy woman, true to my Taurean roots. I love the company of men and romance; it is a big part of who I am. When I'd been out in the world and watching a good movie, during the parts where a man and woman were about to kiss, sexual tension sizzling like electricity, I'd get that warm feeling, my heart would pump a little faster . . . you know. Clark Gable carrying a squalling Vivien Leigh upstairs to the bedroom in *Gone with the Wind*. Or Cary Grant leaning in to kiss Ingrid Bergman on a balcony in Argentina in *Notorious*. Paul Henreid lighting two cigarettes at once and handing one to Bette Davis, their eyes never leaving each other in *Now, Voyager*. Laurence Olivier carrying Merle Oberon to the window to look out onto their heath as she lay dying in his arms in *Wuthering Heights*. Oh, boy. Nothing can touch that feeling. I knew I was a goner when I realized that nothing I saw touched me anymore. And though I observed this change, it didn't move me.

I DECIDED TO GET A CAT, a little female calico I named Nuner. She became my best friend for twelve-plus years. Animals fill the heart of any devoted owner, but become so much more for those who live alone. She was there every morning as I began to rouse from my sleep, sometimes perched above my head on the arm of the couch, jumping onto, then off my chest, meowing to tell me it was time for her breakfast. Nuner was there at night; if I slept in my bed and was lying on my side, she'd crawl up under the comforter at the bottom and lie on the shelf that was my abdomen. I'd fall asleep to the sound of her purring. Unlike most people, who leave during the day at times, I was always there, and we formed an unusually close bond. She needed me, the quiet environment and love I could provide, and I certainly needed her.

CHAPTER 12

She's Listing! She's Listing!/Does This Sheet Make Me Look Fat?

IT WAS EARLY DECEMBER of 1994. I awoke that morning sitting up on my couch, Phil Donahue's talk show blaring on the TV. I slept this way much of the time as I had difficulty breathing lying flat in bed. When I did try to sleep in my bed, it was usually because the circulation in my legs was poor and it did feel good to have them elevated, for a while anyway; my lower back ached when I lay flat on the bed. So pick your poison; any way you sliced it, something on my body was throbbing and uncomfortable no matter what position I was in.

Another Christmas season was upon me. The holidays had meant everything to me. I inherited my mom's love of wrapping gifts. Each package, large or small, was papered beautifully and tied with one of an assortment of lovely silk ribbons. My trees were legendary, each fragrant branch festooned with precious ornaments. I was called on each year to make many of my family's favorite dishes:

candied yams, seven-layer salad, creamed peas with pearl onions and my signature New York–style cheesecake.

We'd gather to open gifts, children's laughter permeating the air and the wrapping paper strewn across the living room floor. We'd eat till we burst, lounge around to recuperate, then play board games and cards till late into the night. Mom and I fought for the title of "Jeopardy Queen" each year. Even if I won, she would declare herself the victor, citing my unconventional all-or-nothing wagering technique, and leave the table before she could be challenged. We'd roll our eyes, snicker and start another round. I missed those days; I missed the people, the silly rivalries and the love.

But nearing the end of 1994, the 25th of December would be just one more day. Perhaps a relative or two would drop by for a few minutes with a gift, most likely only coming after the family festivities were over, bearing a cold plate of leftovers from the holiday meal.

This Christmas would bring change, but not the type I would welcome. I had been feeling a bit under the weather for weeks. That morning, I focused in on Mr. Donahue to get my bearings. He was confronting a guest about some discrepancy in their argument regarding yet another earth-shattering issue, his Irish eyes bulging with emphasis. *Phil, Phil,* I thought, *slow down, buddy, you're going to pop a blood vessel.*

I scooted to the edge to use the right arm of the couch to brace myself and lift up, with my left hand knuckled into the cushion beside me for added support. It was always a big effort, but today my right leg didn't seem to be cooperating. It was asleep, I told myself. I tried to wake it up by wiggling my toes, but still it would not bear my weight. So what did I do? I decided to go back to sleep and wait for the old leg to kick in. I turned Phil off and dozed.

Two hours later I was awake again. This time I *needed* to get up. Nature was calling, and still no feeling in my leg. I had an office-type rolling table in front of my position on the couch to hold the many things I might need in a day. Pens and paper, a book, the *TV Guide,* Kleenex, a beverage glass.

Necessity being the mother of invention, I took every item off the tabletop and moved it onto the couch next to me. Using my good left leg and with my arms grasping the edge of the table, I somehow got myself up. I picked up my enormous belly and laid it on the table, and leaning over it and gripping the edges for all I was worth, I wheeled myself haltingly on one leg to the bathroom. God forbid I should call an ambulance. I'd get better; this would all work itself out. And so it went for nearly three days and nights.

My son, Chris, called me every other day, so when I didn't pick up one night he decided he'd come over to check on me. Sometimes I fell asleep at night thinking of how horrible it would be if Chris were the one to find me dead. Would I be lying there with my hands folded across my chest, my massive body tucked neatly under a sheet, with a peaceful look on my face? Not likely. It was bad enough that I hadn't been there for him in many ways while he was growing up, but this particular thought haunted me most.

Chris opened the door with his key and came inside calling for me. When he saw me, his concern was evident; he wanted to call an ambulance. The whites of my eyes were yellowed. I was pale and clammy. A wheezing cough had developed and I could not stand on my own. I protested. I tried to reason with him, I cried, I begged him not to call.

I was still sobbing when they arrived. My hair was dirty, my body stank, and my clothes were a mess. I had not picked up dirty dishes or anything else for that matter over the last three days; I was humiliated on all fronts. The firemen were the first to get there. Four of them, all young and gorgeous (my weakness, men in uniform), and me without my little black dress and heels on. Next, the paramedics were ushered in; add another four to the mix. As these people were trying to come up with the best strategy to transport my carcass, the irony of the situation hit me and I shouted, "Hey, where are the Marines?" Two cops were now knocking at the door. Lord Almighty.

I remember begging their forgiveness; I said if I'd only had more time to prepare for their arrival, I would have had coffee brewing alongside freshly baked croissants and jam. A couple of them grinned. Most were too absorbed in conversation about how to proceed.

I couldn't use my double-wide wheelchair that night. The "lip" on the lift of the ambulance was a couple of inches too narrow to allow my chair to fit. When I had gone to doctor's appointments in the past, they would collapse the chair, lift it up and into the vehicle, securing it inside with straps to the floor, lower the lift again, let me stand on it and raise me up to get inside the van. That plan wouldn't work this time. I could not stand securely enough to be raised and then seated in the chair. It was finally determined that I would have to get up from the bed and then be lowered with support onto the gurney lying before me on the floor.

Then the unexpected happened. The gurney couldn't be raised. It just wouldn't budge under my massive weight. They had to roll me along the floor to the elevator.

By now it was nearly midnight and cold as hell outside. The

apartment building was nine floors high and housed 207 units. With all the commotion going on, many lights were burning in apartments facing the building's front, and heads appeared as shadows in the window frames. It would give them something to talk about in the morning over decaf coffee in the community room. I was so embarrassed; but it would only get worse.

Next, they had to get me into the ambulance. I sat up on the gurney and, with the help of attendants, was hoisted upright. The end of a tarp had been placed on the back opening of the van, and with one worker supporting me on each side, I managed to scoot my butt onto the edge of the tarp. Three men got into the van behind me and pulled the tarp with its heavy, tremulous load inside.

I rode the entire way to Saint Mary's hospital on the floor of that ambulance, legs splayed out in front of me, oxygen tubes up my nose. I looked out at one point and glimpsed the Amway Grand Plaza Hotel, a much-talked-about project of which our city was very proud. I had only seen it on TV, had never actually eyeballed the thing. In all my pain and even in such humiliating circumstances, it was nice to be outside. It had been more than two years, and back then I had only needed to be wheeled to the elevator and down to the fourth floor to see my mother. It was her birthday, and as my son had been born on his grandma's birthday in 1972, a double celebration had been planned for the occasion.

I DIDN'T KNOW IT YET, but I was to be in the hospital for a month. My thyroid gland was all but nonfunctioning. I was anemic and malnourished, which struck me as funny. After some thought, it made sense. Yes, I overate, but I was not following the four food group recommendations of the pyramid food chart. To discover the answer to the mystery of my numb right leg, they sent in a neurologist to tap on my knee with a rubber mallet. You know, they never *did* come to any conclusion on that matter, at least none that I was ever apprised of. Some feeling returned to my limb over the next weeks, but to this day I have some numbness in my right foot. Initially I couldn't wear my usual "uniform" of home-sewn, elastic-waistbanded ankle-length skirts and 4X Hanes white V-neck T-shirts. I had terrible diarrhea due to the antibiotics being given me through IVs and so needed open garments to afford easy access for hygiene purposes. They had no gowns that could accommodate my mass, and so I sat naked for days, with only a sheet held in front and under my armpits to afford any modesty. Thankfully I was so ill, drifting in and out of consciousness, that I didn't think about it much.

I had been deposited on the fifth floor, in a two-bed room, one of the beds being vacant. I was put in a standard hospital bed, just like the one I had used in my home for years. Some genius decided that it wasn't good enough for me, and so I was told that they had a wonderful new type of bed that was made specifically for people of my size. It was called the "Big Boy" bed. How quaint.

The Big Boy boasted an internal scale, as well, that could weigh patients while they lay in the bed. It registered 600.5 pounds that day. I remember asking God aloud why it couldn't have read 599 instead. It dawned on me later that I had gained 200 pounds between June of 1991, when I had been weighed during my evaluation for Social Security disability, and December of 1994.

The "Big Boy" bed, as staff termed it, turned out to be a torture device. It was a blunted diamond shape; my huge belly prevented my legs from coming together, so they splayed off each side. I had terrible trouble with circulation; my feet and ankles were purple on my best days, and so this added pressure behind my knees was unbearable. It takes a lot for me to complain, but I protested for days that not only could I not sleep, but I was in intense and constant pain; I was given Tylenol 3 in response. I began to believe that their worry was liability. No one would say the word, but even when I offered that I'd slept at home on a regulation twin hospital bed for years, they wouldn't budge regarding the issue.

My sister Michelle came by late one evening and, seeing that I was in great distress, asked what she could do to help. I eyed the empty bed next to mine and said that maybe between the two of us, we could get me into it. She moved a large cushioned chair between the beds as something for me to hang on to while attempting to climb off. My numb right leg was the one farthest from the open bed, so with my sister holding on to my left arm and with the determination and strength that comes only when faced with absolute need, I sat on the edge and put my good foot on the floor. It was all a blur, really. I don't know how, but I ended up in that other bed and had my first decent night's sleep since I'd been admitted. I was so happy.

My nurse was *not* so happy to see me in the other bed the next morning, but she didn't say anything about moving me back into the Big Boy; she just checked my vital signs and IV drips and left the room.

Later that day a young man with a clipboard wandered in. He introduced himself and asked if I might like to talk with someone about my problems. He seemed uncomfortable asking this question, and considering the irony ripe in the picture before him, I came back with "And exactly what would make you think I have any problems, buster?" I said it with a grin. He didn't grin back.

I was all for accepting the offer of help. I said I thought it would be lovely to speak with someone. I didn't know at the time that changing rooms would be part of the bargain.

I was rolled to the elevator in my bed and taken to the eighth floor. There, I was deposited in a room directly across from the nurses' station. This place was called the Psych-Med Unit. They would be helping me with both aspects of needed care, physical and emotional. This was a two-bed room as well, and as no one occupied the other bed in this one either, I had the privacy I needed to feel most comfortable. I was settling in and getting used to my surroundings, when a nurse approached me and told me I was going to be moved back into the *proper* bed.

I don't cry easily, but tears started flowing. My protestations fell on deaf ears. She leaned over and whispered in my ear, "Remember what floor you're on now. We'll make the decisions for you, honey." I was hysterical; she was implying that I was nuts. I suppose I was making her point for her in that moment, in my frantic behavior.

Sure enough, later that day they came to transfer me back into the Big Boy. I felt so defeated, so helpless, so invisible. Here I was sick as a dog; I had come upstairs voluntarily to talk with someone about my obvious emotional problems, and now I felt a captive of *their* insanity. I wanted to go home or die right then and there.

HAVE YOU EVER TRIED to concentrate on a problem when you're uncomfortable or in pain? Imagine trying to talk with a professional about deeply personal things while being hampered by constant worry over how you appear to that person physically, being out of the sanctuary of your home's cocoon after years virtually alone, and on top of that, being in misery physically; impossible.

I was still very ill. I could not keep food down, hadn't been able to since I was admitted. My diarrhea was horrible; they applied what looked like black tar as a sort of sealant to protect my rear end from the caustic flow. One doctor said my skin's condition resembled raw hamburger . . . lovely. My legs were killing me, hanging off each side of that damnable bed.

My sister Michelle came back to visit a couple of days after the move to the eighth floor. She had taken time off work to come stay with me for the day. Michelle had been pleading my case to the nurses for a move back into the other bed, but to no avail.

She had just come back in my room when all at once I felt a subtle shift underneath me. This miraculous, everlasting marvel of engineering genius, the Big Boy, was expiring under my heft. Michelle ran from the room yelling, "She's listing, she's listing!" The flagship was going under with me still aboard. A furious conversation was now taking place outside my door.

It was determined that the first order of business would be my immediate removal from the implement of incalculable torment and torture, my arch-nemesis, the Big Boy. I smiled at my sister from behind my oxygen tubing, not thinking for one moment of my current peril, but instead focusing on the relief I would soon feel in every fiber of my being, if I didn't plunge to the tile floor first. Victory was surely at hand.

Several strong men came into the room to assist in the transfer of my body to the standard hospital bed already in the room. I was making a spectacle of myself, putting other people out to help in the silliest of situations; I should have been able to do these things for myself. But worse for me was the fact that my body was nearly entirely exposed in the process; I was only covered with a sheet and it slid as I was being moved.

The carpentry department was summoned, and in walked a guy sporting a tool belt and looking just like Harrison Ford. Lord; I wanted to die. Why couldn't he be an average Joe? I was still a woman and wanted so much to be attractive to men; fat chance, Nancy. I felt ashamed of just being alive, breathing the same air as this guy.

A second bed was brought in, then a big piece of plywood. I was moved to my double-wide wheelchair while Mr. Ford first zip-tied the two bed frames together in several spots, then laid the large piece of plywood over both beds' bases. Once the mattresses and sheets were back on the frames, I was helped back into bed. The only drawback to this contraption was that it had to be left in one position, with the head at an angle. I couldn't lie flat or anywhere near it, and so I reclined slightly the entire rest of my stay, unless I sat erect without support; I never complained. My legs felt *so* much better this way; at least they didn't feel as if they were being sawed off at the knees.

Now here's the kicker. During the entire remainder of the month I was never on the other half of the misbegotten creation. I sat or reclined on *one* bed; the other held all my writing supplies, magazines and hospital literature. No one other than me seemed to notice this incongruity; I found it hilarious, though I never said a word. The handsome carpenter was also commissioned to create a wooden box with a hole at its center to nest over the room's wall-mounted toilet in anticipation of my catheter line being removed. God knows, I might have ripped that porcelain off the wall and created a flood the likes of which had not been seen since the time of Noah.

NOW THE HEALING COULD BEGIN. I started feeling much stronger soon after the bed episode was resolved, though I was still having trouble keeping food down. My first visit from a staff psychiatrist was memorable for just one moment. I will refer to him only as "Dr. Mengele, Angel of Death." He and his sober-faced clone, a white-smocked female assistant, came into my room. Standing at the end of my bed, this guy informed me that he was leaning toward the theory that I was bulimic. I was frankly astonished and asked him to repeat what he'd just said. I replied, "Well, buddy, if I'm a bulimic, I am the most *unsuccessful* bulimic in human history!" The rest of his ten-minute visit was unremarkable, and his theory about my eating habits was never brought up again.

I still hadn't had a real bath, after about ten days there, and I asked if I could be pushed into the shower stall in my wheelchair. What a wonderful feeling that was. I let the water flow over and over me, and though I was dead tired from the exertion, just being clean and, now that the diarrhea had abated, finally able to wear my usual attire made an enormous difference in my outlook.

My illness was abating and I was eating well now; the staff had been allowing me to eat in my room, but they began encouraging me to go sit with the other patients for meals. I balked. Eating was my "sin." I had rarely eaten in front of anyone for years. After all, eating had turned me into the grotesque creature I had become; why give further evidence to others of my depravity? So for the moment, I dined alone.

The day came when I was to be weighed for the first time since just after my arrival. My nutritionist, Julianne, did the honors that day. She was a little thing, probably 110 pounds dripping wet. The two of us entered the elevator on the eighth floor. The doors reopened on the fourth floor, before we reached our destination. There were four elderly ladies waiting to get on board, chatting as the doors opened to reveal yours truly in all her glory. It was a made-for-Hollywood moment; they all stopped talking and stared. "Come on in, ladies, the water's fine!" I said.

"No, we'll wait for the next one." The doors shut again. Julianne apologized, but I told her not to worry about it, it happened all the time. These old girls obviously thought we would plummet through to the basement with me aboard.

Saint Mary's hospital is joined to a smaller complex, the Mary Free Bed Rehabilitation Center, by a long corridor. The floor scale is located in an alcove on the third floor of the rehab center. The machine was manufactured by the Toledo Floor Scale Co. As Julianne wheeled me onto it, I couldn't resist shouting, "Holy Toledo!" as it registered my mass. We both laughed. I had lost twenty-some pounds already, but I had been so sick that the loss didn't really surprise either one of us very much.

The next step for me was group therapy. I was horrified by the prospect of being exposed. My nurses cajoled me into it, but only with the caveat that we would meet for the first time in my room. I felt safe there. I decided to stay in bed for the event. I could partially cover myself with the sheet; it felt more secure. As the day and hour approached, though nervous, I prepared for my visitors' arrival; I put on some earrings, combed my hair and told myself that this was going to be just fine. I really wanted the help; I'd have to take risks to get better.

And here they came, all shapes, sizes, ages and backgrounds; some walking and carrying folding chairs, others being wheeled into the room. One man's name was Hobbes, a twentysomething guy who'd later become a friend. He looked gaunt, very weak, but he had a wonderful smile for me as he rolled his wheelchair past my bed. I later learned that he had contracted the AIDS virus. One woman in the group was a bus driver. On a winter's day, as she was driving children to school, her bus hit a patch of black ice and she collided with another vehicle, killing a child under her protection. I felt so sorry for what she was going through.

But my personal favorite was a man named Clarence. This guy was about seventy years old, had suffered a heart attack and was currently dealing with bouts of depression. He was pushed inside my room slumped in his wheelchair, emaciated lips curled under into the toothless void of his mouth. He was wearing an old dark-colored robe and slippers and a plaid hunting cap with earflaps.

After we had gone around the room introducing ourselves, the therapist asked, "Who'd like to start out?" Clarence raised his hand. The first words out of this man's mouth were "Hey, Nancy! You mind telling us . . . about how much do you weigh!?" I was no longer the *proverbial* elephant in the room; I *was* the elephant in the room.

I was humiliated beyond imagination; I *did* respond, though. I fired back, surprising even myself, "Clarence, I'll tell you how much I weigh if you'll share with all of us the length of your penis. What do you think . . . fair trade?" Silence. Hobbes flashed a grin. Clarence and I were never again together in a group setting during my month-long stay.

The next time the group met, I was required to go to the therapy room. I sat enthroned in my wheelchair. You wouldn't think that would be so bad, but because my butt was so enormous I sat high above everyone else, a good ten inches above; their elbows rested easily on the table, while I had my exposed belly entirely on exhibit, with nowhere to put my hands; nowhere to *hide*. That's how it felt: on display.

It was nice to be able to talk with the nurses and orderlies who came through every day. I was a smoker, still am, though I'm down to half a pack from my former three-pack-a-day habit. I hadn't had a smoke in days and days. A guy named Jerry came into my room to roll me to the mammography department, and I smelled the distinct waft of tobacco on his person. I asked if he was a smoker; he defensively responded that he was. I grinned and asked if I could sniff his lapels. The technician in the mammography unit instructed me to stand in front of the god-awful machine that all women approach with fear and loathing. Standing erect was hard enough; I was still favoring my left leg, as I had not yet regained much feeling in my right one. Even on my best days, I could stand for only a minute or a little more before I had to sit or unceremoniously fall down. So standing with my bosom flattened in a vise as I trembled to stay erect added yet another layer to an already tenuous situation. I *did* survive the ordeal and was later informed that the test results were A-OK. I would keep hold of these astounding beauties for the foreseeable future. Still, Hugh Hefner never called.

We were housed in very spare rooms. This was by design, of course. We were, after all, patients in the Psych-Med Unit; some of us might want to do ourselves bodily harm. There were no phones or lamps (cords, you know), just harsh fluorescent lighting on the ceiling. When Dr. Mengele noted that I didn't have my light on and only opened the blinds for illumination during the day, he was sure it was a sign of deep depression. And here I thought the harsh glare hurt my eyes; what an unbalanced sap I'd been.

Once deposited in my room after the mammogram, I discovered evidence of my sanctuary having been invaded and called to report what my eyes beheld. In my best maniacal Peter Lorre imitation, I whispered, "Nurse, I think you should come in here right away! Someone's left a pair of sharp, pointy scissors on my nightstand and I'm feeling a little strange, a little out of control!" This was followed by a wild cackle. Three people were standing by my bed within ten seconds. I called the nurse's station on other occasions to casually request a Whopper with cheese, a large order of fries and a strawberry shake. My takeout was never delivered.

HOSPITAL ROUTINE KEPT ME PRETTY BUSY. I spent my waking hours in group, physical or occupational therapy and in my unproductive private sessions with Dr. Mengele. I actually never called him "doctor" at all; I always addressed him as "Buddy" or "Bud." One example of my many exchanges with the man demonstrates why I formed the opinion that his "mind healing" capabilities lacked the gravitas required for the task at hand. He asked me about my childhood. I outlined the early years; the first trip to the monastery, then my second at fourteen. His response? "First time, shame on them . . . second time, shame on *you*." What a dweeb! How was I supposed to trust, process and respect his input when he offered this insane brand of "sagacity"?

There were other activities that filled my time: lab tests, weigh-ins, family visits, meals and some time alone in the evening to read, or to have one of what turned out to be some of the most memorable times, my unanticipated visits with Hobbes.

I had seen him only a couple of times in group, when he began to insinuate himself into my private realm. He would whiz into my room unannounced whenever the mood struck him. At first I felt it was an intrusion. This guy would roll in with a disarming grin, and bags of chips and candy bars resting on his frail lap. He told me as he snacked about how the doctors insisted he eat as much as he could; he was dropping weight so quickly. I was envious of his "perks" until I thought about why he was shedding all those pounds.

One afternoon Hobbes popped in and somehow didn't seem himself. It took some time for him to open up, but finally it came out. He was afraid of dying. What would it be like? Would he be all alone when everything went "black"? He'd noticed my rosary lying on my tray table and picked it up. Hobbes told me he wanted to believe that there was a God and a better life to come. He'd been raised by agnostics, and though he'd always felt that there was something out there, he wanted a more concrete belief to hang on to in the times he was facing.

I reached out and touched his arm. I told him I knew that when the moment of his death approached, the Blessed Mother and St. Michael the Archangel would come to him and escort him to Jesus' throne. The Mother of God must be the best mom in the world, right? Would she leave her child to suffer in darkness and not come to him to soothe his fears, hold his hand and lead him back home? "Just call to her, Hobbes. She'll be there in a flash." I put my beads around his neck and gave him a pamphlet that explained the rosary and how to recite it. Hobbes came to my room the next day and every day after till I left, to talk for a while and say the rosary with me. The two of us exchanged letters after I'd been released; Hobbes left soon after I did. He went home to die among his family. I got a letter from his brother telling me of the wonderful peace Hobbes seemed to have about it when his time came and that Hobbes had asked to be buried with the rosary I had given him.

The topic of further help for me had been insinuated into the conversation early on in my stay. The staff told me about a place I could go where more intensive therapy was available. It was a residential treatment center specifically geared toward those with eating disorders. I knew it would be a good step for me, but the prospect of eating, sleeping, watching TV, going to classes, all the things people do when they live together, frightened me to death. There would be eight of us living in a house there. I would again be exposed to strangers. I had been alone in my home for so many years. I resisted at first, but I could see a glimmer of hope for my future now; I'd lost nearly sixty pounds in a little over four weeks. I finally agreed to go.

Part of the selling point had been that the staff believed that if I went back immediately to my old environment, I'd soon regain the lost pounds. I knew this was true. It's human nature to return to old habits, the same old coping mechanisms, so it made perfect sense to me that I needed to be able to find alternate ways to handle my emotions before I went back home. I made arrangements with my family to continue their care of my cat, had them pack my things and began feeling more hopeful than afraid. My sister Diane, who'd moved to Florida, even made and mailed me five new skirts so I'd look my best. It was the first time in forever that I'd felt like I might be able to touch life again, to really be a part of it. All my nurses were thrilled for me. They told me they wanted me to come back someday to show them the "new me."

The day before I was to be released from the hospital and transferred to the treatment center, the group therapist came into my room. Normally bubbly, today she was quiet. As she began to speak, I understood why. I was not going to be able to stay at this place after all. They had done some further checking and the facility could not accommodate my needs. They had no walk-in shower stall for me (I used a regular bathtub shower at home with a seat and handheld shower head), no proper bed and no one available to push me around campus for classes.

I looked at the woman who was delivering this bad news and said, with tears rolling down my face and a wry grin, "Well, I do understand. It's purely a matter of economics. They can fit four anorexics into the same space as one of me." I was devastated. And mad. I rarely get mad, just disappointed. Not this time. I'd invested so much trust in reaching out and believing again. Why didn't they check more thoroughly before holding out that life-affirming support to me? And why was an eating disorders program not designed to meet the needs of someone like *me*? Certainly, overeating is as harmful, and as much of an emotional dysfunction, as any other kind of oral aberration. I knew that; didn't they? As different nurses came on shift, each of the ones I'd grown to care for came into my room and told me how sorry she was that this was happening to me. Some gave me their home phone numbers to keep in touch. I wasn't angry with them; it wasn't their fault. They were just cogs in the great health care wheel and were nearly as frustrated as I was by the situation.

And so I was released the next day as scheduled, but instead of traveling toward the promise of further help and the possibility of a brighter future, I was returning to my apartment. I was angry; I felt so let down, defeated and dismissed. I was determined to prove their prognosis wrong. I would *not* relapse, I told myself. I lived on the residual fumes of my good experience for a while after my release. During that month's stay at the hospital, I'd felt for the first time in years that just maybe I could grab on to that brass ring and regain a meaningful life, if I could just hold on long enough.

But soon, the sameness of each day set in and the four walls of my apartment again became my world. I regained the weight I'd lost and additional pounds in the bargain.

> *No light can pierce this hopeless place*
> *To bring its warmth upon my face*
> *Despairing hands can't open blinds*
> *To grab life's dazzle locked behind.*

June 1995

CHAPTER 13

Navigating Without a Compass/Going Down for the Third Time

"'Tis true my form is something odd, but blaming me is blaming God. Could I create myself anew, I would not fail to please you. If I could reach from pole to pole, or grasp the ocean with a span, I would be measured by the soul; the mind's the standard of the man."

—Isaac Watts

A NURSE I'D KNOWN from my doctor's office called me occasionally after work to talk. We liked each other, and though she could be stern at times, I knew she wished only good things for me. She always encouraged me to think of my future and to work each day toward the goal of creating a better one. But it was hard to focus on the future when it seemed so remote, so out of reach.

She said she thought it would be good for me to get out more; maybe I should go to the mall and sit in the courtyard area to relax and people watch. She *wanted* the best for me, but, oh, brother . . . "Yeah, I'll bring a cup along with a sign taped to it marked:

'Donations.'" How relaxing would it be for me to have everyone gawking as they paraded by?

My father was diagnosed with prostate cancer in late autumn of 1995; by the time he'd consulted a physician regarding his symptoms, Dad's chances of beating the disease were nil. There was talk among the sisters about whether or not one of us should move in to help him as his condition deteriorated. Most of my sisters either still had children at home to care for or lived out of state. My name was bandied about, but Dad's place was far too small to accommodate both me and the seating I required to be comfortable. And realistically speaking, what could I do to help my father in any meaningful way? I was the dependent one, and I was only thirty-nine years old. My sister Diane made the move back up north from Florida to help my dad through his last difficult days.

In May of 1996 my grandson Isaac was born; Dad called Isaac his little replacement. He was a precious baby, just as his brother had been. One day as I was rocking him to sleep on my couch with a lullaby, his profile momentarily took my breath away. Isaac looked so much like my own son; I felt like I was looking at Christopher's six-month-old face. How different I was now; from the young girl who played with and ran after her own small boy.

CHRIS AND LEANE had been married in a civil ceremony years before; now they were preparing to sanctify their vows in the church. I was pleased to hear it, but sad. Just one more event I wouldn't be there for. His father had moved with his second wife to Colorado by then, and so Chris would have only aunts, some cousins, his maternal grandmother and friends on his side of the ledger to celebrate their special day. These kids were on a tight budget, so I offered to help make some of the food for the reception. I had to have assistance, of course.

Diane did the shopping the day before the wedding and brought all I'd ordered into my kitchen. She then carried in everything I needed to accomplish the mission there at my workstation: already washed produce, knives, cutting board, containers . . . everything. I sat at my heavy rolling table in the living room and chopped vegetables for a variety of salads and sliced mounds of fruit. I still had my huge stainless steel mixing bowls from my catering days, so I used those to incorporate the ingredients. As I would finish something, Diane would carry it away, package it to refrigerate and bring me ingredients for the next item. I plated the cheeses for sandwiches and made relish trays. I knew how to make beautiful garnishes and dressed all the dishes and platters nicely; at least I could do *this*. Knowing that when the food left that day, it was being taken to the church basement for the reception the next afternoon was the hard part.

My father outlived every doctor's predictions; he had been given six months to live when diagnosed eighteen months prior. Diane, who lived with my father for all that time, called me on several occasions to say that Dad was "looking bad," she didn't know if he'd make it through another night; but he always pulled through. He'd bought himself a ten-speed bike the spring before and would take it out on his good days, wearing shorts and with his catheter bag taped to his calf, riding around the neighborhood in plain sight of his appalled neighbors.

If I'd had to live with my father for that extended period of time, I would have put the old man out of his misery well before his clock ran out. I loved my dad very much; he was just a cantankerous man and frugal to a painful degree. He was many times difficult and impatient, possessing few social skills. I think divorcing my mother was good for my father in the long run. I remember Mom telling me that Dad had welled up when he met her in the courthouse hallway after their divorce hearing in 1977, saying that "he had never wanted it to end this way," and tears just weren't part of Dad's makeup. He wasn't one to give up easily, especially on something that involved a solemn vow, but their union hadn't been a pleasant one for the most part over their thirty-two years together. From what I observed, he was somewhat more at ease after the split, even more so once he remarried and was living with a less fractious, less demanding and more encouraging partner. Perhaps the spirit Daddy showed back in the days of Seattle and during his employment as an engineer at Boeing never came back in full bloom, but he seemed to find peace and contentment in his later years, fixing his second wife Marie's car, replacing some shingles on their roof or taking her out fishing in his bass boat for the afternoon, something my mom would have never participated in. He regained some of those rough edges when his second wife died a few years before he did; probably a demonstration of his grief. He softened up during his illness, though. He began calling me "Bluebird" for some odd reason when we talked on the phone, and instead of questioning it, I just tried to enjoy the timbre of the nickname. It was better than some of the less-printable things he'd called all of us as kids when he was angry.

Dad died on the 14th of April in 1997. I've always said he did it to cheat the IRS out of their taxes. I got my love of politics from my father. He'd rail on about waste in government, writing letter after letter to his representative to demand action on any number of issues. I am sure Dad's congressman looked forward with great anticipation to receiving his mail. Dad *did* know what he was talking about; he was not an idiot, far from it. He just lacked tact entirely. He would've made a lousy politician.

His death hit me hard; he may have been gruff, but the memories of the time we spent in Seattle were indelible: camping and salmon fishing off the coast of Washington State. Dad taught me how to scale and gut a fish when I was four. We played pool together on the table in our basement. Dad bought me a Handy Andy tool box for Christmas one year and I'd pound away on the long workbench next to him as he worked. He played chess with me; we liked to sit on the bay window seat in the master bedroom of our home on Queen Anne Hill overlooking the water, with Mount Rainier as wallpaper in the background, while we played on Dad's small, leather-bound traveler's set. He'd never give me a break just because I was a little girl. "You'll never learn to play well if I tell you I'm sneaking up on you. What kind of victory would it be, anyway, Nan?"

When he'd have come home from his engineering job at Boeing and was trying to watch the news, I'd haul a stool up behind his easy chair to comb the few hairs remaining on his shiny-scalped head. He'd try to shoo me away, saying that we girls were responsible for his balding pate and that I should leave what was left alone; I only continued to part and style. I knew he needed my love, even back then. And as was the case with my mother, I was the most vocal of the brood, many times telling him how I felt about what he'd said; I was also the one most often in trouble. My parents were strong people on the surface; Mom in her emotional manipulation, Dad by means of intimidation. I saw through both of these flawed but strangely lovable people, and I think because I stood up to them and kept coming back for more, I held a special and close position with each of them in their peculiar, precious hearts.

I didn't go to his funeral. After the service was over, Diane brought me the collage of photos she'd put together. She also gave me a plaque that Dad had made a few months before he died. He had meant to deliver it to me, but his health was so erratic toward the end that he never knew hour to hour how he was going to feel.

The wood-burned plaque was headed "Mel's Quotes" and featured the following: "You can only stack things so high before they slide off," with the last two words cascading down the edge of the wooden piece. "Don't think, just dance!" "All you need in this world is a strong stomach." "I thought I was leading, but when I turned around, no one was following." "You drew the picture; I just put the frame on it." "Perfect is good enough." "You can be right . . . and DEAD wrong." "When the guns are above water, you might as well shoot!" And betraying his Democrat roots, this observation: "The only difference between Democrats and Republicans is that Republicans don't go to jail." Mel's wisdom; he always had a piece of it for anyone who came within earshot, though it was usually unsolicited.

APRIL OF 1997 came and went, as did April of 1998 and 1999. My life went on as it had for years now, with only the slightest variations to differentiate the days and months. The children in my life were growing up, family members changed jobs and made trips, with smiling pictures taken to bring me as evidence of the times they'd shared; everything was evolving, progressing for them, as it should in any normal life. Mine slid toward an unhappy end; I was resigned to that fact and made the best of what I had.

MY FRIEND MARY LOU called at the close of April of 2000 and asked to come for a visit. She held, still does, a particularly intimate place in my heart. She's my oldest friend; we met within the first couple of years of my return from Tacoma, Washington, in 1978. She'd been there during my divorce and the ensuing melee; she'd watched it all unfold. And though later there were times we didn't see each other for several years at a shot, when we'd be reunited, it was as if no time had elapsed. Yet we are unalike in so many ways. Our tastes in décor, politics, and what we find attractive in men are poles apart.

A big feature of our friendship has always been the "tease"; disparaging comments thrown back and forth, playfully picking at sensitivities to watch the other person's eyes widen and mouth open, waiting for the expletive-laced return-fire rebuttal as consequence. We had been one-upping each other for over twenty years by the spring of 2000. I told her to come over at seven.

She came bearing gifts: a four-pack of wine coolers. She walked out the open door of my balcony more than once and said, "A beautiful evening for a drive, don't you think, Nancy?" I wasn't biting. "C'mon, Nancy. We can have the building sitter open the maintenance door and slip out the back. No one will see us. I can pull my car around the back of the building." She had bench seats in her rickety 1990 Olds Cutlass Calais sedan. I shot back, "Your shock absorbers will never be the same."

"Please, Nancy? Just an hour or two outside; we can go to the park and sit by the river. You can stay inside the car if it makes you feel more comfortable. Hardly anyone will be there at this time of day, especially so early in the season." I still wouldn't budge. "C'mon, you weenie! You know you want to. Just do it! It'll be fine." I finally relented. Mary Lou handed me the carton of wine coolers as I sat in my double-wide wheelchair in the hallway of my building, locked the door, and we were on our way.

I *did* manage to wrestle myself inside the car; I wasn't driving after all, so there was no steering wheel blocking access. My belly was pressed firmly against the glove box. Using a seat belt was out of the question; I prayed that my belly would act as a human air bag if we were involved in a collision. Preventative measures weren't a big consideration for me, anyway. My whole lifestyle was the ulti-mate expression of risk taking. Off we sped into the cool of that spring evening, the skies becoming purple- and orange-tinged as the Cutlass wended its way toward the park. The parking lot was nearly vacant as we pulled in. A lone jogger shot by, dressed in a hooded sweat suit; another young couple walked hand in hand along a path. Mary Lou parked alongside the road's edge to give the best view possible of the river. The change of scenery had done me good; the bonus of having no one ogling me allowed me to relax and absorb the scenery and my friend's company.

She broke out the wine coolers, opened one for herself and of-fered one to me. Sure, why not. . . . It would be my first adult bever-age since 1986. Our conversation flowed, like the wine cooler down my throat. We talked about our kids, funny things that had hap-pened in her workday at the local college, our long-past wild adven-tures and just which of us was responsible for the hilarious and/or embarrassing consequences of our public mayhem. The topic turned to weight loss. Mary Lou was whining about the stubborn twenty-five pounds she was unable to remove from her abdomen. I replied that she had nothing to complain about . . . at least she could do what needed to be done and live among "the normals." And by the way, I informed her, it looked more like forty-five pounds situated at her waistline, not twenty-five. I waited for her protest, which came: "Oh, fine! Real nice, Nancy. What do you think *you* need to lose . . . huh, sister? Give me *that* number, if you dare!"

"Well, I'm guessin' I'd tip the scales at about six twenty or thirty, in that heavy-duty neighborhood."

She snorted. "Ha! More like eight hundred, from the looks of it!"

By now we were roaring with laughter. The irony of an enormous woman, squeezed into a car like a human sardine and quibbling over a mere hundred or two surplus pounds had hit the funny bone. But even then it bugged me. Surely it couldn't be *that* bad? We opened a second wine cooler. "You're full of it, Mary Lou. You never were good at math." I hadn't been weighed in my doctor's office since mid-1996; *I couldn't have gained a hundred pounds plus since then, or could I?* I continued my griping about her "abusive" treatment, her unqualified judgment of my condition. She taunted me. "Well, there's no way to determine who's right here. *There's no scale that can weigh you!*" This slight could not go unanswered. "Yes, there is. . . . The scale at the Mary Free Bed rehab facility has always served me well; the old Toledo." She jumped on it. "OK, let's go! We can put an end to this ridiculous back-and-forth here and now. I'll weigh myself, too!" I wished I hadn't opened my trap. "Nah, I was only joking; I'm not taking that trip voluntarily, Miss Priss. Ain't happenin'."

"C'mon." Mary Lou went on. "Look, it's dark now. Few people

will be roaming the halls at this hour. We can slither in and out in no time. Where's the scale located?"

"On the third floor in a little alcove," I said. I was mulling it over in my mind as she went on. Perhaps it was the wine coolers—my first alcohol in over fourteen years—that gave me the courage/idiocy to take her up on this crazy "challenge"; more likely it was our long-standing adversarial history and a bit of righteous indignation over her laughable assertions that pushed me over the edge. "All right, baby. Let's do it!"

Our entrance was virtually unnoticed; only one employee passed by my wheelchair on our way inside. Mary Lou navigated me down the linoleum hallway toward the elevator, telling me to shut up when I told her to hurry; she was moving as fast as she could given the load. The doors opened on the third floor. We turned toward the alcove that housed the scale. Soon, our wager would be settled; my dear friend's entrée would be a large serving of "Crow à la Nancy." I motioned toward the scale. "You first, fatso," I sneered. Mary Lou climbed aboard, and though she was not pleased with the results, she had been only six pounds off in her calculation. Now it was my turn. I rose and stood to meet my fate on the scale's platform . . . 703. Mary Lou burst into a fit of the giggles. "OK, OK," I said. "I was a little off the mark. . . . But, I was closer than *you* were, you nasty human being; eight hundred pounds, my fat ass!" She couldn't stop snickering. I wedged myself back inside her Oldsmobile and rode along in the blackness to my apartment, then sat alone once deposited back home, to digest the events that had unfolded in our supposedly uncomplicated "stroll" in the park.

CHAPTER 14

An Unlikely Salvation/Rescue at Sea

I HAD ALWAYS had a natural revulsion for anything technical, clinical or machine-like. I detested those electronic gadgets, gizmos and handheld or full-screen video games that gave children that slack-jawed, vacant look of a frontal lobotomy recipient. Seemed to me, these things took us away from one another, isolated us, replacing human nurture and community with a faceless entity that was unable to give love and recognition in return. I enjoy things that require human interaction, an encounter with another soul; eye contact and a smile that send a message of friendship and understanding; communication is vital to living a complete life. Yet, I had become as bereft of that soul-to-soul contact as those children absorbed in their solitary game playing, perhaps even more so. At least they finally turned the thing off and left for school or became engaged in some other communal activity their daily lives offered. I rarely had the opportunity to engage others from the outside world; when it *did* happen, they generally came into mine. And so what happened next was all the more perplexing for me. Desperation does strange things to a person.

The miracle occurred on my forty-fourth birthday, the 17th of May 2000, when my sister Diane purchased a used computer through the local community college as a gift for me. She installed it, arranged for Internet service and paid my monthly bill herself. Diane's always been a generous soul, but I wasn't the most grateful recipient in this instance.

The value of this machine didn't hit me right away. I thanked Diane for the gift, but as she was saying good-bye, I remember asking myself why she would have ever thought I'd appreciate it. And worse yet, it wasn't like I could stuff this gift under my bed and drag it out only when Diane came to visit. I lived in a tiny one-bedroom apartment, so that computer just sat there day after day, collecting dust and staring back at me.

Boredom and curiosity finally got the better of me and I sat down in front of the dark screen. Before I knew it, click, click, click . . . I was out of the dark ages and launched into a wild new world. I visited Web sites of interest, such as the Library of Congress, where I looked up historical documents: Lincoln's Gettysburg Address, the Constitution, the Bill of Rights. I read about the signers of the Declaration of Independence, all the haggling that had gone on, and marveled that we ever *did* become the great nation we now so take for granted.

I traveled to C-Span's Web site and read about bills making their way through committees and laws that had recently taken effect, and absorbed what different legislators had to say on a variety of subjects. I wrote to these men and women, exercising my right to petition Congress. I even wrote to then Senator Joe Biden (D) Delaware to tell him that I approved of his new hair plugs. They made this already debonair man look ten years younger. Joe didn't write back.

Locked away there in my confinement, I saw open to me a whole new world, and I took to it like a starving, drought-afflicted baby, hungry for a crust, anything at all to fill the echoing hole I'd created inside myself. But it wasn't edible food I desired; it was more elusive than that. I wasn't yet completely in touch with what it was I was lacking and what function my new distraction was serving, so numb had I become to real feeling during my decade-long incarceration. But as I typed, I was magically filled, satisfied, in a way no greasy pepperoni pizza or McDonald's fare could ever hope to. I began to approach my keyboard with the same gusto that I had formerly given to a hearty plate of meat loaf and mashed potatoes with gravy.

I soon discovered various political chat rooms and went there to exchange views, learn something, debate issues and stimulate my mind. I found it exciting to be able to touch others with my thoughts. Some seemed bruising for a fight. They were searching for a "something" they were unsure of . . . just as I was.

There were people dedicated to making a difference, to learning more. They were well informed on issues and sometimes made me think about a topic in a whole new light. We didn't share much of a purely political bent; that was irrelevant. It was *them* I liked, not their affiliations.

After a few weeks of sparring, I exchanged e-mail addresses with some of these folks and our communication became more personal. I had no idea where all this was leading me, or why I was choosing this particular fork in the road. I only knew that I was feeling better, more alive and happy to be getting up in the morning to respond to my mail; I felt I had a purpose.

I'd taken my involvement from political debate to a more personal level, an unexpected consequence of my exuberant desire to reach out. At first it frightened me. I was deathly afraid that if I was completely honest with these people, they'd flee. That's the reaction I got from people in person—contempt, disgust—that's why I had isolated myself. I couldn't keep risking the dismissive attitudes of others. I didn't want to tell my new Internet friends the truth, because I was sure I would end up alone in the stifling stillness once more. I couldn't go back now. I'd have rather died.

Think of what my experience had been so far: Most any time I'd been out and encountered another human being, I was met with stares, whispering or the turning of heads in an attempt to mask obvious discomfort. Eye contact with me was somehow painful for people, and even when I'd attempt to engage them in light conversation, their responses were hesitant and awkward, excruciatingly tacked on to the end of their stumbling sentences. I was a beast with a voice to them, a subhuman, and their judgment was keenly felt.

I remember a particular incident, returning from a doctor's appointment, long before I reached my top weight of 703 pounds. I think I was in the 450-pound range at the time. My sister Michelle was pushing me in my wheelchair under the awning toward the front entrance of my building. An old woman was leaving as we were coming through. Seeing what was approaching, she flattened herself against a support column, arms bracing the bricks to one side of the entryway; I thought of an old movie called *The Hurricane*, in which island people clung for dear life to a palm tree lest they be whisked away into an angry sea by the storm's surge. This passageway was at least twelve feet wide, yet this woman appeared to believe that had she continued walking toward the oncoming behemoth in her path, she would have been obliterated under the wheels of my hefty conveyance.

The lobby was packed with old folks that afternoon, seated and chatting on couches and in armchairs; I dreaded having to wheel past their stares. A Hispanic man came forward to hold open the doors for us. He was effusive in his speech to my beautiful and thin younger sister, Michelle. Then he redirected his focus onto me. In his heavy Latin accent he engaged me with "Say, I think I know what your problem is, lady!" I could hardly wait to ask, "Really, sir, and what might that be?"

"Well, I think you eat too much!" I stared, slapped my palm hard against my forehead and exclaimed, "Eureka, mister! You've solved the mystery. Thank you for clearing that up. I will try eating less and see what happens." Michelle rolled me into the elevator and pushed the button for the seventh floor.

This is but one moment among hundreds. I believed from the way I was treated that I was not allowed membership in the human club. But on the Internet, I was looking at a chance to be included, and I was desperate, so I did what I felt I had to do to make the grade: I lied.

I told myself that what I was doing wasn't really lying; after all, the occupation I chose to say I was involved with was a craft I'd worked at for years: cooking. I told my new friends that I drove an old Fiat named Tony; I had driven that model of car just after my divorce from my husband. I built the skeleton of a life where there was none. Who was I without those spare details? Was I someone others would listen to, appreciate and laugh with, instead of at;

would they take me seriously without the framework of some kind of normalcy? I knew what my answer to that question was and I became who I was inside; I was "playing" myself. I was desperately trying to become Nancy.

What evolved by means of these transgressions of mine was an interesting, if unintended, study in human nature. Without the stigma attached to my physical condition, the people I communicated with were absorbing my soul instead of my unpalatable earthly form; and they loved what my thoughts and feelings looked like. Their letters began to speak to me beyond the nouns, verbs and adjectives. Each morning my full inbox gave me what I needed to hear, over and over again, until I could believe it myself, believe *in* myself. I sent letters of support for weeks to a woman whose little child needed to undergo heart surgery, from which he made a full recovery, thankfully. I encouraged her along the way, yes, but mostly I made her laugh; laughter really *is* the best medicine. I sensed loneliness in some; I wrote to a middle-aged man who, over time, shared that he was estranged from his grown children. Regardless of fault or the genesis of the breach, he told me that my letters made him feel that he had something to offer the world after all, and shortly thereafter he wrote to say that he'd become a Big Brother, and how that new relationship had changed his life.

And their thanks for my support was causing change in *me*. I put on a new skirt every day, even if the one worn yesterday wasn't dirty, just to have something different reflected in the mirror. I put on earrings every morning, something that had seemed useless until then as no one but me would ever see them gracing my face. I lotioned my hands; though my sister Diane brought me exotic varieties often as gifts, these lotions had, until then, just sat unopened on a shelf gathering dust. I suddenly stopped biting my nails, a habit I'd had since I was ten. I now saw fingernails, instead of remnants of nails, bitten to the quick, sometimes to the point of bleeding, when I looked at my hands as I typed out letters to friends every day.

I was a valuable person, regardless of my size or ability to move about freely in the world. Just by sitting at that keyboard and expressing my thoughts, I was being accepted, loved and nurtured and was reaching back out to care for others in return.

The vital love I speak of is the "agape" version of the word. Its root is Greek and its meaning worlds apart from the sad, artificial brand that Hollywood so often throws at us as something that will fill us and make us whole. Agape is selfless love; the care and feeding of another's spiritual and core needs for the other's benefit alone, although the person on the giving end receives great unintended benefits. I am no saint; I am not trying to portray myself as the on-line Mother Teresa, not even close. But, the thing that renewed me, that began my healing process, is the agape form of love. To me, real human interaction is supposed to achieve this selflessness, a basic component of our makeup that often gets forgotten in our reaching for the unattainable. That other, exciting, titillating "love" (infatuation), which once captured dissipates through our fingers like so many grains of sand, leaves us feeling lost and cynical and many times unwilling to trust again. Those "things" and "feelings" are not real, not what we are truly looking for; we need one another in very profound and elemental ways. Romantic love *can* be wonderful; agape love is essential.

I soon found myself communicating with people all over the world. Through these e-mails, by sharing my thoughts, humor and my attempts at expressing myself through writing poetry and prose, I began a healthier focus, venturing outside my limited world and reaching out to discover what had seemed far beyond my grasp.

I received tremendous feedback from others, from places as far-flung and people as diverse as a factory foreman in Saudi Arabia, a retired investment banker from St. Petersburg, Florida, a computer software saleswoman in Montreal, a social worker in Omaha, an industrial parts buyer in the UK, a commercial shipping container leasing agent from South Carolina, a homemaker and mother of six in rural Tennessee and a roofer living in Great Britain.

The roofer, or "tiler" as they call themselves in England, sent me numerous lovely photos of ancient castles, double-decker buses, narrow and quaint brick-paved alleyways in rural English villages, a photo of the Lion Hotel in England, which dates from the seventeenth century and is where one of my favorite authors, Charles Dickens, stayed for a time to write. He sent pictures of cottages in the Welsh countryside and of himself skiing in the French Alps. These pictures, these people, their touch, fed me over these many months, so nurturing were they to the vast emotional chasm that a lively spirit used to inhabit.

I wrote horrid limericks to a guy in Britain and he to me; some were bawdy and foul and hilarious. It became a case of one-upmanship, each one worse than the previous sent. He wrote poetic verse regarding the illusive and dastardly "Shropshire Slasher," a mythical highwayman who ravaged the English countryside with his ever-present sidearm and pint of mead, laying waste to hot-on-his-trail authorities and innocent maidens alike along his depraved, hilarious and unlikely path. He'd pen a chapter; then it would be my turn to "stand and deliver" some outlandish continuation of Shroppy's wanton exploits.

These hours of writing dialogue and sharing brought irreplaceable memories and profound changes in what I thought of myself and my capabilities. This man, this grandfather many times over, brought to the table pieces of his humanity and vast experience, setting them on my empty plate to be lapped up as if I were an overworked border collie at the end of a hard day's travail with errant sheep.

There was a single mother in Tennessee who bemoaned her circumstances; her husband had cheated on her with her best friend and she was left with four small children to rear alone. She was sure she'd never find another man to help ease her load. Men simply couldn't be trusted. Her e-mails sounded like a droning "woe is me" country song; the only thing missing was her ne'er-do-well husband running over the family's hound dog with his rusty pickup truck on the way out of the drive.

"Balderdash," I countered. "There are rotten apples in every barrel, no doubt; but throw the tainted one away and rinse off the others. You'll be sure to find one that tastes great underneath the bad. Come on, lady. . . . You've got the life you have right now, and if you keep this attitude, you'll never be open to good things when they come into view; you won't even notice that they're there."

After a short period of time I told her my whole story. I hoped that if I shared my current obstacles, she might see a glimmer of hope in her own case. I honestly didn't believe yet that my outcome was going to change, I only wanted her to see that others had difficulties, too, and still had the ability to laugh apart from their pain. I don't know how much my tale impacted her decisions moving forward; I only know what her reaction to my openness was. It was wonderful. She told me she cried when I sent the letter explaining my situation and that it opened her eyes to some defects in her thinking about her own life.

Over time she began taking steps to raise the quality of life for herself and her kids. She enrolled in a nighttime nursing course, leaving the children with her mom while she went back to school to improve her lot. She met a man in class that she started dating, and it was obvious in the tone of her letters that she looked at life and her future in a far more hopeful light.

Our correspondence became less frequent as her outlook improved; it drizzled to once a month to update me, then to nothing at all. She was spending her time loving a man and her children, improving her life, not sitting at a computer to bleed her angst out onto a page. I understood her silence completely; I was happy for her.

As my online relationships developed, there was now little mention of the logistics of our lives: our jobs and cars, our travels, etc. But I still felt like a fraud. Those with whom I was closest at times heard me say that someday I would be able to tell them just how profoundly they had changed my life for the better. It must have sounded to them like only a compliment, that their letters had cheered me when I felt blue. Until the day I could finally feel free to open up—and I ached to do it—they couldn't have imagined the true import or depth in my words of gratitude.

Those people now know me fully and are amazed that they couldn't see through the mask I held to cover my shame and fear of rejection. But none that I eventually opened up to were angry or felt they'd been deceived; knowing me then and now, knowing my character and soul, they told me that they understood what I had felt compelled to do and what a miracle it was that I had emerged from my self-imposed hell. I didn't have to "play" Nancy anymore; it was the real McCoy that now smiled back in the mirror's reflection.

My spirit started to bloom again; I began to blossom. Food no longer held a death grip on my being. Food was still delicious, but it was not the focal point in my life. I fed instead on other people's happiness and excitement, their letters telling me that I had brightened their day and made them smile, made them laugh and feel better when they'd been down; and they filled me. Lord, what a wonderful feeling. Then that feeling became my reality: I was worth something.

I was a diabetic, no surprise there. I had to take a pill called Glucophage to regulate my blood sugar, but amazingly, even at my top weight of 703 pounds, I was not yet insulin dependent. I sometimes typed for hours on end and would suddenly begin to feel dizzy. Then I'd remember that I hadn't eaten a bite since breakfast and would have to stop to find something to eat. I ended up putting a Post-it note on the corner of the screen with the admonition *Eat, Nancy!* so I wouldn't forget and become ill.

There was never a particular diet plan I followed; I'd been on all of them at one time or another over my lifetime. Before my "awakening" I felt that there was never enough; I would eat till I was very uncomfortable and then immediately add a heaping portion of self-criticism on top for my piggish lack of control. I didn't want to feel that way anymore. I didn't *need* to feel that way anymore.

The obese are not necessarily gourmets. I did not require filet mignon and beluga caviar, a fine English trifle or Belgian truffles to be satiated. I wasn't picky at all. I simply ate more than I needed to accommodate my energy output, far more. I was an emotional eater.

Period. There was no rhyme or reason to my eating habits. I can remember standing at the refrigerator door one day before the computer came into my life, looking inside and not wanting to expend the effort to make a meal. Not that I was really hungry; I just wanted to eat something. I grabbed a fork, and half of a cold baked acorn squash, mindlessly eating it out of its shell just as it was; this was common for me to do. Presentation, garnish and the perfect seasoning rarely entered my mind back then.

Food is the obese person's "tool" to stuff feelings. . . . It has little to do with what we consume or even whether we're truly hungry at the moment; we rarely allow a natural tummy rumbling to occur as an indicator of our body's need for fuel. We eat to avoid a hellish "reality": the thought that we are worthless, for whatever reason. Food, for a moment, becomes the nonjudgmental friend that will soothe that harsh reality. It's the obese person's heroin, but instead of track marks left defacing our arms, we sport stretch marks and double chins.

Again, my turnabout away from this was not something I decided to do in any conscious way; it just happened. I think I now know why. When you love someone, you give that person the best of everything, true? You feed the loved one well, make sure he or she has clean clothes to wear and crisp sheets to sleep on, and you give that person little unexpected gifts to show how much you care. I was now treating myself like I was someone that mattered; I was a lovable human being and it was beginning to show.

I remember distinctly the moment I became aware the weight was leaving me. I was sitting in front of my computer, on my oversized ottoman, and believe me, darlin', I covered every inch and more. And on this day, about four months into my online adventure, my loyal and neurotic feline companion, Nuner, jumped up on me. Her action was so stunning that I stopped my tapping and looked down. I laughed at my reaction; jumping up on things is what cats do. *What's so astonishing about that, Nancy?* Then it hit me. There had never been room before to allow for such a thing to occur. She didn't fit on my ottoman with me aboard. I had never *had* a lap for her to sit on. I was so wrapped up in my new distraction that I had been oblivious to its effect on my body. I filed away this new information, but it really didn't impact me as you might think it would have. I was still so heavy; I had dug myself a bodily Black Hole of Calcutta to try and climb out of and had lost all hope of ever again seeing the light of day. I wasn't trying to lose weight; the thought never entered my mind at that time.

One Sunday morning my priest, a very learned, age-bent and holy man came to the door to pray with me and offer Holy Communion. He'd done this every Sunday for years. Father would perform his priestly duties, and then knowing my love of politics and Sunday morning TV news shows, he would shout out, "All right, Nancy, turn on the tube. . . . Let's see what the heathens are saying today!" In the past, I'd left the door open and would call for him to come in, as it was difficult to move quickly and embarrassing to me for others to watch; this time I went to the door. As I opened it wide, my elastic-waistbanded skirt fell off my hips and down to my ankles. Thank the Lord I was wearing a slip. From that day forward, I used a safety pin at the waist to gather the excess fabric.

MY MOM WAS more than usually irritated with me during this period of time; I was online a lot and she was feeling neglected. I always checked in at some point during the day, but my new routine was screwing up our normal pattern of speaking several times daily, and Mom was having trouble making the adjustment. I felt resentful; I was not content to play bingo on Thursdays, or go to the monthly community room potluck to exchange pictures of the grandchildren and talk about the old days; not just yet, thanks. I was forty-four years old and had an opportunity to touch life again, and by God, Florence was not going to guilt me into giving up that injection of spirit no matter how much she pouted. What happened next would make me feel that guilt acutely.

She called late one night to say she felt woozy. I knew what that meant; her blood sugar was going wacky on her. She sounded really drifty, just out of it. I always felt so helpless when Mom called like this. I should have been able to run down and help her, but in my condition there was just no way. Now she was crying. I told her to get a grip on herself and grab a cracker and some peanut butter; it's one of the things doctors say help raise your blood sugar quickly when it's dangerously low. I could hear her groaning to get up and then the sound of her voice (still talking to me, of course) drifting off, I knew toward her kitchen.

Mom always kept one can of regular Coca-Cola in the fridge, not its sugar-free, diabetic-friendly cousin. This carbonated shot-o'-sweetness was the last defense when her blood sugar went reeling out of control; it really gives a jolt to the system. I hoped she'd thought of downing that as well as the peanut butter/cracker combo. I waited, praying she'd get her butt back on the line soon; I was worried. Finally, I heard Mom coming, mumbling, whimpering and panting. *Speak to me, Mom,* I thought. "Oh, honey . . . I grabbed the jar and a tube of crackers; I'm going to eat it now."

Mom had a habit of talking to you even when she'd have to put the phone down to attend to something momentarily. You'd hear her prattling on about whatever came into her head; she'd even ask you questions. And she was doing that very thing now as she prepared her life-saving meal. Her statements were odd and disjointed, making little sense.

I made a radical decision: I hung up the phone. I thought it better to call an ambulance, though I knew Mom would berate me for it later. I told the dispatcher what was going on and that my mom's phone was probably off the hook. After giving her the address of the apartment building, I disconnected and waited. Perhaps Mom was still talking to me while munching away on her perfectly coated crackers; worse, maybe she was unconscious. Minutes later I heard sirens outside the building and knew Mom would have help; I prayed I hadn't waited too long to call.

My unease ended with the ringing of the phone twenty minutes later; it was Mom on the line. She sounded a bit drifty, but much more in control; she interrupted my questions with a string of sentences being offered to somebody else. "Excuse me, honey. . . . No, you'll find a pan under the counter next to the stove, dear. And, yes, the juice glasses are in *that* cupboard. Thank you so much, angel! All right, I'm back, Nancy. Yes, I'm going to be just fine; I only needed a little help. These nice people are doing just that. Now, go back to sleep and don't worry." My persuasive and charismatic mother had commandeered the two emergency workers to make her fried eggs, toast with jelly and orange juice. Mom was in her element; I was no longer needed.

The emergency medical team ended up insisting that Mom go into the hospital that night anyway. After all her efforts to mitigate damages by ingesting breakfast in the wee hours, she was unhappily sent on her way to be inspected further; her blood sugar numbers didn't lie and they were still critically low. Mom never came back home to live. What was thought to have been only huge blood sugar fluctuations upon admission to the hospital turned out to be a urinary tract infection as well. Part of the delirious sound of her speech in that final call from home was due to an infection running rampant through her bloodstream; it had turned septic. She was next confronted with a series of mini-strokes, which were at first undiagnosed. They left her unable to communicate well, and she must have felt very frustrated and without hope.

She was sent to another hospital, geared toward recuperation, and there, in the middle of the night and disobeying orders, Mom got up alone to go to the bathroom, slipped on the slick linoleum and shattered the femur and tibia of her left leg. The fall was disastrous for someone of her size, approximately three hundred pounds. The surgery to repair the damage was difficult to perform, and with her diabetes, renal deterioration and congestive heart failure added to the equation, it was very serious indeed. But it had to be done, and the old bulldog pulled through. She'd added the new piece of steel inserted in her leg to her wardrobe of the season.

On the heels of that catastrophe, she had a massive stroke. God sometimes uses blunt methods to redirect our focus toward our ultimate goal of eternal paradise. Mom always spoke of heaven, its beauty and majesty, and how she longed to be there in Our Lord's glorious presence. It looked like she was mighty close to getting her wish.

As Mom was moved from the hospital to a nursing home, I kept in contact with her by phone. It was horrible for me to hear the tone of her voice; so defeated and afraid. Her speech had somewhat recovered from the depredation of her strokes, but none of her feisty nature was present anymore; I wondered if it still lived somewhere within or had left her completely.

But life went on, and a few months later I woke up one morning and decided that my hair needed cutting; this was an understatement. I had worn it pulled back in a ponytail for years, leaning my head over a small wastebasket placed between my knees to snip off the ends with a pair of scissors every six months or so. In my twenties, before all my self-inflicted calamities had occurred, I had been close with a married couple, Sally and Dennis, both hairdressers. As with almost anyone else you could name, I had allowed communication with these two to first trickle and then end entirely. I hadn't spoken to either of them in a long, long time. I surprised Dennis with a call and he said that he'd be happy to come over to cut my hair. It's interesting to note that at this point I was still an enormous woman, but because of what had transpired over those months online, my newly held opinion of my value helped me in overcoming my usual fear of rejection, at least to a degree. Dennis is a very kind person by nature, a compassionate man. He made me feel like a million bucks that day. I was beginning to overcome the worst obstacle to my future happiness: myself.

I started making mini prison breaks, sneaking out late at night and crossing the hall to the stairwell door in my building, slowly and carefully descending seven flights in my bare feet, gripping the metal railing as I went and then taking the elevator in the empty lobby back up to my roost. I didn't do it for the exercise; I was doing it because I *could*. It felt wonderful to be able to use my body to get someplace other than to the fridge, a toilet or a bed. I was a giddy child doing something forbidden, clandestine, and getting away with it.

And I danced! I did a clumsy samba holding my cat, poor thing. Nuner was used to my being still, but she soon adapted to her owner's new activities. Music has always sparked me, has meant a lot to me. I had loved to go out dancing in those distant days when I was "normal-sized." And now I could release all that wonderful energy and expression through movement again, even though ungracefully and at the time only in the discotheque of my tiny living room.

I felt more comfortable going places now, though still very selective in where I chose to be seen; and I chose to be seen as little as humanly possible. My outings were mostly to a sister's home or to sit with my son in a less-populated park to watch the kids play early in the evening. And I spent more time with Mary Lou.

She invited me over for a backyard weenie roast. Her daughters, Patty and Therese, were going to be there, and it had been years since I'd seen them. I waited on a bench outside my building to be picked up. It still felt odd and wonderful to be able to get inside a car's front seat without any feelings of fear or humiliation; I could now get in and out on my own without great difficulty, though my belly still nearly rubbed the glove compartment. I sat in my friend's backyard that late afternoon and talked with her girls, reminiscing over times when they were young and their experiences with my little boy, Chris, while holding my hot dog over the open flame and watching it sizzle away.

These simple things, these everyday events that people take part in without a second thought, were wide-eyed moments for me. I felt like a modern-day Lazarus, self-proclaimed as dead as a doornail, now inexplicably resurrected into a new and wondrous life. The three of them stood up to take the dinner dishes into the house, and as I sat there watching the sun going down and listening to the crackle and hiss of the declining fire, I thought about how different my life was now, less than two years from the date that the computer had been delivered to its unwelcoming and suspicious new owner.

CHAPTER 15

On to Valhalla/Mom Goes Under the Waves

MOM WAS DYING in earnest now. She had been taken to the hospital again due to a medication foul-up at the nursing home. By the time the staff had figured out their mistake, she was hallucinating, sometimes seeming herself, other times making no sense whatsoever when I'd call, and according to my sisters, periodically pulling out her IV tubes and trying to get out of bed unassisted. The nurses finally tied her wrists to the bed rails. This was causing us great torment; to see your mom so helpless and out of control will break your heart.

Mom and I had many times been adversaries, but she and I knew that great love was there as well. I thought back on the occasions when my sisters would witness our little explosions and stand aghast at our fractious behavior. I'm sure some of them thought I was terribly disrespectful at times. But, they saw through Mom's ladylike veneer as well. I simply pointed out her outrageousness more often than they chose to.

Appearances had meant everything to Mom; what people thought of her was paramount. She had even told those in her building that her husband was dead, rather than admit that a "good" Catholic would be involved in a divorce after thirty-two years of marriage. I never measured up to her standards; the harder she tried to get me to, the harder I fought her. But somehow, instead of turning that rebellion outward, I took it out on myself. I beat myself up instead of using that energy to move my life forward. And there's no bigger waste of time than beating yourself up. It doesn't change anything that happened in the past; it doesn't help you not to make the same error in the future. It takes up all the time you should be using to make real changes. It's a common mistake so many of us make, but an understandable one. Children of critical parents, even grown children, are always striving, looking for the loving approval of those they hold most dear. I wanted to be held as "good enough"; that designation was never fully given me.

And now here Mom was, so "imperfect," so not in command of her environment, her bodily functions. Her eating and breathing were now facilitated by tubes, and she drifted in and out of consciousness, unable even to give orders from her throne anymore. Poor Mom, and poor me; was I going to let her die without seeing her, as had happened with my father? I determined then and there that it would not be the same this time.

A sister had given me a pretty caftan a few weeks back and I had not yet worn it. Mom was aware that I was getting better, that I'd already lost a lot of weight, but as of yet I hadn't felt comfortable going to see her in the nursing home; I had kept in contact only over the phone. But I had been taking my nocturnal excursions down the seven flights of stairs in my building, so I knew I was capable of walking down the long hospital corridors to my mom's room. This outing was important; I put on my new caftan and called my sister Diane to ask for a ride.

I wanted to see Mom late in the evening, when the fewest visitors would be around. We got there about ten; I was nervous to be walking such a distance on my own, but I knew there would be wheelchairs available if I really needed one. I did make it the whole way under my own power; when everything you've tried to do has met with failure and/or embarrassment for so long, it is second nature to assume the worst.

Mom didn't look like herself. She was so frail. Her hair was a mess and her demurely colored nail polish chipped. I'd never seen her like that. I sat rubbing her hand and reaching to stroke her brow, talking to her in the soft tones a parent uses to comfort a sick child. Mom's silence was punctuated only by the hum of monitoring equipment stationed nearby. I stayed overnight to spend some quality time with my old sparring partner. I soothed myself and her by singing oldies that we both loved: Frank Sinatra, Tony Bennett, Ella Fitzgerald, Glenn Miller, Cole Porter. "*Pack up all my care and woe . . .*"

And so it went throughout the night, singing, weeping softly in her ear, holding her soft hands and apologizing for any pain I'd caused, of course reminding the woman as well of how obstinate and insensitive she could be and that she was a poor loser when playing games. It was my way; it was *our* way of showing love.

By the next afternoon, Mom's condition had deteriorated even further, and she was now deemed brain dead. She wasn't in there anymore; only an exhausted shell remained. We were going to pull the plug; Mom had wanted it that way.

Diane and I sat on my balcony in the warm sun and talked about how sad, how odd it would be not to have Mom there; her irritating, disapproving, why-can't-you-be-like-me, manipulative, vulnerable, lovable, childlike-at-times, complex, vexing self. In my grief, inside all the wild emotions that swirled around in my brain on that hot summer day, something came out of my mouth that both shocked and horrified me. I looked at Diane through tears, and knowing how it would sound just before saying it, I still found myself unable to stem the tide, and though strangled, it came: "I don't think I can ever fully heal until she's dead. Oh, my God! Isn't that a terrible thing to say? How could I even *think* of something so bad! I will miss her so much. I love Mom, Diane. You *know* I do."

My sister was not shocked; she understood my meaning completely. And though neither of us elaborated, the message rang out as loudly, clearly and finally as church bells at a funeral. Though as an adult I'd rebuffed Mom's slights each time they were thrown, I still felt her harsh verdict's sting to my core, and the pain of that thoughtless rejection of me as a child. And I was *still* her child. Mom's love and approval meant so much to me that until I couldn't feel her harsh judgment only a telephone call or disapproving glance away, its effect could never fade; not as long as she had breath to speak.

Two days later found me just before sunrise walking toward my computer chair to write a letter, copying all the friends I wanted to let know as soon as I heard she had died. Mom had breathed her last at 4:23 A.M. on the 23rd of July 2001. And though I wasn't with her at the moment she exited her tired and wasted body, I knew she was with me then and there, hovering over me at the keyboard to console and probably cast a disapproving look at my typing skills.

We six girls were now orphans, for all intents and purposes; old, wrinkly ones, granted, but the pain attached to Mom's loss amazed me in its acuteness. You don't know how it feels, the "lost" element attached to a parent's death, now both parents, until you've experienced it. We were going to have to bury Florence now, as Dad would have said in his delicate and genteel way, "if not for love, for stink!" What a charmer.

The day of Mom's funeral was warm, cloudless and bright; most people like that kind of thing, but I like to avoid sweating whenever possible. Besides, it wasn't like I was heading for a happy, anticipated gathering, a potluck dinner or a baseball game; Mom was dead. . . . It was hard getting that idea to take hold. I rode with my son and his family to the church. Little Isaac looked so cute in his black suit with a yellow rose on his lapel; Ian wore one, too. He was eleven now and starting to look less boyish and more adolescent. I was proud to be out with both of them; it had been such a rarity for me.

The doors of Saints Peter and Paul Catholic Church were left open to allow a light breeze to flow into the main area where the service would be held. My sisters were already seated up front when we arrived, so I ushered myself in next to Diane on the end and waited for the soloist to begin. Mom's casket was at the front of the center aisle, resting on a fabric-draped bier, its top strewn with beautiful flowers. And then the unthinkable happened.

Out of the corner of my eye I spied a small mongrel dog standing near the entrance of the church, panting from his drifter's travels out of doors. He looked to be smiling, his tongue draping from his open mouth, and he was now heading in our direction. This vagabond beast made a beeline across the front of the pews. He stopped dead in his tracks at the side of Mom's casket and began to sniff. "Oh, no. Please, God . . . don't let him lift his leg on Mom," I whispered to Diane in mock indignation. Mother would've died of mortification if she already wasn't so (in)disposed. An usher snatched the dog away nearly in mid-lift.

At the cemetery, I stood with my son, holding the back of one of the seats set out for family near the open grave; I wasn't sure the chair would hold my weight. I was shoeless. I'd taken off my slip-on sandals to walk through the lush grass; any unevenness of the lawn could have thrown me off balance unless I was barefoot. I had progressed enough in my weight loss that if I'd fallen down, at least I could have gotten back up. And though I was somewhat uncomfortable with my appearance, especially in front of so many relatives whom I hadn't seen in forever, I was not as concerned with what they thought as I'd assumed I'd be. I was there to honor my mother and to prove something to myself as well: It was my place to be there and I was *worthy* of being there. I was validating my humanity. And odd to think that Mom had died just as I was truly coming alive.

CHAPTER 16

Scraping the Barnacles off My Hull/ Rechristening the Good Ship *Nancy*

NEWBORNS AWAKEN TO life in increments. My rebirth was much the same, crying, flinching; fearing the loss of my cocoon. If an infant could speak, perhaps it would beg to reenter the birth canal, to travel back to a soothing darkness, to a comfortable and familiar place. I had a hard time giving up the familiar. I was excited and scared to death all at the same time.

I began to ponder what losing weight and being back out in the world would mean. There were then and are now a series of what I call "firsts." They are each landmark events in my reemergence from that dark, isolated space.

Apart from the occasional visits of my dear friend Mary Lou, whom I had long ago dubbed "Florence II," in light of our loving yet ofttimes adversarial relationship, I hadn't seen most of my friends in fifteen years or more; this was my choice. I was ashamed of what I'd become. A rare exception was Cindy, who sometimes stopped in with her husband, David, to visit. She never lost contact with me completely.

I felt comfortable with her. We were fellow "devotees" of compulsive overeating, but more than that I connected with her personality. She was and is a very open and loving person, a "give you the shirt off her back" type. Besides, she laughed at my bad jokes and my horrid, black humor. In my isolation, I knew Cindy would accept me as I was, as she, too, was quite overweight.

Cindy invited me to go on a visit to Howard City, a small town north of Grand Rapids, where she and David had moved a few years prior. I had been out, yes, but had not left the city limits; the prospect was exhilarating. I remember shaking as I stepped out of my apartment door without the aid of a gurney or wheelchair to facilitate my departure. And more exciting was the thought of leaving Grand Rapids. I hadn't been farther than ten miles from home in years. Now I would be taking a forty-five-minute drive.

No one else would give a second thought to getting in a car. You are, after all, only stepping into a vehicle, true? Not so for me. I didn't have to worry anymore about wedging myself in and getting stuck, but old habits die hard and I still thought about it. For so many years, I had had to think ahead, anticipate the next step. Every movement has to be calculated when you are morbidly obese; nothing is easy, nothing.

I was still very heavy, but by the standards of what many Americans look like these days, I wasn't that much different. Even so, I was still afraid that I didn't measure up. The woman who had once had to call ahead to the doctor's office to have all six doors measured from the front of the building to the exam room in order to determine whether or not her double-wide wheelchair would fit, was now sitting comfortably in the passenger seat of Cindy's midsized car. The seat belt actually reached around her sagging abdomen and clicked.

A thousand million thoughts raced through my head as Cindy drove us to her home. My eyes drank in everything around me as we whizzed by the traffic, houses, a child on a bicycle, a park full of flowering shrubs and then the on-ramp to the freeway. Cindy was talking to me, but I wasn't fully listening. We were on the freeway going north, when she starting laughing. She said that my head should be on a pivot, that I reminded her of a small child, agog with wonder over the silliest things.

Howard City is a very small town. At the time it boasted a couple of gas stations, a like number of bars, a grocery store and a pole barn used for auctions. It appeared to have been refurbished last in the 1950s or before; the décor of the few mom-and-pop eating establishments bore this out. But the shop I wanted most to enter was the Dollar Store. I'd heard of these odd emporiums from others during my years inside, but had not yet ventured out to one. So in I walked, and I went mad.

I found a carousel of sunglasses and proceeded to gather eight pairs in varying hues and shapes. I bought several bottles of gaudily colored nail polish, as one of my newfound loves was painting my toes—now that I could reach them. I grabbed packages of copper scrub pads for washing pots and pans, gift wrap and a package of padded mailing envelopes. I needed none of these items, but everything was one dollar.

We spent the rest of the afternoon at Cindy's home visiting, and when it was time for the return trip, Cindy's husband, David, joined us. He suggested that we stop at Bob's Big Boy for dinner, and though I was hungry, I was extremely nervous about going inside a place where so many people would be gathered. I hadn't been inside a restaurant in more than eighteen years. Did I *deserve* to be in there? They would all be staring at me.

I was so frightened that I found myself immobile. David has never been one to mince words, and in response to my concerns he said, "Damn it, Nancy, you're going in! It'll be just fine!" Next thing I knew, I was walking up the sidewalk muttering, "I'm walking into a restaurant, like I'm normal or something."

"Just shut up and walk, for God's sake," David quipped. The man loves me, I know this. He just has a low tolerance for the ridiculous. Without him, I'd never have made it inside the door that day.

ANOTHER "FIRST" OCCURRED while I was sleeping one evening. As I lost weight, I could finally recline flat on my couch or lie on my side when I chose to, the ever-present drone of the TV set in the background as I drifted off to sleep. One night, I drowsily lifted my head, fluffed up the pillow and turned over. As I was reentering my dream, I suddenly realized I'd just done something I hadn't been able to do for a very long time. I sat up, fully awake now, to absorb what had just happened: I had turned over. I practiced the process, back and forth, flopping like a fish on that couch.

And my cat Nuner lost her usual perch. She liked to sleep on my belly when I was turned on my side, but now when she tried to lie down, she slid off. She tried again with the same frustrating result, finally going off in search of a more secure resting place.

[207]

* * *

CHILDREN HAD BEEN such a lifeline during those many years inside; they were always as glad to see me as was I to see them. The five main characters were two small nephews, a niece and my two grandsons. We'd spent many days together over the years and so they knew me well. There was a certain protocol they followed at my place. Immediately after entering through the door, all shoes came off and were put in a corner out of the traffic pattern. Only the toys currently being played with were allowed out. There was a little stool in the kitchen each used to climb on in order to put empty dishes in the sink after eating. The children knew where the large comforter was kept, so at nap time they could retrieve it and spread it out in front of my large aquarium to rest. I softly sang their favorite tunes while they drifted off to sleep. They each had jobs as their price of admission, and there was never a question as to why it had to be that way.

When I would have to get up and move, either to go to the bathroom or to the kitchen to get them something to eat, there was another kind of protocol put into action. After the announcement was made that I was rising, they would all quickly scurry up and out of the way onto a piece of furniture. A person of my former size—seven hundred pounds—isn't exactly agile on her feet. Movement of any kind is a hazardous procedure; balancing that much weight is harder than you can imagine. The slightest misstep could have landed me on my butt. I could have killed one of these precious lightweights if I'd toppled over. Not alarmist; it was true.

When the children came to visit me now, there were so many more things that we could do together. I could get down on the floor to play with them, racing large plastic cars from one end of the apartment to the other. Things were so much more relaxed, more normal.

But my transformation and all that had come before it had left its mark on those children as well. My niece Lydia came to spend some time with me. It was close to Christmas, and I was standing at the closet in the hall looking for some gift wrap. I became aware that she was standing next to me, and when I turned to look at her, she was distressed. When I asked what was wrong, she broke into tears. "I'm afraid you're going to fall over and hurt yourself, Aunt Nancy! You've been standing there too long! I think you should go and sit down now!"

I held my niece. "Things are different now, honey. If I need to sit down, I will. Promise."

CHRISTMAS OF 2002 was the best I'd had in nearly two decades. So many things were making a reentrance into my life, but we all had to make adjustments. My grandson Isaac, a little more than five at the time, spent the night with me while his mom and dad were out doing some last-minute Christmas shopping. We always made blueberry bagels as part of our breakfast; it was an unwritten law. I had given away my toaster years before, as it was hard for me to stand long enough to butter toast, and it took up precious counter space as well. I owned two ottomans; one was in the bedroom near my computer, the other stationed in the kitchen opposite my stove. I would sit there and watch the bagels toasting underneath the broiler, turning each when ready and then buttering them on a plate, using the open door of the oven as a countertop. I'd hand the prepared bagel to whichever child was waiting to carry it to the table in the living room.

Isaac was standing beside me as I sat that morning watching his bagel toasting. He noticed that there was a foreign object on the broiler pan; it wasn't round, but square. He asked me who that other "thing" was for. I told him that it was mine; that I chose to eat something better for me and that I liked how it made me feel. Isaac broke into tears. "What's wrong, sweetheart?" I hugged him. "It's nothing bad. I *like* my toast!" Through sobs he told me that my new "skinny toast" was going to change me into someone else, someone he didn't know. "You won't be my grandma anymore." Over time I proved him wrong, but my bread was now dubbed "skinny toast" and was eyed by Isaac with suspicion for quite some time.

A COLD DAY in January found me walking up the path to my son's home, the crunch of freshly fallen snow under my boots. This terrain would've been impossible for me to cover only a year before. Isaac had come with his father to pick me up from home that day. He sneaked up behind me, letting loose with a snowball and landing a direct hit on the back of my coat. For a lifetime, his only memory had been of a grandmother who hobbled and teetered, saying a Hail Mary that she'd reach the end of her fifteen-foot trek without falling on her enormous keister. These babies always knew that they could attack without fear of retaliation.

The tables were about to be turned. I swiveled and wearing vengeance's sweet grin bent over and packed a mean powdery bullet, then let my icy missile fly. Isaac's ruddy-cheeked face bore the look of a man doomed. He beat a hasty retreat, but got his comeuppance right where his jacket collar met his tender exposed earlobe. Nothing would ever be the same; nothing.

One morning a few months later I walked outside onto my apartment complex's grounds. I wandered back behind the building's gazebo and sat down alone to drink in the atmosphere on a small rolling hill of green among the flowering crabapple trees. I'd brought my notebook and pen; they went with me everywhere. I watched spring's newborn squirrels frolic and laughed at the birds all atwitter over a scrap of food. I felt the warmth of the sun on my smiling face and marveled at God's gracious gift. I had dreamt for years about this very moment, never believing that it would come to me again. Yet there I was, cool blades of grass pressed against my exposed lower legs, naked toes wriggling through them, and with hands that could now stroke the surface of this green swaying sea surrounding me. It reminded me of the texture of a newly barbered man sporting a brush cut. I grabbed up a handful and felt its tickle under my eager nose.

Then lazily I turned and looked behind myself and up, up, up toward the top of the nine-story structure at my back. For the first time I was looking at the back of my apartment from the *outside*. Those few bricks that had held every joy and fear, every sad, desperate moment and hopeless sigh for more than a dozen years, looked so small, distant and far removed from what I now experienced. In that instant I was free, and I wept.

While I was still writing letters to my online acquaintances, the new developments unfolding in my life were taking up more of my time and energy. Some of my online retinue felt slighted if I didn't pen a long e-mail every day. I wasn't neglecting them; I was taking better care of myself.

Many, however, took my absence in stride, and though our communication was not as frequent, these were the friendships that last to this very day. As my overuse of food had been supplanted by my online friendships, my online time was being slowly replaced with being able to live a full life.

The little things we take for granted were all changing for me. I hadn't taken a bath for years. Let me rephrase that. I hadn't been able to *sit* in a bathtub for years. I'd lost hundreds of pounds by this time; I'll never know exactly how much, as I still hadn't gone into the doctor's office to be weighed. I was brushing my teeth one morning and glanced over at the bathtub. There it sat: my shower seat. This contraption had been my only means of keeping clean. I remember always having to be careful of my wet sides pulling the shower curtain away from inside the tub and allowing the stream of water to spill out onto the floor instead of onto me, because my body hung over the edges of the seat and onto the rim of the tub.

I turned on the water to prepare for yet another seated shower and all at once had the most astounding thought: Perhaps I could fit in the tub. I approached my mission like I was scaling Mount Everest; I brought the phone with me just in case. I stepped into the water and swirled my toes through the wet heat. Using my right hand on the tub's edge to balance my body, I dropped to one knee and voilà! I was sitting easily with room to spare. Sir Edmund Hillary would have been proud. My mind now drifted to the future, not the past. Bigger events and changes were on the horizon; the prospect of them both thrilled me and left me with feelings of trepidation, but these challenges were inevitable steps along my new path.

CHAPTER 17

Sea of Opportunities/The World Is My Oyster

I WAS NOW at an unexpected crossroads. I could go back to work. I'd been notified by letter that recertification of my eligibility for Social Security benefits was coming up soon. This time I knew I wouldn't qualify. The clock was ticking on my meager government subsidy; it was either sink or swim.

Julianne, the nutritionist I had become acquainted with at the hospital during my monthlong stay in 1994, gave me a call one day and asked if I could help her out; she needed a cleaning woman badly. She sometimes went on the road, lecturing on nutrition issues around the country, but with three toddlers, she was feeling overwhelmed. Her call surprised me; I was taken aback at the thought of it, but with all the bravado I could muster in my fledgling spirit, I agreed to give it a go.

Mind you, I was still heavy. I hadn't been weighed, that would be coming soon, but looking back now, I believe I had lost about 350 pounds over those last two years. Considering my top weight of 703 pounds, I was still carrying around a significant amount of excess cargo. Cleaning is a strenuous activity, but I knew I was good at it and enjoyed doing it. I was eager to start. Julianne offered to pick me up and drop me off at home after each workday; I gratefully accepted, and so it began.

Julianne would pull up in her white van, all children in tow engaged in various degrees of conduct, some giggling as I approached, or fidgeting in their car seats, another wailing, having dropped a bottle or badly in need of a late-morning nap; there was never a dull moment in our travels. The children liked to help me; I'd hand them wrung-out rags and give them each a mission to accomplish. I had to go over everything they cleaned of course, but it made them feel a part of things. The eldest, Meg, age four, called me "Cinderella," much to her mother's horror. Kids are so honest. It only endeared her to me.

"Cinderella" was lugging buckets of ammonia water up and down stairs, her long, flowing skirt tucked at a corner into the waistband like a scullery maid's, crouching low to dust mop the hardwood floors under beds and reaching for cobwebs hiding near the ceiling. I scrubbed Julianne's kitchen floor on my hands and knees; Mom would have cursed me from the great beyond had I done otherwise. "How can you properly clean a floor if you're not down on it to feel when it's clean? Your hands are your best tools." I agreed with Mom on this point.

I was sweating like a plow horse for those fours hours each week, and though I was exhausted at the end of my shift, I was content. I was doing something meaningful, something that propelled me out into the world and on my way to better things. Julianne's mother soon got into the act and offered me work as well, along with the cab service perk Julianne had given me—I didn't have a car.

Another old friend, Susan, who had been one of my art teachers during my Walden school days, but with whom I had long since lost contact, told me that she'd be interested in using my services. Susan's boss, Jim, then asked for my help as well and everybody offered transportation.

I could feel the pounds melting away. My tops hung on me now; my skirts had needed taking in at the waist again and for some unknown reason, I kept tripping over the hem. Lord, was I getting shorter in the bargain? I was already of near-munchkin stature; I couldn't afford to become any lower to the ground. This mystery both confounded and frustrated my smooth movement. Julianne came up with the answer: My rear end and abdomen weren't sticking out as far as they once had. My circumference was shrinking, thus the fabric fell toward my ankles with less impediment and now nearly covered my toes. I wasn't getting any shorter, I was getting thinner.

The excess skin really weighed on my mind. I would shower in the morning and catching a glimpse of myself in the mirror naked, stand there waggling my arms back and forth like wings, ready to fly into O'Hare Airport unaided by jet fuel. This wasn't a case of "granny arms"; this girl was sagging. My abdominal skin was worse; I had to "tuck" it inside my leotard to give a smoother, more firm appearance. Problem was it also gave me the look of someone six months pregnant. I wanted so much to feel normal; I didn't expect to look like a supermodel, I just wanted to feel *whole*. The skin was a constant reminder of the grave damage I'd done to myself. I called it "the haunting."

I needed to get in to see the doctor; it was required as part of my recertification for Social Security. I hadn't been weighed since my outing with Mary Lou the month before the beginning of the computer adventure back in May of 2000; I hadn't been in my doctor's office since 1996. But, in order to have the skin removed, I'd have to be deemed a healthy candidate for surgery. So I made an appointment and in I went.

I stood to be weighed and measured. The nurse's aide who did the job was a lively, thirtysomething black woman with a cheerful demeanor. I was telling her my story as the weights slid and clunked under her index finger's nudge at the top of the scale. She wrote the number registered down on her chart, and only then did it seem to dawn on her: "My God! You've lost four hundred and twenty-six pounds. . . . That's *three* of me!" She hugged me and then ran off shouting the news to anyone within earshot; she came back and escorted me to the exam room to wait for the doctor.

The door opened, and in he walked. He stopped, looked at me, down at the chart, then pardoned himself and exited the room. I had already waited for fifteen minutes in this room; I really didn't appreciate having to wait any longer. He reentered within a minute, apologizing and saying that he hadn't recognized me. I thought, *Say, buddy, you try losing four hundred pounds and see if you look any different!* He weakly congratulated me and then proceeded with the usual exam. When he was done, I asked if he thought I might be eligible to have the surgeries I needed. He said he'd do some checking and write his analysis of my case for the insurance company.

I waited for weeks on end, pestering his nurse on many occasions. When his evaluation finally came through, I sent it off to my insurer and waited for their answer. When it came, it wasn't what

I'd hoped for. They had denied me on the basis that it was not a "medical necessity," only "cosmetic," and so would not be covered. They weren't looking at what I was looking at. This wasn't cosmetic; what I needed was reconstructive. I decided to appeal their decision.

I wasn't going to miss any angle. If my insurance wouldn't cover the surgery, perhaps a teaching hospital would. I wrote a letter to the University of Michigan, asking if their school of medicine might perform my surgery. Their students would have a willing guinea pig, and they'd get a ton of excess skin to use for burn victims to boot. I was told that they could not only not help me, but that my skin would be "undesirable" as I was still diabetic and a smoker; not only that, fetal pig skin was now being touted more highly than human skin for grafting purposes.

I went online and researched my condition. The hanging skin at my abdomen was called a panicullus. The literature said that this condition can cause grave infections in those with diabetes; these infections can become septic and result in death. If that didn't qualify as a medical necessity then I don't know what did. As the date of my appeal hearing approached, I was nervous, having already been disappointed the first time and knowing that I'd be facing a panel of doctors, never the best of friends in my experience, with a judge present via phone. I typed up my research, had a nurse at the doctor's office take some photos of me naked, lifting my belly "flap" to expose sores that bred there due to chafing, and wrote a six-page letter, making copies for each panel member, detailing my story and offering arguments as to why I should be allowed this surgery.

On the day of my hearing, I walked into the insurance office, and a lady who'd been so helpful to me in phone calls regarding my case came up and hugged me and told me she hoped I would be success-ful. I walked into the conference room and introduced myself to the six-member panel and to the judge, just a disembodied female voice echoing from a box on the table. The panel did not appear welcom-ing; one member smiled when I shook his hand, but the rest wore poker faces. I hoped they were bluffing.

I started out just fine. I read them the results of my research, even questioning one doctor as to the validity of my findings regarding infections in diabetics. He agreed that they could be fatal; *could* be. Then I read from the letter I'd written. I didn't know till that moment how deeply what I'd gone through still affected me; when I began to weep, it took me by surprise. My leg was shaking under the table like a flea-infested dog's. My hands trembled. The doctor seated nearest me grabbed my wrist and said, "It's OK, Nancy, I think we've heard enough to make our decision. We'll let you know within a few days. Thank you for coming." I smiled weakly, apologized and walked out of the room and out to the parking lot to wait for my ride.

I sat on the curb and pushed the rewind button of my perfor-mance in my mind. *What an ass! Can't you do anything right? Where the hell did all that weeping come from? You've really blown it.* About ten minutes later; my ride still hadn't come, and from be-hind me I heard a familiar voice. It was my friend from the insurance company. She sat down next to me and, seeing that I was crying, put her arm around me and said, "Nancy, please stop crying. I need to tell you something. The usual protocol with these things is to send out a letter stating the panel's decision. They didn't want you to have to wait. It was a unanimous decision: You can have your sur-gery. One of the doctors told me to tell you that you are an amazing woman and should go into public speaking or the law. Two doctors teared up while discussing your case after you'd gone," she added. "I've never seen that happen."

This was a great first step. I knew that the abdominal surgery was only one of many I needed; I had a lot of restoring to do, but I'd eat this elephant one mouthful at a time. My victory didn't really sink in for a while; I'd waited for it to become real for so long. It felt like a fantasy.

I was still wearing skirts, never any kind of pants. I wore what are called "broomstick skirts," ankle-length and flowing, the kind you see gypsies wearing in the movies. On top, I wore leotards. I was thrilled to be able to get into them again; I'd worn leotards years before and liked how they looked.

I was heaviest from the waist down, so the tightness of the leotard accentuated the smallest part of my body, sucking in the excess skin hanging from my arms and lower abdomen, while the voluminous ankle-length skirt masked the figure flaws below. My ankles sagged, giving the alluring appearance of an epidermal pant cuff. The skin hung on my legs like dripping candle wax.

I met with a surgeon a few weeks later. I was so excited at the prospect of not having what I called "the baby" with me anymore. He lifted my sagging belly, examining every disgusting nook and cranny, but I didn't care. I was long past being ashamed in front of a doctor; I wanted this "thing" gone in the worst way. I liked my surgeon. He was young, not hard on the eyes and had a sense of humor. He said I was going to be his *Mona Lisa*. If that made him Da Vinci, then he'd better live up to his reputation.

Then came the letdown. I had to lose another eighty to ninety pounds before he performed my abdominoplasty. What a silly girl

I'd been. I'd had my head in the clouds and wasn't thinking realistically. Of course it made sense; the doctor explained that if he did it too soon, once I *did* lose more weight, I'd end up with a sagging abdomen all over again after all that effort. Though a bit deflated, I left feeling hopeful and even more resolute that those pounds were going to melt off me one way or the other. So I continued doing what I had been doing: eating well and working (exercise) and looking to the future. At least I had a goal to reach, and had no doubt I'd get there.

Someone must have squealed, and while friends and family denied it, the news was out. The tale of my resurrection from the dead had reached the ears of a writer with the *Grand Rapids Press,* and he called to ask for an interview. I agreed and we met at my place soon after. He was getting the bare bones of the story from me while pawing through a small stack of photos that had been taken during those years inside. He was shaking his head, and you could tell what he was thinking before he said it. "This is amazing, Nancy. I've never seen anything close to something like this. I really want to tell your story. Will you let me?" I didn't see any harm in it; perhaps it might even inspire someone. I said, "OK, let's do it!" Later, a photographer set up an appointment with me to take a few shots for the article, and that was that.

MONEY WAS TIGHT. I had been allowed only a few months of further Social Security payments, based on the analysis of my recertification information. Soon, I wouldn't be able to depend on those few hundred dollars per month at all. I was paying a reduced rate for rent at my building, based on my income, but it was still difficult to make ends meet. I needed to make more money; perhaps another set of eyes looking at the problem would help. I decided to take advantage of the resources the city offered to help people in transition. There was a place in town specifically geared toward helping women in getting back on their feet.

I am no fan of gender politics, or even of identity groups formed to further a particular agenda. I believe that we can bring about more change *together,* acting as one, not in creating artificial walls that tend to leave those outside the barriers feeling resentful. So going into a "women's" center that day was a stretch for me. But I needed the help. I believe in women's rights, don't get me wrong. A woman should be paid a rate commensurate to a man's. But so much of the women's movement became ridiculous to me: bra burning, rallying lines like "A woman needs a man like a fish needs a bicycle"; it made these women look like fools, too militant. I liked men; still do. I, personally, wouldn't like to try and live without them. What a boring world it would be. And childless as well.

I was called into the office of a career counselor at the center. Her name was Barbara, and I knew immediately that I would like this woman. She was about my age, in her late forties, with faux leopard-skin eyeglass frames and lush, wavy brown hair, and an impish smile to boot. We made our introductions and settled into discussing what I needed her help with. I gave her a brief overview of where I'd been and what challenges I now faced. We talked about expanding my housecleaning business, and my new desire to branch out into public speaking. I enjoyed people, loved a crowd and hoped that recounting my story might help inspire others. I'm afraid my love of the limelight and a captive audience sidetracked us a bit during that first meeting; my fault, not hers. Every stumbling block that was introduced for discussion was answered with a joke. We would work on the speaking angle as my finances became more stable. For now, we decided my cleaning business should be my primary focus. Barbara suggested that she could have some cards made up for my cleaning business and that I could place them in hair salons and on bulletin boards of grocery stores in the more affluent neighborhoods in town, along with other promising locales.

"Say, Nancy! I know how you can get some practice with public speaking. Why don't you go do stand-up at the comedy club in town? I'll come and sit in the audience for moral support!" Barbara had another client waiting in the wings, so we scheduled our next appointment and said good-bye.

We got down to business, the "numbers," at our next meeting. Barbara had asked me to make out a budget to give her an idea of how far behind the eight ball I was. It looked pretty bleak to me; there was about a four-hundred-dollar-a-month shortfall. I was terrified by the deficit, but Barbara reassured me, saying that "in no time at all" I would be wondering why I had allowed myself to become so afraid. "You can do this, Nancy! If you're good at what you do, others will come!" I knew in my head that she was right, but my present circumstances and immediate need for cash caused my emotions to take over my thoughts. I couldn't see the forest for the trees at that moment.

Everyone's been there in one way or another. You're in some dire situation and someone else offers support, a silver lining seen just over the horizon, and though you appreciate the effort, no matter who that person is or how much you respect his or her opinion, it doesn't entirely stop the angst you're feeling. But lo and behold, my mentor/cheerleader was right. Only two days later, something happened that would accelerate my ability to make money in a big way.

Jim, my latest client and a stocks and bonds financial whiz, was home one day for lunch. He often came in, wolfed down some food, and then lay down for twenty minutes or so before heading back to the office. I was busily cleaning his tub, attempting to remove a stubborn rust stain with chemicals and a little elbow grease, when he called out, asking how the "car hunt" was going. I had told my clients that I was saving as best I could to purchase a car I could afford.

I had my eye on an '89 Plymouth Reliant K-car that was full of rust holes and sounded a bit like a Huey helicopter when you started it up, but it ran. I was nearing my goal of six hundred dollars. "No! No! No!" Jim shouted. "You're thinking poverty consciousness!" Rolling my eyes and still scouring, I shot back, "No, Jim. I'm thinking *reality* consciousness!" Jim jumped up from his bed and, now standing behind my hunched, sweaty figure, went on to say that image was so important. He knew I wanted to do some public speaking and felt that the car I drove could influence what prospective clients thought of me. I knew Jim had a point, but at that time I felt that I had little choice in the matter. I had to play the hand I was dealt.

There was silence for a moment, interrupted only by the sound of the scouring powder and rag's convergence over the offending orangey stain. "You need my Saab!" His exclamation caused me to drop my rag with a splat and turn toward him, still on my knees, "Have you been drinking, Jim?"

"No, no," he bellowed. "Nancy, be serious. I mean it! You need my car!" We discussed the particulars for a few minutes, Jim saying that he had been looking at new Saabs, and as he had told me, appearances meant so much, so he, too, wanted to "upscale" his wheels. I thanked Jim profusely but told him that he should think about it for a week or so and then come back and discuss it with me again if he still felt the same way. Since I was almost done cleaning his apartment, he offered to stay around till I finished and give me a lift home.

Soon we were walking down the three levels of stairs leading away from his loft apartment in a lovely old turreted Heritage Hill home and out onto the sidewalk near his car. He handed me the keys to his Saab and told me to give it a try by driving myself home. Imagine, try to imagine, how I felt at that moment. I had not been behind the wheel of a car since 1987, sixteen years before. And here it was; my moment had come.

I literally had goose bumps as I grasped the keys and situated myself in the driver's seat of this beautiful silver machine. It was a dream, some crazy delusion, I was sure. I took off into the flow of late-afternoon traffic on College Avenue and at the bottom of the hill turned right onto Fulton Street, toward my home. Though a bit nervous, I was all smiles as we proceeded west. It was like riding a bike, and soon Jim was showing me some features of the car, turning on the CD player for me, telling me that it was located in the trunk and could be loaded with six CDs at a time. Remember, when I went inside, CDs were a brand-new technology; I'd certainly never had a car with a CD changer in it. I felt a little like Rip Van Winkle.

I parked in the lot behind my building. Jim and I went upstairs for a drink. We went out onto my balcony, and looking over the railing at the parking lot, Jim said, "Look, that car will be yours." Of course I focused on a "rust bucket" instead of what I failed to see parked next to it, Jim's car; it was such a surreal thought. When it sunk in that he was referring to his own vehicle, a very odd feeling shot through me, one I'd not felt in forever it seemed. I still didn't dare believe it could truly be so. I reiterated that he needed to sleep on this business and that we'd talk further next week.

The onus was now on me as I sat that night pondering the day's events. Jim seemed to really mean it. And if he was sincere, this Saab could be mine. Oh, my Lord. We had already vaguely worked out that I could barter with him, cleaning his apartment twice a month, doing his laundry also, and providing him with a home-cooked meal once a month, as he rarely had the time or inclination to prepare anything to eat after a hard day's work besides perhaps a microwaved frozen entrée.

If I took him up on this offer, I'd then be under the gun to secure other clients, to cover costs. All sorts of defeatist thoughts entered my mind; with all that pressure, the prospects seemed insurmountable. How would I find these clients in such short order? I found myself full of self-doubt and wanting to crawl in a hole, pretending the offer had never come.

The next week Jim was back in my apartment and we were about to cement the deal. He threw out a number more than twice what the car was worth as a trade-in. He wasn't the type to go through the trouble of putting it in the paper to sell it. He'd take the loss of the "trade-in" value. I'd researched his car online, knew its Blue Book value, and countered with what I thought was more than fair; I would pay the Blue Book "private sale" quote plus three hundred dollars.

I think I took him by surprise; I *know* I did. I could hear it in his chuckle when I handed him my research info on the car. He looked over what I'd typed up and tacked on an additional seven hundred dollars to my total, reminding me that I wouldn't be able to get financing anywhere else, and knowing he was right, I agreed to the terms after a few minutes of thought. We made a toast.

I HAD BEEN SHUT AWAY for so long that now I sometimes had to pinch myself to realize that I was back in the world, not merely watching life go by on a television screen; then something even more profound hit me. I was waiting for a ride from Leane after I took my driving test and realized it would be the last time I'd have to wait for a ride. I'd never have to ask someone to work me into their schedule or wait for a time when someone else could accommodate my needs. I would be able to go wherever I wanted, whenever I wanted.

I drove with Jim to the secretary of state's office to transfer title and pay the necessary taxes a few days later. I handed over hundreds of hard-earned dollars to facilitate the transaction, nearly every penny I'd saved for months. Being momentarily poor that day was the best feeling I'd had in the longest time. I drove Jim back to his office.

I had no obligations that day, and I sat for a while in Jim's parking lot thinking about what I would do first. It was sprinkling that morning, but I drove with the sunroof open and the driver's side window down. I was reveling in the moment, wind and rain whipping through my hair; I felt so alive. I turned on some Stevie Wonder. In fact, I still remember the song. It was "For Once in My Life." I knew then where I wanted to go.

I pulled into my son's driveway and blasted the horn. At first no one opened the door, then Christopher's head popped out to see who was causing such a ruckus. He was in shorts only, so he lifted a finger to say "just a minute" and soon reemerged wearing a shirt. He hopped into the passenger seat smiling ear to ear. I was so excited. I showed him what every button did, raised the volume of the stereo (men are so impressed by woofers and tweeters) and even made him climb out to view how the mini windshield wipers on my headlights worked. He hugged me and wouldn't let go. I felt him sobbing against my shoulder, this six-foot-tall, strapping thirty-one-year-old man.

For all those miserable, hopeless years, he'd suffered, too. Chris had had to watch the mother he loved sink further and further into an abyss from which there seemed to be no escape. I knew the pain and frustration he'd felt; what I'd put him through. Now his sobs came from a place of great relief, pride in me and happiness that I was finally going to be all right. "I thought this day would never come, Mom. I'm so happy I was wrong!" It was wonderful for me to hear. I love him so.

I had six dollars and change left in my purse with which to make my wheeled entrée into civilized society, and so I sped off to meet my future. I pulled into McDonald's drive-thru and ordered a Diet Coke. My next stop was the grocery store; I bought three cans of cat food, along with a small bottle of vinyl cleaner for my car. And I named my Saab Sven.

For the first couple of weeks I'd wake up, and thinking it had all been a dream, I'd go outside to the parking lot to see if Sven was really there. I'd walk down the hall on workdays and whisper, "You have a car, Nancy!" I couldn't really absorb it for a while. I remember running out of Coke one night and thinking, *Man, I'd like a pop right now!* but then thinking I'd have to wait to get a ride to the store. Ha! I threw on some clothes and went out at midnight just because I *could*. My first solo trip to the gas station was another Rip Van Winkle moment. I walked inside to ask the attendant, "Say, can you tell me, does my car take unleaded fuel?" The guy looked at me like I was from Mars. "Well, lady, if it was produced after 1979, I'd say it's a sure bet."

"Sorry," I said sheepishly, "I've been away for a long time."

I could now go and pick up my grandsons for an overnight, or take them to the park to feed the ducks. I drove to Coldwater, a small rural community in southern Michigan, near the border with Ohio. I went to scour their renowned antique shops with a guy I'd gotten to know online. I could take flowers to a friend in the hospital or ask a sister out to dinner. Everything was new and exciting; it still is. I pray that I never lose that sense of awe over the simple things. To this day, whenever I start the engine, I rub Sven's dashboard and tell him I love him.

Anxiety disappeared as word of my legendary floor-scrubbing skills and acumen with a stiff-bristled toilet brush spread. One new client was a lovely woman, somewhere in my age range and a professional, harried by her work schedule and finding little time or energy for major home upkeep. Her young daughter, Elizabeth, ran in and out, happily injecting herself into the conversation as we sat talking in a sun-soaked sitting room at the back of their beautiful antiques-filled home. This woman said that my referring client had told her the bare bones of my story and she was amazed. As the details of my "recovery" were elaborated on, her face began to light up. "My goodness, are you *that* Nancy?" What? My mind reeled to capture what she meant by her question. And then it dawned on me; I *knew* her unusual first name had rung a bell when I first heard it. This woman had been an administrator at Saint Mary's Hospital during my stay there in December of 1994 to January of 1995. I couldn't have escaped her notice, what with the "Big Boy" bed catastrophe.

It was a weird moment; I was sitting with a woman who knew intimately just how precarious my health situation was back then. If she'd thought of me since, it probably wasn't in a hopeful way. I sat in that room with her, smiling, feeling satisfied to have been able to demonstrate hope to someone who must've seen many examples of cases like mine going bad. She hired me and introduced me to her husband the next time I came. He sat on a stool at the kitchen counter and smiled, shaking his head as he looked at the pictures of my "former self" that I'd brought with me to remind my long-lost administrator of just how far I'd come to serve her now.

I TOOK REAL PRIDE in anything I did; Mom and Dad were responsible for that. Now that I had wheels, my business boomed. Soon my schedule was packed with as many jobs as I could or wanted to handle, with clients often asking if I happened to have time available for a friend of theirs. After all those anxious months and moments, it felt great to be able to say, "Sorry, I don't have any openings right now."

I was now a busy woman and dog-tired as well. One particular workday had been long, but productive; two homes scrubbed and glistening and then the long drive back into the city from the burbs. I had barely shut the door to my apartment, kicked off my shoes and grabbed a cup of java, when I heard a knock at the door. I swung it open and there before me was this wisp of a woman. I thought that I was short, but the top of this old chick's hairdo didn't make it past my eyebrows. She had beautiful Mediterranean blue eyes and didn't dress like many of the ladies around the complex; you know, frumpy or, worse yet, trying to look twentysomething at seventy-plus. She had a certain élan, and though it wasn't my style, I sensed something different about her, something I was drawn to immediately. She introduced herself as Marty and asked if she could come in for a few minutes. I led her into the living room.

She told me that the Resident's Association at the complex needed new blood. The current officers were nearing the end of their term, and so she was calling on people to see if they might be interested in helping out. I nipped the idea in the bud. I told Marty I was sorry, but that I had a very busy schedule and didn't see how I could possibly fit any other commitments in. I soon learned that this old broad (she'd like that term!) had a velvet touch, more like a beautifully wrapped sledgehammer, in her arsenal. She convinced me to become secretary.

And so began a wonderful, close friendship. Marty was an amazing woman, who'd lived a full life, though one with more than her share of tragedy and heartache. But she still knew how to have a good time, and perhaps that came from understanding the difference between the two. Marty died on April Fool's Day in 2007; no joke. I miss her every day.

One night after work, soon after our introduction, I was acclimating myself to the "state of the art" tape recorder (a twenty-dollar model) that the association had provided for my use as secretary at the upcoming monthly meeting. It would be my first, and I wanted to make sure I was prepared. Marty had given me a shopping bag full of old cassette tapes to reuse. I was told to listen to each to make sure they didn't hold any current information and, if they didn't, to tape over them. I put one in the machine and listened; might need that one. Tried another; nope, not that one either, and a third, dated October 1991. . . . I listened as the old tape scratched and whirred to life. . . .

THE MEETING RECORDED on this particular tape was called to order by the then president; the Pledge of Allegiance was solemnly recited and attendance taken. Then the participants broke into business details. An old woman's voice rose in the audience and said, "Say, has anyone met the lady who moved in at the end of the hall on the seventh floor?" Mutters all around . . . "Nope, not me." "Not me either." Another voice: "I hear she's as big as a house!" Giggles and twitters. "I see a young woman come to her door each week and leave with big garbage bags. I think it's her laundry!" Yet another voice was added to the mix: "Hey, maybe it's just her kitchen garbage, if she's as big as they say!" Amused laughter . . . "She's so unsocial; she never comes out!" Another woman laughs, "*Yeah, we call her the monster in the corner!*" More laughter . . . The president bangs the gavel, calling the meeting back to order.

This old back-biting session, the focal point of which had been the "old Nancy," was taped over at the first meeting I helped officiate.

I HAD NEVER TAKEN my son and his family out to dinner. I had a full roster of clients now, so money was not an issue; neither was getting me there. We decided to meet at Brann's, a local steak house where I used to love to go in days gone by. As we sat across from one another in the booth, I drank in the moment and listened to the hubbub surrounding us. I heard children squealing while slithering under tables and parents admonishing them to stop, and wondered if they all realized how happy they should be to be able to share one another's company; probably not. It is human to take things for granted. Why be thankful for what is expected?

We all had a wonderful meal, and as we got up to leave, my son, who was now standing in front of me at the booth, put his arms around me to tell me I was beautiful. Chris had always been on board to cover my difficult entrances and exits from places I had to go, trying to shield me from the stares and snickers that had invariably occurred when I was out in public. This time, I just stood, not seeking cover, and was able to proudly walk out of that room with my family.

Parking lots had been a nightmare for me, and cars the bane of my existence. Imagine being so wide that your clothing brushed vehicles as you walked between them, no matter how far apart they were parked. Obese people are resourceful. We think ahead and plan for obstacles; they are everywhere in our world. I learned to walk sideways between cars, and usually came out unscathed. As the weight left me, the habit did not. I was walking with Chris and his family through the parking lot after dinner, when he asked if I was demonstrating some new dance move. I looked at him strangely and then realized that I was sidestepping my way through the cars. The four of them broke out into laughter.

All that cleaning was paying off; on my last visit to the surgeon's office to be weighed, I'd reached the magic number and beyond. My diabetes was now officially gone and I felt like a million bucks. My surgery was scheduled for the 27th of February 2003. I'd been saving for the event, so knew I could easily float till back at work—it would take a month to recover.

Every client was thrilled for me, and my jobs were secure. Christopher would take care of Nuner. I would be in the hospital for only a day or two if everything went according to plan. These things were never precise; so much of it depends on the patient: blood loss, finding something unexpected once the incision's been made, or any number of other variables. We'd just have to see how everything went, but I was not nervous in the least. The surgery went off without a hitch.

Four hours later I woke up in the recovery room, having an odd, vague recollection of a dream that included Clint Eastwood and paragliding.

Recovery was not as bad as I had been told by others it would be, but I arrived home to a howling cat. She was strutting around laying out her case for "alienation of a feline," and I was the guilty defendant. I made my peace with the animal litigator and settled in for the duration. There were cold packs in the freezer, pain pills on the coffee table in front of the couch and a couple of new books I'd asked Chris to pick up so I could escape the pain and tedium by distracting my mind.

The part I found most uncomfortable was the drainage tubes. There were four; two on either side of and just above the pubic mound and one within inches of each hip bone. The tubes were each stitched to a hole in my body, and if they got tugged even slightly I winced. They were also attached to bulbs that resembled the rubber end of a turkey baster. These would fill with fluids rapidly, especially for a few days after surgery, and I'd have to empty them, then reseal the cap on the bulb. They also made unsightly and disturbing bulges in places where a lady's clothing should have none.

I was moving around my apartment easily within a few days. I held the rail in the building's corridors and walked the halls for circulation and exercise. I wanted to heal quickly and be able to leave my place when I felt like it; I was feeling a little isolated, as I had for all those years, and it wasn't a feeling I liked. When I returned for my first checkup, the surgeon told me he'd taken sixteen pounds of flesh from my abdominal area. "Whoa . . . that's a big baby, doc. . . . Where is he now?" He told me that the "infant" was on a slow boat to China. I hoped the boat sank.

I had one more question; it was a mystery that was driving me crazy. I used to have a single small freckle located approximately three inches above my navel; it now resided about three inches *beneath* the navel. He told me that it was a medical secret and that once he'd divulged the answer, he'd have to kill me to ensure my silence. We moved promptly to another topic.

It was time to remove the drainage tubes. He said I should look the other way and that "this might pinch a little." I love euphemisms. . . . Pinch? As I screamed, I thought of far better words to describe the procedure. Some of those tubes nestled inside of me were at least eighteen inches long; small wonder they'd been "uncomfortable."

I was back to work ahead of schedule. Though a bit swollen at first, my stomach now lay flat and tight against my ribs. I hadn't known I had hip bones and ribs for a long while. I sometimes found myself feeling them just to make sure they were still there. It was so foreign to have a shape, where for so long there was only a "mass." And pretty soon, I had my first pair of jeans. Like the casing on a sausage, they squeezed the folds of skin sagging on my legs and at the same time gave the impression that I was heavier than I was. I hated this bodily distortion, but knew that someday, *someday* I'd be able to afford the surgery to rectify the disturbing illusion.

I SPOKE ABOUT my journey before a weight loss group at Holland Hospital, with many audience members coming up afterward crying and saying that if I could lose so much weight, then they were sure that they could lose that stubborn twenty to fifty pounds. A young nurse working there named Kris was a real peach. I liked her enthusiasm and sincere wish to help others. She thanked me for coming and that was that, or so I thought.

A few weeks later, Kris called to ask if I would be willing to go visit a person who was homebound in a nearby town; her name was Geneva. As I had a few years before, this woman weighed in the neighborhood of seven hundred pounds. The nurse had received a call from the fire department, as they had been called to this woman's home when she'd fallen on the floor and was unable to get back up on her own. The fireman was concerned enough with what he saw to ask for further help. I have found that emergency workers and fire department personnel are the exceptions to the rule when it comes to compassion for the obese. I was always treated with as much dignity as possible by these brave and loving human beings.

I told the nurse that I would be happy go visit this homebound woman to offer support, but asked her to really listen to what she was asking me to do. She was requesting a civilian go "support" a person with grave medical and emotional needs, a person who would surely die if she didn't have serious intervention in some form. There was a long pause on the line. She was as frustrated as I was.

As I was leaving Geneva's home that first day, I turned to smile and say good-bye. Instantly I was transported back to the many times that family members had come to see me in my apartment and were preparing to leave. Tears welled in my eyes as I recalled the feeling that as they had come and brought a piece of life with them, they now were taking life away as the door pulled shut; it was the silence that smothered you. It's what I used to term "the sameness." When you're inside every day for years, each day becomes the same.

I gave Geneva my double-wide wheelchair so that she could get outside, and I called Kris and asked her if the hospital might be willing to donate a computer for Geneva's use. Kris told me she'd investigate and let me know. The powers that be decided that they would fork over the money, and soon a new computer was delivered to Geneva's home. I thought that this could be another way for me to keep in contact with her on a more regular basis. She didn't end up using it much, unfortunately; the same thing that worked miracles for me may not work for another person. Everyone's path to healing will be a different one.

Unfortunately, I noticed another trait in Geneva that I felt would keep her from taking back her life if it didn't change. Geneva was a "victim"; she blamed every obstacle she faced on somebody or something else. There was always a "reason" this or that didn't apply in her case; *she* was unique. It's a very human thing to do, and if anyone could understand that this woman had huge hurdles to climb, it would be me, but complaining and deflecting blame doesn't get you where you want to go, *if* you want to go somewhere else. I'm not sure Geneva knew what she wanted at that time.

I've known a number of people in my lifetime who seem to thrive on chaos and in relating the most recent installment in the ongoing saga of mishap, injustice and tragedy that is their life's fabric. I was born happy, an optimist, and have never truly pitied myself, so it's not part of my makeup to wallow in misfortune. I drew the long straw; I am the fortunate one, because without the ability to accept our part, to own what we are responsible for and laugh at ourselves and situations to *some* degree, change cannot occur. Things can only stay the same or get worse. We must each ask ourselves what it is we truly want, and if we want it badly enough to be willing to step outside our self-erected barricades to grab it.

Change is a scary thing, sometimes causing us to retreat into our old places, habits and ways of thinking. It's more comfortable there in the familiar, no matter how unpleasant the familiar is. It is at least known to us. It's said that no one does something without a reason; I believe that is true. We are getting *something* out of everything we choose to do or allow. Sadly, we many times employ the most destructive method in an attempt to meet our needs, needs that can never be met with the faulty tools we use.

CHAPTER 18

Getting Back My Sea Legs/Thighplasty

MY CLIENTS WERE the cream of the crop, and they ran the gamut of occupations and positions in life: financial planner, portrait artist, nutritionist, public speaker, a young widow, hospital administrator, retired public relations rep, expert home renovator, social worker, an innovative guy whose dot-com business served as a conduit for renters and landlords, hairstylist, college professor, bank officer, director of community events planning, music store owner, publishing VP, retired instructor at a correctional facility, marine specialties rep, retired state policeman, elementary school teacher—a wide-ranging cross-section of American skill and ingenuity.

I took pride and pleasure in keeping their homes in shipshape condition. Some left to-do lists; others left it up to me. Some homes were easier to maintain than others; several needed only "the usual": bathrooms scrubbed, vacuuming and dusting, countertops shined, some laundry done and perhaps a few suit jackets taken from backs of chairs and hung up in the closet.

Other homes were more of a challenge. Some people drop everything where they finish the task: wet towels on bathroom floor; dribs and drabs of pasty food debris on counters, stove, and door handles. Kitty litter pans sometimes needed attention; wet laundry would be left overnight in the washing machine and now need an additional cycle to get rid of the musty odor. I'd find fast-food bags strewn over the garage floor, someone's idea of cleaning out the car, or once beautiful and expensive steaks bought for a party that never came to be, now rancidly gracing the bottom shelf of the fridge.

Everyone's different and it wasn't my place to judge. My job was to make it look like the catastrophe had never occurred, and that's exactly what I did. Some find cleaning toilets an ignoble act; I never have. I was leaving people glad that I'd been there, and that gave me purpose. Most of my clients and I became quite close. I was occasionally asked to whip up some hors d'oeuvres for a party they were hosting that evening, or to take in their dry cleaning for a last-minute trip. It didn't matter how I spent my time; I was theirs for the hours they had been allotted. Ours was a wonderful reciprocation: You scratch my back and I'll scrub yours.

ONE OF MY CLIENTS was a widow; her husband had died of undetected cancer soon after retiring from his VP position at the company he had helped found. She lived in a sprawling, lovely home with an in-ground pool, set in the woods on several acres of prime property far from the hubbub of the city. She had three dogs—two *real* ones, large breeds, and the other a mite of an animal, no bigger than a coffee mug and a breathing ball of nervous tension—as well as a cat named Max, with whom I became fast friends. I could relate to Max; the aging cat's abdominal skin swung back and forth, like a fur-covered pendulum, waggling from side to side as he briskly padded down his mistress's long, blond wooden-floored hallways.

Max's mistress missed her husband; this was obvious to me. She seemed like a ship without a rudder most of the time, not knowing which way to turn, and consequently spent much of her time in superficial pursuits, trying to avoid thinking or being alone for any significant length of time. The things that occupied her mind weren't always petty, per se. She devoted some of that time to helping others, buying food for the underprivileged during the holidays or raising funds for a soldier's family in need. But if you looked closely, and I had that opportunity in being on the scene six hours every week, you understood that this woman felt alone even when laughing with others and offering to buy the group another round. *"Uno mas!?"* It was her rallying cry, as she bellied up to the bar alongside her friends to throw back another one.

She didn't want to be alone; she hadn't been able to come to grips with the fact that her dear husband was really dead and not just off on another business trip. What was her purpose now? This was not the way she'd imagined it would turn out. She often confided in me, sitting out on her spacious deck that was carved into the woods, and when asked my opinion on this thing or that, I tried to give her my brand of "wisdom," such as it was. She asked me to join the American Legion post she was a member of. I tried my line on her, purloined from the fabulous Groucho Marx: "I'd never join a club that would have me as a member!" I finally relented, however, and paid the measly twenty-dollar fee to join.

Occasionally after work I would meet her at the post for a libation. It was fun to be with people in a social setting, but I still felt like an outsider; plain and simple, I wasn't comfortable with men, and it wasn't because I didn't love the boys. A man would approach us sitting at the bar and engage me in conversation. He'd even tell me that I was pretty, which is never hard to hear. But once his eyes fell below the countertop my arms were resting on, the bottom half of me would sometimes cause him to change his seductive tune and begin making his excuses; he had to see a man about a horse.

My godforsaken legs. I was small on top, looked perfectly normal in that regard now, perhaps a little heavy in the upper arms due to the squeezing in of excess skin inside the leotard, but within the realm of reason; my legs were a different story. There was no way to disguise this grave abnormality. When I took a bath, my thigh and calf skin floated aloft on any ripple or shift created by the water's disturbance. It looked like some decaying fish, undulating, awash in a sea of fragranced bath salts. It was quite depressing to look at.

In the early spring of 2005, I was sitting on my couch watching an old movie on a Sunday afternoon. Saturday was "errand day," but the Sabbath, that day was set aside to relax completely, as dictated by God Himself or not, knowing that Monday morning was coming hot on its heels and another strenuous week was about to begin. The phone rang; it was my widow client. She had just gotten back into town from a day at her brother's place and wanted me to meet her for a drink at Bob's Sports Bar on Michigan Street. I so much wanted to just sit on that couch and vegetate, but something in her voice told me to go. I rarely took her up on her offers anymore; there had been a lot of them turned down over the last two years, and so accepting this time wouldn't hurt. I liked her, even loved her, but man, I was just *not* in the mood to socialize. Still, I threw on some clothes and headed out the door.

We chitchatted about anything you could name for a while, but she soon grew uncharacteristically serious. Her speech followed something along these lines: "Nancy, you know how devastating my husband's death has been for me. I always thought that after all his hard work and my efforts to keep the home fires burning while he was out slaying the dragon, we'd have time to travel, be alone, just enjoy our remaining years together. He, we, never got that chance. And now what am I left with? My kids are all grown; off on their own and well on their way. I have a huge pile of money with little real meaning attached to that legacy. I have enough to last ten life-times. I need to do things with what my husband worked so hard for that will honor his life and our love. Will you allow me to help you get the surgery done on your legs?"

I was uncharacteristically silent; I sat staring at her in disbelief. "Do you know what you're saying?" I whispered, not wanting to share this private information with others around us in the pub. "We're talking thousands of dollars here." She replied, "What's money? What's it worth if you can't use it to help someone else? Nancy, please let me do this for you. I know how badly those legs make you feel, how much they hold you back from a lot of things you'd like to do or even wear. Please help me find some meaning in my husband's absence; you'd be doing me a favor. Please?" After my regurgitation of all the facts about cost, about how she didn't need to do this to show me her concern, how I never expected such a thing from her, and then her rebuttal as to why it was important to her to do and how she knew it was something I never dreamed would be coming from her, I accepted. The only element of her offer that caused me concern was her insistence that I recuperate in her home. Not only did she live a distance outside of Grand Rapids and far from possible help from my family, but she wasn't exactly a homebody. It was rare to even have her hang around for the entire six-hour period I was cleaning for her each week, if she was there at all. How could she provide the kind and amount of care I was bound to need? Still, how could I say no?

Later, driving home, I thought about what this would mean for me, how wonderfully odd it was not to have to be thinking about "someday" anymore. The "someday" I would finally have saved up the money to repair my damaged legs. It had been one of my jokes: "Yeah, I'll have the money saved for the surgery just in time to be fitted for my new mobility scooter at the retirement village. I'm going to have myself laid out in a tight, short black leather skirt and stiletto heels for viewing at the wake. I'll be dead cold, but, honey, I'm going to look hot!"

LOGISTICS WERE NOW my only worry. I would have to take time off from work to get the surgery done. My benefactress had said that my part of the expenses would be to save enough money to float for the time I'd be off my feet. That amount of moola would take several months to put together, but I was up for the challenge. I made an appointment to see a surgeon; the guy who'd done my abdominoplasty had moved to Las Vegas and now had a booming business doing implants for would-be showgirls.

The surgeon I chose to consult with had a great reputation for his artistry; his suite of offices was located on the sixth floor of a luxury hotel in Grand Rapids. The reception area was beautiful and everyone I encountered there very pleasant. I was given the requisite hospital gown and a pair of paper, thong-type panties, and told to strip and put them on in preparation for inspection. These guys must see thousands of bodies over a lifetime. I've noticed that while consulting with another surgeon in your presence, they examine your battered body almost like a car mechanic would when attempting to ferret out whether that "clunking" sound you're describing is only a symptom of some minor difficulty, and easily repaired, or instead signifies the death knell of the ailing vehicle.

My surgeon examined what he had to work with, lifting and pulling the sagging skin in order to determine his plan of attack. He was frank with me; he'd never worked with this amount of flesh before. The consultation was sobering. The muscles in your legs are used for many movements, some you wouldn't think of, and because of that fact the patient has a difficult time healing properly after this surgery. The stitches would pull when strained, sometimes causing them to rip apart, like the fabric of a garment under stress. There would be internal and external stitching needed, and I would be in far more pain than I had been in when my abdominal skin was removed. I could figure on two full months for complete healing, and even after that, I might be limited for a while in how much exertion I could withstand.

With all the caveats just presented to me, I didn't hesitate one moment. "Let's do it, Doc," I said. "I want this stuff gone." I had the surgery slated for August, when many of my clients would be on vacation abroad or off to their summer cottages on Lake Michigan. I then set about putting into action my austerity budget, saving every possible penny toward the blessed event.

Again, my clients came through. Two even offered to pay me while I was laid up. My son drove me to the hospital around five-thirty the morning of the surgery. The operation was set for seven, but there was paperwork to fill out, a weigh-in and all the other pre-op stuff. I hadn't really had a problem with being "put under" for my prior surgery; somehow this time it all felt a little more serious. What if, just what *if*, I didn't wake up at all?

My surgeon had me stand next to the gurney with another physician in attendance. They began drawing all over my legs with Magic Markers. As they pulled, tugged and prodded my flesh like seamstresses trying to make a misshapen pattern fit together, the emotion kicked in. I was trembling, and suddenly tears started to fall. The gravity of what I had done to myself hit me like never before. *You are going into a very long and difficult surgery because you so abused and distended your body that it now looks surreal, like some Daliesque raisin.* These men were lifting, twisting and trying to imagine how the seams of my newly hewn flesh would finally come together to form what would pass for a reasonable facsimile of legs; it wasn't a pretty picture.

AFTER THEY'D FINISHED with their artwork, my son, Chris, came to sit beside me. I told him to tell my grandsons and my daughter-in-law, Leane, how much I loved them all, and then went into how sorry I was for all I'd put him through over his lifetime. He could tell by my speech that the weepy discourse was code for my fear, a feeling of dread that perhaps I wasn't going to make it back from the other side of that anesthesia mask. He hugged me and told me that I was going to be just fine and that it was normal to be a little worried before serious surgery. I'd made it this far, Chris said; this "little procedure" wasn't going to end it all for me now. My surgeon peeked inside the curtain and told me he'd ordered a little something to calm me down a bit. I didn't argue. In a few minutes, I was drifting off to sleep in my dear son's arms.

Well, I *did* wake up; I vaguely remember doing that much. A nurse was looming overhead and telling me that I'd pulled through like a trooper and that soon I was going to be moved out of recovery and into my room. I was pretty drifty for a few hours there, and can't remember being in a lot of pain, but once I was fully conscious, Holy Lord! I was feeling a lot of things and none of them were good. Lying still was excruciating, shifting position was a nightmare; my legs were sutured 360 degrees around the tops directly under my butt cheeks, with an "inseam" extending from my crotch to eight inches below each knee. I had an internal as well as external layer of stitches holding my legs together; no wonder I felt a little "pinched."

A FEW HOURS AFTER being planted in my room I was told that I needed to get up and move. I remember laughing through tears at the nurses' commands. Are you insane? Surely this was just some crazy kind of mental exercise; shock aversion therapy, perhaps? No, my two caregivers were dead serious; I was expected to hoist myself out of the bed to stand for a moment. *Got to get that circulation flowing, sister,* I told myself, so with the nurses' help, I painfully rocked and shifted in minuscule increments toward the edge of the bed. I was still somewhat groggy, but aware enough to feel the horrible tightness of each stitch as it pulled at its moorings; childbirth was a breeze compared to this.

After I was back in the bed and left to myself, I gazed over at my tray table and saw an exotic bouquet of flowers displayed with a card lying next to it. It was from a client, Mark, and his friend Frank, and the text of the card was punctuated with black humor. Laughter was painful; anything that caused tensing of the muscles brought on an agonizing reaction, and so I lay there laughing inside, my room's silence speaking volumes.

I was told that the surgery had lasted far longer than expected, nearly twice as long, and that I'd lost a lot of blood and had needed a transfusion. Before the operation, my surgeon had hoped that I would need to be hospitalized for only one day, but now I would be in the facility for three more days. I was blessed with six drainage tubes: the "sextuplets." The bulbs constantly filled with wound-site fluids and had to be drained many times a day; it was ugly to look at and the contents stank. The bulbs had measurement lines on them, and the nurses would chart the volume every time they were emptied to be sure my wound sites were draining adequately. I was being given morphine for the pain, from a self-dispensing unit that fed into my body from an IV attached to my arm. I kept thinking that the pain would subside over time; I guess I was being a little optimistic. I had been carved up like a Thanksgiving Day turkey and was expecting to heal as if I'd scraped a knee on the playground.

I was determined to get out of that place, so after the first day-and-a-half, my single-minded resolution took the form of gingerly walking through the halls, both during the day and at night when the pain prevented sleep. I'd plod along, using my IV drip pole for balance. As I ambled past the nurse's station, I'd yell, "This is my fifth time around the block, ladies and gentlemen! Ain't I amazing!?" I'd sometimes be told that I was getting a little ahead of myself, that I had to alternate time with my legs elevated to prevent swelling, then ambulate for a while to increase my circulation. But lying in pain for hours on end will drive a person crazy. Breaking up the monotony in any way my mind could imagine became the number one goal.

The "go ahead" was finally given and I was released from my sterile prison. During my extremely painful convalescence at my client's home, as predicted, I was left to my own devices much of the time. One day, I caught a full-length glimpse of my likeness in a sliding door's glass. Who is this creature!? What I saw reflected was no one I knew anymore; she reminded me of the "old Nancy" and I began to cry. I lifted my long gown to reveal what I began to call the "mighty oaks"; my legs, nearly as thick at the ankle as they were at the knee. I was swollen beyond self-recognition, and the feelings attached to that transitory image took me back to my days of isolation, alone and resigned to what I had left to me; very little life at all.

Late one night, I got out of bed to go to the bathroom, my client's little dog following along behind me. I've never been drawn to the little ones; they generally yip and nip, nervous Nellies the lot of 'em. But over time, this tiny creature and I had formed a bond. My drainage tubes were connected to the waistband of my underwear with a safety pin, so when I had to pee I could just pull them down "en masse," and the tubes would be out of the way but secure. I sat there in the semidarkness, half-asleep and hurting; just sitting down on a toilet seat caused a grimace. My tiny friend liked to put her paws on my knees, hoping for attention by letting me know she was there; it's hell being little. I looked down at her, tiny paws perched and waggling tail, and noticed something hanging from her mouth in the dim light coming from the bedroom. It looked tubular and long; what *was* it?

I was wide awake now. . . . It was my drainage tube; the *internal* end! The pooch seemed to be grinning. A quote from Winston Churchill during World War II came into my head: *This is not the end. It is not even the beginning of the end. But it is, perhaps, the end of the beginning.* It couldn't get any worse.

LABOR DAY WAS here; I was just waking up and turned down the blanket to put my feet on the floor. I'd fallen asleep after my shower the night before without putting on my panties and "girdle," an incredibly tight, knee-to-waist garment that was supposed to help limit tearing of stitches. I had been tired already, and pulling that damned thing up over my lines of sutures was exhausting and painful. . . . It felt so good to lie there without the constraint. My nightgown was just to my waist, exposing my naked body from there on down. My skin didn't seem to have that normal, overall fair-skinned Irish look to it; what was amiss? Upon closer inspection, I realized that there was a huge gape, an opening in the flesh at the juncture of my crotch and left leg. This was no small hole; it was enormous and exposed the "meat" of my body. I had been given an emergency contact number for after-hours calls and reached over onto the nightstand to retrieve it. If anything came under the heading of an emergency, this would be it.

A doctor answered right away; it wasn't my doctor, but at this point, I wasn't being picky. He said he'd been out doing some yard work when I phoned. "Don't worry about it, Nancy, that's what I'm here for. What's the problem?" I was frantic and crying.

"Well, I have a gaping wound; my stitches have come completely undone. . . . I can see big, black wiry loose threads sticking up and out of me!"

"Calm down, Nancy. . . . How big is the opening? . . . Is it bigger than your fist?"

I didn't want to look at it again, but I had to. "I'd guess it's about that size exactly, Doctor. . . . All I know is that it looks like I'm falling apart and it's rather disconcerting to look down and see your insides on the outside!"

"It's going to be OK, Nancy. There's really nothing that can be done; re-suturing is not an option now. This happens more often than you'd think. Stitching together parts that move as much as legs do is a very inexact science; it will heal. Please trust me. Just keep applying the antibiotic cream and try to keep it covered as much as you can. . . . Your scar will be more prominent than it would have been otherwise, but other than that—"

I interrupted him. I was very grateful; the information and his reassuring voice were so consoling to me in those anxious moments. Now I felt compelled to lighten up the conversation. "Doctor, I fear not the devastating scar. . . . I haven't had many opportunities to share that vicinity of my body with anyone worth mentioning, so whether I'm badly scarred is really irrelevant. All I care about is whether my legs are going to fall off or not. Get back to your gardening, Doctor, and God bless you."

He was right; I didn't fall apart, and soon saw evidence that my body was healing, making real progress. These mortal coils of ours really are amazing things. My recovery was far from over, but I finally felt like I was going to make it back to "the real world." My swelling was still pronounced, but I felt more able to walk around, and over the next few weeks sleep began coming somewhat easier for me.

* * *

IT WAS ANOTHER couple of weeks or more till the doctor gave me the thumbs-up regarding resuming my full schedule, and he gave me stern warnings about "overdoing it" by vacuuming (not seemingly strenuous, but the movement involved is the reason for the taboo) and picking up heavy objects, so I rolled my eyeballs at him and told him I'd do my best. How do you clean without straining something? It would take a long time till the swelling in my legs was completely gone, due to my being on my feet so much of the day. But I felt like a million bucks—I could fit into Levi's two sizes smaller than before.

At my final checkup I talked with the nurse before the doctor came into the room. "Look at this!" I was pulling at the skin that still overlapped my knees and sagged at the ankle. "Is this going to firm up suddenly? Is that going to get any better?" The surgeon soon answered my questions in "doctorese." He offered, "Well, your case was an unusual one, Nancy. . . . I told you that before we went into this thing. We were working with an exorbitant amount of flesh here." He was yanking on my knee flap as he went on. "It's impossible to predict exactly how it will all come together as the patient heals. In a case like yours, the best we can do is to try and pare off as much as possible while contouring the leg, and pray for the best results." (Here comes the special lingo.) "You will need some 'revision.'"

"Lay it out for me, Doc," I said. "I'll need more surgery, right?"

"Yes, Nancy," he said, "that's exactly what I mean." My legs were now a vast improvement over the former models, but though my pants size was smaller, I still had excess skin hanging on my thighs, kneecaps and calves, right down to my "pant cuff" ankles. . . . Capri pants would not be gracin' my wardrobe for the foreseeable future. At least not till my next appointment with a scalpel.

SOMETIMES WE JUST have to get on with it; with our lives, that is. If we live with the constant and irksome emotion of feeling "incomplete," not being fully "there" yet, we miss a lot of the things and events that, if really absorbed, make a far bigger impact on us than all our wishing for perfection can ever achieve. I was not completely thrilled with my "new" body; who would be? I was still limited in what I could wear; I wore harem pants to go swimming in a friend's pool, but I could go swimming. Sleeveless tops were not for me, but I looked pretty good in something with tight longer sleeves. I had to see that damaged view of myself in the mirror, naked after bathing, but I now accepted that my physical form might never change much more than it already had; I was and am part of the "package" of my life's experience and choices. The difference came in learning to love and revalue the soul within that school-of-hard-knocks encasement. It's that simple; and that intangible to many who struggle with image each day. I believe that the struggle is caused by our not having discovered our innate worth.

AFTER MY SECOND SURGERY, I went back to the life I'd created for myself, and it wasn't a glass half-empty or even half-full for that matter; it was and is a *good* life. I was no longer an outsider; someone standing with her face pressed against life's window and wishing to become a participant. With the rare perspective I'd gained in having existed for years without much human touch or healthy interaction, I could see just how lucky I was to be alive. I wouldn't take back one minute of the suffering and humiliation of my past if it meant losing the zest I now possess in being a part of all the little things we see and feel each day; I know now, in a huge way, how good life is, without the trappings of a yacht, pâté de foie gras on toast points or a perfectly sculpted derriere as evidence.

I celebrated standing in line behind someone with forty-seven coupons to redeem for their food purchases. So what!? I could now *stand* in that line. Traffic jams, noisy kids in church, waiting for an extra few minutes in the dentist's office—hell, I hadn't been able to fit in his chair for years.

I eventually got involved with men, dating on a sporadic and not-too-serious basis. I even copped a midnight ride on the back of a friend's Harley. What a trip that was. Some of these men didn't think I looked too bad for an old broad and accepted my body faults. The ones who were appalled, well, they just weren't into digging that deep—their loss. I never did attach myself to any one guy; after two decades–plus of living on my own and having gained some wisdom with age, I found myself a lot more picky about whom I'd want to share a bunk with for the rest of my life. I haven't found him yet; perhaps I never will, but the thought of being alone does not horrify me.

I love men; that is an understatement. I love their brains, confusing and vexing as they are at times, just as women's brains must be to them. I often find myself agreeing with their take on things. Go figure. We, both sexes, are in this "thing" called life *together.* We might as well join forces and try to get along.

Funny, the physical form of the men I've grown fond of has not been what society would call "eye candy." Antonio Banderas is a hunk, no doubt. I could drool for hours just looking at the boy, but what really attracts me, what holds my interest and enthralls me, is the mind. A man's mind captivates me, and that's as it should be; men will always be some of my best friends, if nothing more. Being in their company is more than enough for this woman.

CHAPTER 19

Out of the Blue/Media Storm Approaching

IT WAS A workday like any other of the past several years. Another summer would soon be coming to a close. It was mid-August of 2007, and though the clock read only six A.M., the warm, humid air drifting in the open door from my balcony forecast another scorcher on its way. As I sat on my couch drinking coffee to nudge myself into full consciousness, I glanced over at my end table and noticed the red light blinking on my telephone base. *I must have had a call while I was out yesterday*, I thought. I am notorious for not checking my landline messages in a timely manner. I picked up the handset to check the last call received: "Harpo Productions." My heart jumped. The woman on the voice mail said she wanted to talk with me. She had read my letter, congratulated me on my success and asked me to return her call. It was only five A.M. in Chicago, so I left her my cell phone number to reach me during the day. I couldn't stop thinking about it as I scrubbed and polished at my client's home on Lake Drive.

My cell phone rang around eleven o'clock, and I fumbled to remove my faux leopard skin–cuffed rubber glove. Sure enough, the telltale area code, 312, was staring back at me; the same bubbly, energetic voice was on the other end of the line.

It was hotter than blazes already; I stood in my client's yard on that August day, with sweat pouring off the tip of my nose onto my chest, and wondered what had possessed me to go outside to take the call. We talked for more than forty minutes . . . and then it was over. No commitments, no nothin', just more congrats and good wishes for a happy future.

August of 2007 became history, as did September and most of October. The ads in the previous day's Sunday edition of the *Grand Rapids Press* had been filled with last-minute sales offers on Halloween costumes for the kiddies. And not another peep from my enthusiastic friend in Chicago. I was taking a smoke break on a client's apartment balcony above Fulton Street around noon when my cell phone rang. I didn't recognize the number, but picked up nonetheless. There was a guy's voice on the other end. "Hello, is this Nancy?"

"Sure is. Who are you?" It was a Harpo producer: "I've got a few more questions for you, Nancy. Do you have a minute?" he went on. *Shoot, mister . . . I'm game.*

And so standing in the stiff autumn breeze of that overcast late October day, I went over the basics for this man with a radio announcer's voice; its timbre was amazing, the kind that could cause a woman to turn her own mother in to the secret police. "OK, Nancy," he finished, "I just wanted to get a better picture from you. I may be calling you back. It's been nice speaking with you!"

"Same here . . . ta-ta!"

A few days later my angst was put to rest. This was real all right. That semitruck-load of letters had gained traction and I was headed for Chicago. I had to be on a plane on Sunday afternoon; it was already late Friday. I wouldn't be back home till late the following Thursday, so I had clients to reschedule, I needed someone to water my plants and feed my fish. I needed to borrow my sister's luggage, take stuff to the cleaners. I sat alone and cried. I cried for the stress I was now under and cried because I'd finally have a podium, a fine podium, to shout to the world that there is hope. I had for so long wished that everyone could hear about my rediscovery of self, but there was a certain population that mattered more than any other. I needed to reach out to those hidden in their homes as I'd been, people who'd shut themselves away to blunt the pain of rejection, of thoughtless stares and cutting comments.

Those who breathe free can't possibly imagine how many of these precious souls, our brothers and sisters, hide themselves away behind doors and wait to die, without help or hope. I was now being given the kind of exposure that could touch these human beings and maybe spark that elusive something that I'd needed to reignite my life. If I could reach beyond my smothering prison walls, then they could as well.

IT WAS A whole new world out there, and I was about to find out in one more way just how different it was. The last time I'd flown had been in 1975, when I'd brought my three-year-old son, Chris, back to Grand Rapids from Tacoma for a brief visit during the air force years. A grinning middle-aged man behind the counter quipped that there had been some changes since then in air flight. You actually got to fly inside a windowed craft and didn't have to wear those pesky leather goggles anymore.

After I had begun working, I would often sit for my break on a client's deck in Cascade Township to enjoy the peaceful setting. Her house abutted a wooded area, and sometimes you could catch a glimpse of majestic hawks circling overhead. Other times, the tranquility would be broken by a jet engine's roar. I'd look up and see it piercing the clouds, off toward somewhere, anywhere, and whisper to myself that I would someday be on one of those again, going somewhere, too.

My father, a Boeing engineer and former navigator in the army air corps during World War II, had he still been alive to be aboard on this trip, would have been sitting next to me explaining the physics behind air flight. Sometimes Dad instructed, not explained, and was quite impatient with brains less mathematically inclined than his, but I still wished he could see me now. I missed my grouchy father as we tore a hole through the air that day.

My producer and I rode into town together from O'Hare, discussing philosophy and a bit of religion among other topics along the way. He asked me for my take on how a person who is suffering great difficulties handles it all without going insane or becoming an animal, losing his or her humanity entirely. Some events aren't brought on by our behavior. They are foisted upon us unjustly, as in the case of the horrors of the Jewish Holocaust, for instance. In my case I'd been a party to my own near demise. I thought I got through hard times, my isolation and shunning by others, by not attempting to make sense of it. It was just the way it was. I accepted my lot in life during those years and tried to make the best of my circumstances. Humor had long been my ally; it took away some of the sting from the ignorant actions of others. My companion told me that he'd been given a very insightful book on the topic that had opened his eyes through those of one who'd suffered indescribable pain and torment; he thought I should read it. I wrote down the title and author and told him I'd be sure to get a copy.

The limo driver dropped me at the Omni Chicago Hotel. The doorman held open the door for me at the entrance—this was all such a treat. The hotel was opulently appointed: gorgeous chandeliers, thick, lush rugs and fine, polished wood for as far as my dazzled eyes could see.

My room was very nice, too. All the toiletries you might have forgotten to bring were displayed on the counter in the bathroom; plenty of fluffy towels were tightly rolled and waiting as well. Cleaning women notice how things look; if a job has not been done perfectly, we can spot it lickety-split. This place passed with flying colors. In the bathroom mirror I could see my bedroom through the open door as I washed the weariness from my face. I went in to lie down on the bed for a moment and almost didn't get back up it was so comfortable. There was a safe in the closet, a plush bathrobe on a hanger, even a slacks hanger for the scarves I'd brought with me.

Room service was delivered promptly; what a luxury. I had already showered and changed into my pajamas and robe, so after eating my delicious salad and putting the rolling cart outside my door, I cracked open the window next to my bed. I was exhausted. I felt like a well-wrung-out washcloth . . . nothing left to give. I'd been promised the next morning to myself to recuperate, and so with the cool of evening's approach embracing my face and drinking in the sounds of the city beneath me, I fell asleep wondering what tomorrow would bring.

*   *   *

THE NEXT MORNING I opened up the drapes to let the day come inside. Slivers of vacant space between high-rise buildings allowed only a glimpse of nature from my sixteenth-floor perch. Thin ribbons of white blew across the autumn sky. The Windy City.

The previous few days of preparation had been far more emotionally draining than I'd expected. Probing my bank of memories for what I wanted to impart to the audience about my journey lanced some old wounds and left me feeling spent and stunned. Looking through old pictures and journals written during my years inside brought those times, those feelings, all back into focus. . . . I was somehow wishing I'd left it all a blur. Rewinding the tape of not being at my dad's funeral, and the one of missing my son exchanging wedding vows and celebrating his happiness had caused my hand to shake as I held the photo of Chris and Leane smiling at the church on that long-ago day. I hadn't looked through those pictures or journals for years, not since I'd been back out in the world and able to participate in life again.

I had hidden the pain, buried it with shovels full of humor and neglect, pushed it down deep in my mind's pockets so that I could move forward in the new and unexpected life granted me. And that morning, there alone in my hotel room, the penalty for my recent bold excavation was making its presence known to me.

I found myself afraid. I had always dreamed of being in big cities: Dublin, Istanbul, London and Rome. My reading had taken me to many far-off places; I'd longed to walk the soil where history was made and touch the ancient edifices that other souls had brushed against thousands of years before.

But mixed with the happy agitation of being in the heart of Chicago, a fabulous, vibrant city, was the sense of wanting to withdraw from it, to isolate myself. I thought, *You picked a fine time to crumble, you fool. Are you going to break under pressure and unmask the real Nancy, the fearful little girl without verbal armaments to shield her from barbs thoughtlessly thrown her way?*

I was afraid of what people would think of me as I walked outside the hotel room door and onto the bustling street. I had no one there but me to draw from. I was on my own; entirely alone. Odd, these were the same emotions I had borne all those years while shut inside my self-made prison. My body was so changed; scars remained, but I'd been told by others that I was acceptable, even pretty. I'd always think, *Yeah, so you say! If I took off my clothes and unmasked my reality, you'd run in horror and never come back!*

I had to stop this, I told myself. *Blow your own horn a little; hell, blow it a lot! You know you've got Fanny Brice and Ethel Merman living in your brain and voice. . . . Let 'em out! Everything's comin' up roses and daffodils. Order two pots of coffee and some eggs, drink in the scenery and focus on what you need to do.*

It wasn't long after I'd swallowed the last bite of breakfast that a ringing phone broke the tranquility of my sanctuary. I needed to come to the studio earlier than expected to go over a few more details. I wasn't ready to leave, but I had to "get on the train." I rushed to the closet to find a color to match my mood: vivid red. I managed to shower, get dressed, find some jewelry that matched, brush my wild hair and apply lipstick in record time, and I left my room to face the music. *Don't think, just dance, Nancy* was trilling through my head.

I stood underneath the canopy overhanging the front of the Omni, my long black trench coat and hair flowing behind me like flags flapping in the cold breeze. I found myself wishing for a weather guy with a chart and pointer to explain the phenomenon that creates the Chicago wind. Whatever the cause, I was lovin' it.

My day had begun in angst and self-doubt, but now that I had been pressured out of my cocoon, exhilaration began to take over. As I stood there on that cloudy, windswept day, watching the flow of humanity rushing past, "Fly Me to the Moon" came on over the loudspeaker, the sun choosing then to make its brief curtain call. A tingling sensation washed over my cloaked frame and my toes began to tap; my body swayed back and forth with the tempo, and my arms crossed, embracing each other. I couldn't stop grinning, and I didn't fight to do so.

A sense of belonging washed over me like a windy baptism into a community of believers. Feelings and fears I had thought securely, deeply buried or dead in me had reemerged that morning. I hadn't thought much about "the dark time" in a long, long while. Those emotions of uncertainty had taunted me, tried to stare me down to shake my composure. In that moment outside the hotel I suddenly felt a weight, one that I hadn't been fully aware of, lift off my shoulders, sent where monsters go as the sunlight creeps over the horizon. I felt fully alive and here to stay—maybe for the first time in my life.

There were a number of other guests on the show with me who had come to share their weight loss stories, too, and we traveled together in limos from appointment to appointment throughout the time we were in Chicago. I rode up front with the driver to forestall the nausea I had experienced while riding in the back. Their conversation after our visit to the hair salon went something like this: "Oh isn't this all exciting? Look at my nails." "I love your color, too! Your hair is to die for; you look ten years younger!" "I can't believe this is all happening . . . and national television to boot! What an amazing trip it's been! We went out last night, did you?" "Yes! My friend and I ordered Chicago pan pizza." "Oooooh! You bad girl." "I was bad . . . and you know what else? I ate two bites of a second piece!" "Oooooh! You are a bad girl!" (Nervous giggling injected.) "But I got up this morning at four and exercised like mad in the hotel gym!" "Well, I only had a small plate of steamed veggies when we went out," another woman went on. "I wouldn't *dare* get near a pizza. I don't ever want to go back to how I looked before" "What's *your* food plan?" "Oh, mine is set in stone. Each morning I measure out a half cup of steel-cut oats for my carbs, with a quarter cup of skim milk and a sprinkle of artificial sweetener. I have half a medium banana and allow myself one cup of decaf coffee per day." They went on and on about their particular food and exercise regimens; it all sent a shiver down my spine.

I would never want to burst their bubble, this was their "moment," and I truly wished each of them the best, but I didn't think they understood what I heard them *really* saying. These ladies were holding on to their "success" by their teeth. They each had some formula that they rigidly clung to, almost like a religion. Every waking hour was spent thinking about the next precarious step along the imaginary tightrope they had to tread upon to keep the slimmer form they now so admired in the mirror. Their worth seemed based on their newly attained societal stamp of approval, and they were filled with trepidation over losing favor if the scale registered even one pound more than the day before. In my opinion, they had not yet discovered the nugget that would keep the weight from reemerging on their thighs, as so commonly happens.

My companions were still basing their worth and happiness on the transitory evidence demonstrated in the *appearance* of their outer shell, not on nurturing the damaged image within that had been the original cause of their weight gain. The new figure they woke up to each morning did not equate with the uneasiness they still felt regarding their God-given capabilities and worth. With all the measuring of oats and limitation of caffeine, with all the inflexible, sweat-producing appointments with a treadmill or elliptical machine to keep their bodies in bikini-model form, I wondered when they found the time to enjoy life, to just relax and *live*.

I had a different formula for my time left on the planet, so without commenting on theirs, I called to those seated behind me. "Hey, y'all! I haven't been out to see the sights of the big city; I've been staying in and ordering room service. You know what I had the kitchen send up the other day?" "What, Nancy . . . what!?" "I devoured a twenty-six-ounce piece of Argentinean beef, fat-laced and glorious, and I sucked the bone dry. It was magnificent." The driver chuckled. Dead silence from the back of the limo; I didn't have to turn around to know what the expressions on their faces were saying. *Poor Nancy. She's going to be as big as a house again any day now. What can she be thinking?*

What I was thinking then and what I still think to this day is that I learned a huge lesson during that crazy incarceration of mine; I learned to just *live* my life. I no longer obsess about anything. What we obsess over, we fear. If an old way of thinking tries to make a comeback to set me off course, I send it off to the place the thought deserves—the trash chute area of my mind. That huge hunk of meat cannot harm me unless I choose to eat it on a very regular basis. Food is not the enemy; it is a life-giving and wonderful blessing from God, and He intended for us to enjoy the act of eating it, not to feel guilty and less than human when we decide to consume one more forty-calorie bite than required to maintain our hard-won image. It shouldn't have to be so hard-won, anyway.

I worked every day cleaning homes, and so I got my exercise naturally. If it hadn't been available in the way I made my living, I would have walked more places or done something else I enjoy doing. To act otherwise makes you a slave to yet another obsession. I no longer felt the need to "binge" to comfort myself, but if I had gone overboard during the last week or so, eating a little extra nibble here and there, my monitor was and is a pair of Levi's. If they felt snug, I'd just look in the mirror and say, "Nancy, you slipped off the saddle a bit this week, pardner; get back on that horse, dig your spurs in and ride." And I wouldn't say it with derision in my tone anymore; I didn't scold and berate myself about my imperfections. I had learned to cajole myself back into reality with a grin and a gentle nudge.

I weigh myself only at the doctor's office now, and that's about once every six months, and I'm always within a three-pound range, up or down. I'm not what society would deem as perfectly thin. Now, ask me if I *care* about what they think? "Frankly, my dear, I don't give a damn." *They* don't live my life and I'm not after anyone's stamp of approval. I know what I am, who I am and what's important to me. *That's* what matters, and that's *all* that matters. I will not have my daily mood determined by a specific number on a scale. I am far more than a number; we all are. If food's role is truly in perspective in our lives, we do not need to monitor every move we make. Our core, our rediscovered, inborn spirit, will begin to radiate outward and become evident in *new* actions—e.g., not over-eating to stuff feelings—and in our new treatment of ourselves as a valuable person. That moment only comes with the "Eureka!" awareness that we have arrived, that we are worth treating well and that nothing and no one will ever again wrest that belief from us, including the person who was always our harshest critic: ourselves.

If we have faith in *our own* judgment, if we trust that we will now care for our bodies, spirit and emotions because it is the *natural* thing to do for someone who is of value, there will be no need for hyper-vigilance. We will have no worry over the outcome, because the out-come is preordained; we will flourish. Only with the reconstituted belief in self can we truly get on with living a full and more contented life, focusing on what really matters in the end—the love and service we give to others and the natural blessings we receive in return.

Surgeries, prepackaged food programs, overly rigid exercise reg-imens, and water pills are only cosmetic applications that don't touch the real problem in any lasting or effective way, and in some cases, these tools can cause us greater harm than good. Anyone can lose weight doing almost anything under the sun. That's exactly what we do in America to the tune of more than thirty *billion* dol-lars per year. So why are we as a nation getting only fatter as time waddles on? The answer is held within each of us, there for the tak-ing at no cost to the owner of that vital information. It's been there since birth; it's God-given. We are just so programmed to listen to the experts, hanging on their every word as to which path to take, believing ourselves victims and helpless to change our situations, that we've overlooked the key to happiness we've possessed all along: our humanity.

In this age of enlightenment, with the acquisition of material goods and eternally youthful bodies as measure of our value, we've forgotten about the very nature of the human creation. We are valuable *because* we are human. If we are allowed to touch the beauty within each of us, our outside shell reflects that self-assured, more positive state of mind. I learned that the hard way, and it is a lesson I hope to never forget. I doubt that I will, though I am watchful for signs of habit and complacency attempting a rebound when I'm in stressful situations. I have better tools for coping now.

Lord knows, I've had my share of odd, sometimes painful occurrences over a lifetime. My mom and dad were decidedly not Ozzie and Harriet. I could point to any number of events that some authority could pronounce as *the* cause of what I ended up choosing to do to myself to express my pain and uncertainty. But no one is God; no one other than God, that is. Authorities can be as fumbling and fallible as the next guy in line; I've seen 'em in action. In my case, I have not found it productive or necessary to spend hours, days, months and years of this second bite at the apple in a quest to discover what I can never be certain is the seminal event or events that sent me careening like an off-course missile toward disaster. Even if I *was* able to point to a single trauma from my past that caused everything to unravel, what would it change?

I can look only to my future. Dwelling on missteps or injuries in my past will not heal me; at least that is my assessment. I now inspect what happens more carefully, however, and what I do. I am even more cognizant of my effect on others, wanting to preserve their dignity and sensitivities as much as I can without compromising myself and my value as a person. I still stumble in that pursuit and try to make amends when I'm made aware of unintentional pain

I've caused. I am far from a perfect human being; just ask those who love me.

I now think about why I am feeling the way I do in any circumstance and therefore am better equipped to forestall possible harm by being proactive instead of reactive when my internal "quiet voice" tells me something is off-kilter. I really listen to myself these days and trust my judgment. I value my opinion. I don't live in a fog anymore; I am more self-aware than ever. I don't yearn to be young again and recapture those glory days; they weren't so damned glorious in hindsight. More years on the planet give people perspective and, with that new outlook, a hunger to taste every experience with true attentiveness and a desire to let its flavor linger on the tongue, to not swallow it ravenously and whole and then wonder why they don't feel full.

There are times I ponder what I now know were not optimum choices made by my parents and that their decisions certainly must have impacted all of us kids in many ways and each of us differently. But I take it all for what it was and still is; they were the acts of flawed and wounded human beings, with demons of their own, making decisions based on faulty, illogical thinking while trying their best to nurture those under their guidance and protection. I've grown enough to look at my parents as people, just like you and me. I love my mom and dad, warts and all.

I SMILE ALL the time. Some think I'm crazy, but I smile because I know a secret; it's as clear as the nose on my thinner face. Life is sweet and always worth living no matter the tempests that blow through it. There will always be a sunrise and a second chance if you believe. I believe. I believe in me.

THE TAPING WAS at one the next afternoon. I had packed my bags upon returning to the hotel the night before. All I left out were the things I'd need at the studio and for my flight back home later on in the day. I sat at the desk in my room near the open window to listen to the bustle of the traffic below while eating my final Chicagoland breakfast of Western omelet, fresh berry medley and toasted English muffin.

I had been on television as a child in Seattle, approached on a walk with my sisters one morning on our way to church. A local celebrity, a clown named J. P. Patches, whom I watched every morning before breakfast, was filming on the sidewalk that day and pushed a microphone in my face to ask me about my hat. It was a type popular in those days; it had a Russian look to it, a Cossack-type affair. It was white and furry and I guess it stood out from the pack. My sisters had backed away when he came toward us, but not this little girl. I answered the clown's questions, threw in comments of my own, and then he asked me to dance with him. J.P. and I did the twist, with strains of Chubby Checker's rousing tune trailing through Seattle's autumn air.

Some forty-odd years later, I was set to appear again before the lens of a television camera. Would I be nervous onstage, faltering in my words and betraying my anxiety, or would I take to it like a duck to water and splash my way through, waddling off satisfied, knowing that I'd delivered my message in a meaningful way?

I said good-bye to any staff I met on my way through the hotel lobby and took my place under the awning in front of the Omni to wait for the final ride to Harpo Studios. Though I'd been pampered and treated like royalty during my stay in Chicago, it hadn't been a "joy ride" for me; hardly. I found myself feeling very apart and intro-spective during this trip. I felt I was there to learn things in a course I hadn't been aware I'd enrolled in. So many evolutions of thought about my place in the world, of what my past had *really* meant and what the path before me held had come roaring out from within, catching me off guard, and though still standing after the onslaught, I found myself needing time and space to digest this heavy meal. Hul-labaloo for my fellow guests and the rest of the world, I didn't know about, but my personal hullabaloo had been jarring indeed.

My "debut" on stage went swimmingly; I *did* take to it like a duck to water. The instant the audience laughed in response to some-thing I said, any lingering nervousness left me and my tale unfolded as if I was sitting in my own living room swapping war stories with old friends. I left the stage that day, tail feathers dripping wet with acceptance and content that I'd delivered the goods as best I could given the time constraints of television production.

Two FRIENDS OF mine, Mark and Frank, had decided at the last minute to drive from Grand Rapids to Chicago to be at the taping. After my exhausting day, I wasn't looking forward to walking through O'Hare and climbing aboard a plane to fly back east over Lake Michigan. So I took my friends up on their offer of a lift home. I'd had a brief moment with my producer inside, but with so many people and so much activity going on around us, our farewell was short and sweet.

But as I was waiting for Mark to wrestle my luggage into the trunk, here came my dear producer, running over to the curb to tell me to wait for him; he had something upstairs on his desk that he wanted me to have. It was a book, one we'd discussed in the limo on our way into Chicago; a second printing circa 1963 of *Man's Search for Meaning*, by Viktor Frankl, a survivor of the Holocaust who wrote the book to explore the reasons behind how and why man survives under the direst of circumstances. I've since read the book; it holds profound insights. Experience can be an amazing teacher, if we survive to tell the tale. Perhaps my producer said it best in the short note he enclosed inside the book's cover:

N—— *There is a lot of wisdom in here . . . More than 700 pounds worth!*
Fondly,
C____

Once home from Chicago, I tried to settle back into my normal routine. I say "tried," because there was nothing routine about what was happening around me. My friend Mark had set up a Web site for me prior to taping the show to accommodate any possible public interest stemming from my appearance. My Web site received hundreds of e-mails from people around the globe, from both those seeking help and those requesting an interview for print or other media. Somehow, my private phone number wasn't "private" anymore.

One such caller made an impression on me, and not a *good* one.

She identified herself as a reporter calling from London, and her queries were of the general sort at the beginning of our conversation. How had I gained so much, and over what period of time? The all-too-familiar question of what I ate at any particular meal came up; I didn't like where this conversation was taking us. She seemed to be heading for the sensational. Her questions became invasive: Could I bathe at all? Could I even reach to wipe myself? What kinds of physical maladies presented themselves due to my massive tonnage? Any boils, oozing infections that I could detail for her readers? I hedged each time, not giving her what she obviously wanted. I should've hung up then and there, but I was naïve and thought I could somehow navigate this interview into less turgid, more hopeful waters. Just minutes before, I had answered the phone as only a woman, a normal human being, and now with this reporter's insistent probing for more personal, and more demeaning, information, I felt unmasked as being, or as having *been*, some kind of alien creature. And in response to her dogged, unexpected, debasing and humiliating attempts at exposure, I instinctively reacted like a mama hyena protecting her pups. I cut the broad off mid-sentence . . . and *exploded*. I swore like a sailor. I then gathered myself and my thoughts and went on.

"Madam, not only is it painful, horribly humiliating, to talk about such intimate things, but the main reason for wanting to get my story out there is propelled by my desire to reach out to those who are *now* like I was *then*. These souls are already treated as if they are lepers, perhaps worse. Most people believe that the obese are pigs, slovenly hogs that gorge themselves out of some bottomless slop bucket. They believe that the obese have no willpower, no ability to feel emotion, pain, nor do they possess any other recognizable human trait. I know; I've felt these instant judgments myself too many times to number.

"If I choose to open that door, unnecessarily betraying the hidden shame of these already tormented and maligned human beings, it will give those judging so harshly one more reason to cement their feelings of disdain and superiority. You *say* you want to bring better understanding to the public, that because you paint a detailed picture for them, they'll suddenly cry rivers of tears and change their attitude, welcoming these ostracized people into the greater fold of humanity; it won't engender empathy, lady. Your readers will only be disgusted and feel further vindicated in their ignorantly held opinions. Let these fractured souls have a modicum of privacy in such personal and painful areas. I feel I am standing up for those who have no voice." She tried to calm me down (the chick wanted her story) by saying that she totally understood, apologizing for delving too deeply and taking me out of my "comfort zone." After a few more innocuous questions and a little general banter, she went in for the kill. "I have only one more question before I ring off, Ms. Makin. . . . Have you had sex since the weight loss?" Lord Almighty. Being the uncultured Yankee that I am, I "rang off" without saying good-bye to my high-minded interviewer across the murky pond.

I didn't see the show I'd taped in Chicago when it initially aired; I was on a plane to New York at the time. The next morning found me sitting on a couch in a studio in Manhattan with Diane Sawyer on *Good Morning America*. A British magazine (not the one of muckraking phone call fame) ran a feature article; I also appeared live by satellite on Britain's biggest morning show. I received offers to speak locally as well and did so as my work schedule permitted.

Late in December of 2007, two publishers made contact, asking me to write my memoirs. I was bowled over by the prospect of having some concrete way of reaching so many other human beings with my message of redemption. Along with the excitement came anxiety; I was simply overwhelmed. I knew I wanted to do this, but just how to accomplish it? I had attempted to write this book over the previous few years, but somehow working long hours of strenuous physical labor left me feeling so drained by the time I was back home, that my story was only in bits and pieces, both in my computer's guts and in my mind. I would be burning bridges, those financial bridges I'd created to support myself. *You say you want to find a way to help others. Put your money where your mouth is, Nancy.* And so I did. I hung up my rubber gloves and toilet brush and never looked back. I needed expert advice as to how to proceed.

I CALLED A literary agent in New York City and left him a thirty-second message, just the bare bones of what I had been through and what I now faced. I received a call back within hours. I now had representation; a contract was negotiated. I would receive an advance to write the book. This would support me financially, giving me the latitude and time to get my story down on paper.

It took me a week or two to really get into the writing full-bore. I missed my daily routine, I missed my clients, and I missed their children. Hunkering down to write had an unexpected effect that nearly threw me into a tailspin. I have always been an upbeat person, but many times during that period, I found myself quickly drained. All I wanted was to lie on the couch and drift off to sleep in the middle of the day. I was never the type to nap during the day, and so I didn't understand what was wrong. It wasn't the aftermath of the media attention; it wasn't the stress of being out in the public eye. I had gotten plenty of rest and I should have been at the top of my game. Yet I just couldn't shake this crushing feeling that I was somehow doomed.

Writing had always been such a pleasure for me, a great release, yet now it seemed like a tightening vise. I shut myself off from others, not accepting invitations to go out for dinner or to a party, many times not even taking phone calls. A dark cloud encased and blurred my vision. I plodded along with the text, but it was like pulling teeth without anesthetic. With each vignette transposed from memory to page, it felt as if my emotional airways were constricting in kind, like some form of emotional asthma attack.

I thought perhaps my malaise had something to do with my not having anyone to serve, no one's home to keep in order, and the resultant praise attached, and that may have played a part in my unease, but it felt like so much more. I was unable to control the feeling that I was being dragged back into the dark and isolated cavern I'd miraculously escaped from, and the thought scared me to death. How many times would I have to expel these demons before they evaporated once and for all like so much morning fog? Would they ever, ever truly be *gone*?

The bleakness of winter didn't help my somber mood. I decided that I had to take steps to shake this thing before it did permanent damage. I was weaving myself another stifling cocoon, and all while still living in the same place I'd inhabited during the years of my imprisonment. It dawned on me one morning that it had been more than two weeks since I'd walked outside my apartment door. Then and there I promised myself I'd get out of the building every day if only briefly, to break the rhythm and rupture the malevolent vein of thought that was pouring its poisonous blood into my system.

Sven (my Saab) came to the rescue. I'd load some tunes into the CD player and head out on the road. It didn't matter where I was going; sometimes I wasn't going anywhere at all. A cool breeze through an open window and Eric Clapton on the CD player were enough to break through my melancholy, if only for that hour. I saw other faces along my path, those in their cars who were off to work or running errands, and I thought back to the time when I could see them only from my balcony's roost. The difference now was that I was out among the travelers; I was one of them. *See, Nancy, you're still one of them.* I vowed to keep it that way.

One cold, gray morning I pulled into Schnitzelstein's, a bakery on Fulton Street that I'd so often frequented on my way to a client's home; I would leave my clients a loaf of bread or other goodies to enjoy when they returned from work. A guy named Larry who manned the counter could always make me smile, and I needed that boost about now. On my way inside I noticed an old black woman resting her bones on the curb; her "home," in the form of a rusty grocery cart, stood sentinel beside her small, hunched frame. She had her life's possessions inside that cart, covered by black garbage bags to keep out the inclement weather. She raised her knit-capped, life-battered and line-etched face to meet mine and smiled. There was something in her joyful expression that drew me to stop and talk with her.

I saw something in the basket area of the old woman's cart that would start our conversation; a gallon jug of bleach. I told her that I cleaned houses and that bleach was a mainstay in keeping things looking their best. "I wouldn't be caught dead without mine," the old woman responded. "I find a lot of useful items that just need a little sprucing up. There are a lot of germs in this world, but they don't come into mine," she offered, tapping on the handle of the tarnished cart, softly smiling. It was then that I noticed that her gnarled, chapped hands were uncovered and told her to wait a minute, I'd be right back. I always keep an extra pair of winter gloves in the car. I sometimes run out the door without remembering them, and this way I never find myself stranded with cold hands. Leaning inside to retrieve the red leather, fur-lined gloves, I opened my wallet and slipped a ten-dollar bill inside one of them.

Her eyes lit up when she saw my arm extend to hand the gloves to her. "How did you know that red's my favorite color!?" she exclaimed. "Isn't it *everyone's* favorite color?" I threw back with a grin. "I adore red." She laid them atop the cart and grabbed one of my hands. "You are a blessed person, miss. You have more strength in you than even you know about, and so do I. People look at me," she continued, "and believe that they know who I am, but they don't know nothin' about me. I've lived a good life and had more than my share of blessings; heartaches, too. But I wouldn't take back one thing that brought me to this place. Look, if I hadn't been sitting here this morning, we never would've met. It's the little things that keep you goin' . . . every one of 'em's important. You remember that, miss." I told her my name was Nancy. She nodded. "Mine's Merlene. So good to know you, Nancy." I angled my head in the direction of the bakery door. "I'm going in to buy a dose of caffeine, Merlene. . . . You want a cup, too? How about a donut?" "Bless you, honey. I'll have a cup, yes, black and strong like me! You pick the donut; surprise me!" she replied.

I came back out after a short conversation with Larry at the counter, holding a bag and a cup of coffee for each of us. She looked in her bag, then up at me, and smiled. "You're trying to make me fat, aren't you, Nancy?" I smirked, "Yeah, Merlene, that was my plan. You can't fool a fooler, sister." She picked out one of the donuts and dipped it in her Styrofoam cup. "Nothin' like it on this earth, an apple fritter dunked in hot coffee . . . delicious! Thank you, Nancy." "My pleasure, Merlene."

I believe in angels. I think we encounter them everywhere; we just don't take the time needed to notice them in our harried midst. They are God's emissaries on Earth; He sends them to us when He senses our need, our child-like angst along the riddle-strewn path of life. As I was pulling away, my sojourner friend was picking up her gloves to put them on. I hoped they warmed her hands and spirit. She had certainly given me what I needed on that cold, wintry day.

I smiled the whole way home, and over the next few weeks my melancholy ebbed, then disappeared, and the writing of my tale became a joy once more. I called friends and met them for dinner. I went to the bookstore and picked up something new to dig into, putting aside my "employment" for a few hours, just to relax and escape into another world, one painted with someone else's words. I pampered myself by buying expensive bath salts to scent my daily soak. The text flowed out of me, no pain, no wanting to hide by napping in the middle of a perfectly good day. Life was calling to me again and I was answering its welcoming heartbeat.

CHAPTER 20

Food for Thought/Some Hearty Fare

NOW THAT THE process of telling my tale is nearly at an end, I am able to better understand the darkness that came over me during those long months of writing it all down. Hour after hour at the keyboard, I was reliving those painful years, both those in my early childhood and then teenage life. I expanded on my list of failures as I traveled back to times when I felt hopeless and alone as an adult, regurgitating the missteps, poor choices and defective tools I used to dig the colossal hole I created to exist within. I relived every painful, insecure moment I had caused my son, Chris. I had to rethink every nasty stare and inconsiderate comment thrown my way as well.

Once paroled from my long confinement, I had gladly and glee-fully put that past behind me. The more months, years and new experiences that had come between that old existence and the now, the more those memories were fading. It seemed I couldn't really place myself inside that situation anymore. And I didn't want to try. We are each an amalgam of our experiences and choices. By painstakingly re-creating every emotion and pivotal event held during those years of self-destruction, I was falling dangerously close to reentering my former existence. Or at least that's what it *felt* like as these memories poured out and onto the page, and perception is everything.

These sensitivities can become our reality if we do not closely inspect their intrusion into our thoughts. Why are they there? What value do they give by renting space in our cranium? Are these thoughts trespassers to be treated accordingly or guests to be embraced and welcomed? Not asking myself these questions and more is what allowed me to slip into that emotional chasm. Being more aware of my imperfect thinking is what now gives me the comfort of knowing that I am capable of pulling myself back up from the doldrums that come into each of our lives. For memory is a powerful thing.

The events that have unfolded over the last ten years have been magical, yes, but it has not been smooth sailing since the day the computer arrived in my life. Along with the thrills of this new chance at living a better life—my exciting "firsts," my rediscovery of driving a car and the amazing freedom that brought with it, making a living, slipping into a pair of Levi's, getting down on the floor to play with children, taking a bath, painting my newfound toes—came feelings of fear, anxiety, worry and self-doubt. I am just like you; I am a human being, full of conundrums and of uncertainties.

The puzzles life sends our way are the variables; situations and events that will or won't affect a person to a wildly varying degree, based on each personality, how we each see our life experience and then in how we translate that impression to others. Humor has been my tool. I really *do* enjoy a joke, but for me some of that laughter has masked what I could never face entirely before I wrote this book. I've never tried to hide the details of my life. Anyone who knows me well is already aware of the great majority of what's been written here.

But I'd never *owned the pain* before now. I had never personalized those experiences, the experiences of a child who was abandoned not once, but twice in her formative years. When I'd occasionally recount those stories, I felt removed from the scenery, almost as if in an out-of-body experience, and they were always told with humor. I never felt sorry for that kid; because that kid was *me* and Nancy can handle anything. She just laughs it off. Nancy is tough and no one and nothing can hurt her.

I FINALLY CRIED for that kid out on my balcony. I was on the phone with my friend Barbara, and we were discussing what a draining process it had been initially to open up my "Pandora's box" of memories, but how theraputic it was to have it all come flooding out of me. And all at once it happened. The tears came out of nowhere and just wouldn't stop. I cried because I could finally attach myself to the child in the stories, now in the role of a protective adult, and look at that kid and think, *She didn't deserve that. She was just a little kid. Ah, don't do that to her. . . . Can't you see you're hurting her?*

Something clicked in that unexpected moment of emotional dam-bursting. But I'm not sure the healing is complete; in fact, in light of the impact of that unforeseen moment, I'm more sure that it's *not*. I do know this: My past doesn't scare me anymore, and whatever does come to face me from my store of memories and experiences, I will be able to handle it with more grace and security than at any time previous to this moment, this very moment as I tap out these words for you to examine.

In finally acknowledging the injustice done to "that kid," to *me*, I've turned an important corner and believe with all I'm worth that I will be just fine. That is an empowering feeling. It's not a matter of placing *blame* for what happened to me in life, not at all. What *is* important comes from the sudden and freeing realization that what happened to me when I was dependent on another's guidance didn't come about because I was somehow defective and unlovable. It happened because it happened. I always *was* lovable; I just didn't think so for the longest time.

I will still find humor around every corner in this crazy life. But what caused the explosion out on my balcony will never be lightly dismissed again. I will now give honor to that pain, to that valuable little kid, and wear my scars discreetly, but with pride. For not to give honor to the pain is to devalue the person who lived it. It would be tantamount to saying that all of it was no big deal. No joke; it *was* a big deal.

The certainties that bind us as one are the framework we all face: our mortality, our limited minds, our imperfect ability to reach the best conclusions when fielding choices along our way. But if we can start from a place where we at least believe ourselves to be of value, born to love and be loved, and nurture *those* thoughts, then I believe our reasoning is surer to bring about a happier finale as our ultimate curtain falls.

Laugh at your foibles, your imperfectness; even relish these flaws, for we are only human. Then examine and learn from these examples. Take berating yourself out of the equation when you make mistakes. How do children learn and absorb best? They reach their

highest potential with kind admonition and the gentle encouragement to do better next time when they falter. Forgive yourself, just
as you forgive other imperfect souls who have harmed you. Be your
own best confidante, cheerleader and shoulder to lean on. Other
loved ones will fill in the gaps at times, sometimes total strangers,
but beginning from a place of self-love is your finest assurance of a
life of contentment.

Reaching out to touch someone else is vital in·rediscovering that
true value and beginning the process of fully loving ourselves as we
were intended. By redirecting your focus onto another soul's needs,
by not obsessing over whatever stumbling block in your own life is
currently causing you distress, you will not only be helping another
suffering human being, but as a result of that selfless act, you will be
restoring your own God-given value. The impediment you once
found so overwhelming, such a struggle to deal with, will lose its
grip on your being and gradually become impotent. It was only fear
all along . . . and you won't be afraid anymore. You will know your
worth.

There is no template to determine who that fellow traveler will be
or where you will find the one who calls to your heart; you will
know it when you feel it. It's up to you to trust and follow the small,
still voice that urges you on. To deny its resonance is to reject your
innate need; by doing so you are wounding, neglecting, your own
humanity. To answer that inspiration is to honor your best motivation; we are built to function as parts of the "body human" and are
most fulfilled when giving to that noble effort.

Just as there are billions of people populating the planet, there
are an equal number of gifts and sensitivities that will guide each of
us on the path to helping whoever needs it. Listen to the call and act.

It may be only one person who calls to you; it could be millions. Each person's mission is equally important. The effect of that act will astound and amaze. I know.

I have crow's feet and laugh lines, perhaps more than most women my age. The map of my life on my face blesses me with its presence. Each line bears witness to having laughed more than cried, smiled more than frowned and having embraced the love sent my way far, far more than the sad ignorance I've encountered.

The human spirit is indomitable. It can be crushed, ground to a pulp by self-hate, ignorant and emotionally frail loved ones' or unfeeling strangers' barbs, only to be reconstituted by the miraculous waters of love and belief in self. Belief is more powerful than memory. It can conquer what wise and pragmatic human beings see as impossible hurdles. None of us knows what the future holds, but I face mine with joy, optimism and belief. What more can anyone ask for?

Finis

ACKNOWLEDGMENTS

To my parents: I mourn the loss for you of dreams never fulfilled, emotions you wished to, but could never bring yourself to express, and the remorse, regret you were incapable of giving voice to. I thank you for giving me life, for my insatiable curiosity, my deep love of books and of nature. But, your most precious gift by far has been an immutable belief that God loves us, even when those surrounding us falter in the translation and intact delivery of that precious emotion. Yes, God loves us even when we find ourselves unlovable.

I've always said that once your mortal coils were shed, your communal purgatory would be sitting on a lonely bench, side by side, nitpicking and rebutting arguments like petulant children, thus forestalling ascension to Heaven's majestic plane. . . . Have you learned nothing? Cut it out. Write me when you get there. . . . I love you both dearly and miss you every day.

PS: Oh, yeah . . . and Mom? I also thank God for the color of my eyes . . . just like Daddy's.

Acknowledgments

To my precious sisters: This is my life's story. It charts my path through my set of eyes, both those of a child and those in adulthood. It gives my perspective and memory of both good times and bad. It is my voice reaching out to be heard and hopefully understood. Some of what makes up the fabric of my life, however, are necessarily memories that include each of you. Some of you decided to blot out entirely or reshape our family history's pivotal events into a form you found acceptable in order to live the life you chose to lead. I have done my best in the writing of this book to tell my tale fully and honestly, while at the same time endeavoring to honor your path, to shield you and your choices. But I was not raised as an only child. My life did not unfold in a vacuum, but among six other sisters, all of whom I love dearly. I loved you all then, I do now and I will forever.

To my daughter-in-law, Leane: Thank you for loving me and for allowing me to love you back. Leane, I am a mother-in-law, after all, and a woman. Though I've raised your hackles a time or three over the years and vice versa, I've always felt a wonderful bond and a wish for only good things to unfold for you, much love and success. You are a beautiful lady, in and out. But don't forget: I was voted as having the best lips at our holiday celebration a few years back. Kiss, kiss.

To my dear grandson Ian: You have brought me great joy; more than I can express in words. I think it was your special love that saved me during all my years inside. You will always hold a special place in a corner of my heart where no one else need apply. I will be there for you in every way, every day, till they throw the dirt on top of my pine box; maybe even after that if I play my cards right. I am so proud of you and love you unceasingly.

To my wondrous grandson Isaac: I always smile when I think of you. You are my heart. You remind me of myself as a child, a real pistol, full of life, full of jokes, eager to please and with a generous heart and loyalty that will serve you well in life. You have a gentle spirit that follows me whenever we're apart. My love for you is endless, sweet boy.

To Barbara Cooley: For your invaluable contributions to the development of this book in its preliminary stages. For the many hours spent wielding your gentle red pencil over reams of printed text, your fine eye for detail in "plucking the author's eyebrow" here and there, that is, of course, when your contact lenses were perfectly aligned. The technical skills you possess took the memories of someone who had little understanding of the proper use of semicolons and paragraph structure and left her with a manuscript graced by flow and continuity. You were my rock; a comfort in the times regurgitated memories overwhelmed me with emotion. You believed in me and in my story's impact when I had my doubts. What a good, good friend you are, Barbara. Saying thank you just doesn't cover it. And this mention for Jim, Barbara's dear husband: The epicurean delights that Barbara is wont to create for your eager palate were put on the back burner so that *my* needs could be met. Thanks for the sacrifice, Jim. Hope all is back to normal in the Cooley manse.

To NGH: For your dreadful, merciless, interminable and undeserved torment and supercilious disdain. (These slurs, you ofttimes note, are intended "in the most loving manner.") For the vapidity of your arguments that can at times drive me to heights of apoplectic proportion. For your third grade puns that always leave me feeling stratospherically beyond you; my Oscar Wilde to your Soupy Sales. For never having grown up, instead remaining an annoying, nasty, yet oddly lovable little boy; thank God for that much, 'cause you

Acknowledgments

sure ain't cute no mo', bubby. But most of all, for loving me, though you will never say those scary three little words, unless you've poured yourself a second healthy dose of Glenfiddich. . . . *I love you* anyway, bozo. I even love your goofy, untrained and ne'er-do-well heathen chocolate Lab, Nell.

To SS:

There was an odd bloke from Manchester

Sent girl limericks, thought 'e could best 'er.

Return volleys they flew, 'cross the briny twixt two.

Most were foul, worthy of sequester.

To Steve: For the midnight rides on your Harley and all the cups of early-morning coffee before heading off to work in the "toilet fields" of greater Grand Rapids. I brought the donuts; you ate 'em.

To Jeffrey: You are an amazing human being, such a rare creature and a privilege to know. I stand in awe of your treatment of those around you. Unfortunately, God *did* break the mold with you. Thank you for all your kindnesses and trust over the years.

To Leslie: For your dear Swedish ear, for your no-nonsense advice, for your love and belief in me. Give Winston a kiss for me.

To Mark F. and Frank M.: Mark, I love you like a brother. You're one of the finest, brilliant and most loyal people I know. Your friendship means the world to me. Frank, oh, Frank: You are truly one of a kind; a very creative and talented guy with a heart as big as the Continental Divide. Your sense of humor ought to be enough to have you thrown in a facility for immediate rewiring, which is saying a lot comin' from me. I love you, mister.

To Mary Lou: Man, oh, man . . . What a long, neurotic trip it's been, eh? You know me inside out, milady . . . know where all the bodies are buried. I'll pay you off if I make a buck. I'd run through fire for you . . . I take that back. But I might give you half of my only sandwich if we were stranded on a desert isle . . . nah, scratch that one, too. I'll think about it and get back to you. I love you. If anyone finds out I said so, I'll deny it to the death.

To Sally and Dennis: For each and every kindness extended to me and my family over many years. I love you both.

To Cindy and David: You stuck with me through fat and thin. I love you guys.

To Ruth: For all your help and thoughtfulness and most of all for your love. Though we don't see each other often, the closeness remains. I love you.

To my own Doctor Mengele, Angel of Death: For making me feel vastly superior to a man with numerous diplomas hanging on his sterile wall. Thanks, bud.

To all the doctors and nurses out there who have chosen the road less traveled; I've met a few of you: It is you, your brand of thinking, compassion and creativity that will change outcomes for millions of forgotten people; those who count on their doctor's knowledge but are prescribed archaic, inadequate treatment in many instances. We know there is a better way.

To Coca-Cola and Maxwell House: Your constant dosing of caffeine, day and night, sustained me. Without it, this book would've never been written. I will gladly accept samples in the mail.

To Mel Berger, agent extraordinaire: You are my personal caped crusader, doing battle for and protecting this fledgling author from dangers lurking in the back alleys and dives of Gotham City's publishing world. Your valuable time, advocacy, effort, long-distance hand-holding and encouragement have made all the difference. I couldn't have weathered it without you, Batman. You are the best.

Acknowledgments

To Graham Jaenicke: You are The Boy Wonder, Graham. You've listened to my concerns in angst-filled moments, turned checks around faster than a speeding bullet and always forwarded on my needs ASAP to the Big Kahuna in the Cowl, Mel. The way you're going, you'll soon be known as The Man Wonder . . . keep it up, fella. Thanks for everything, Graham.

To Amy Hertz: Your finely honed editor's scalpel is renowned in the publishing field; after dealing with me, it should be bronzed. I initially sent you my life's version of Tolstoy's *War and Peace*; I thought five-hundred-plus pages were perfectly reasonable. I didn't even include the narrative of my time spent milking domesticated yaks on a windswept plateau during my brief novitiate as a Tibetan monk. . . . You're *so* picky. After days of coaxing me off the precipice with the startling revelation that only two people on Earth, with me being counted as one of the two, would consider the purchase of such a tome, I allowed the radical surgery to commence. I am very happy with the results. You may have missed your true calling, Amy. You could have gone into psychiatry. Thanks a bunch.

To Melissa Miller: You took the bullet for Amy (preserving her mental health) by taking my phone calls many, many times during this lengthy process; you deserve a gold medal, woman. As you well (and painfully) know by now, my computer savvy and technical acumen are foul beyond understanding. You would've been better off tutoring a chimpanzee. Your time, patience and in-depth knowledge of the industry and computerese were great comfort and essential ingredients in seeing this thing through to completion. And, you bore my black, sickening humor with dignity, with even the courtesy of laughter attached. What a gem you are, Melissa. Thanks for all your help.